Trial by Fire

Science, Technology and the Civil War

By
Charles D. Ross

 WHITE MANE BOOKS

This White Mane Books publication
was printed by
Beidel Printing House, Inc.
63 West Burd Street
Shippensburg, PA 17257-0152 USA

In respect for the scholarship contained herein, the acid-free paper used in this book meets the guidelines for permanence and durability of the Committee on Production Guidelines for Book Longevity of the Council on Library Resources.

For a complete list of available publications
please write
White Mane Books
Division of White Mane Publishing Company, Inc.
P.O. Box 152
Shippensburg, PA 17257-0152 USA

Library of Congress Cataloging-in-Publication Data

Ross, Charles D., 1958-
    Trial by fire : science, technology, and the Civil War / by Charles D. Ross.
        p. cm.
    Includes bibliographical references and index.
    ISBN 1-57249-185-X (alk. paper)
    1. United States--History--Civil War, 1861-1865--Science. 2. United States--History--Civil War, 1861-1865--Technology. I. Title.

E468.9 .R67 2000
973.7--dc21

99-042228

To Caryn, Dylan, and my wife, Paige

Contents

Illustrations

Preface

The American Civil War was a war of transition. While in many aspects it was no different from wars fought several centuries earlier, it also contained the seeds of modern total warfare. As the war began, most commanding officers were prepared for what was then traditional battle. Such a conflict would include Napoleonic frontal assaults on open ground, respect and chivalry toward the enemy and avoidance, when possible, of damage to civilian life and property. By the time the war was nearing its end, gallant charges had given way to the grim reality of slow attrition in the trenches. Prisoner exchanges had long ceased and men by the hundreds were dying unromantic deaths in military prisons on both sides of the Mason-Dixon Line. William Sherman and Phil Sheridan were teaching Southern citizens early lessons in total war.

As the nature of war changed from 1861-1865, another transition from old to new was occurring in a broader sense. If one looks sixty years on either side of 1860, the differences in the typical human's way of life are astounding. In 1800, people traveled on foot, on horseback, or across the water by sail. Information traveled from place to place by the same slow methods. But though life was much as it had been for hundreds or even thousands of years, dramatic changes were bubbling up from just below the surface. Men were gaining the first crude control and understanding of electricity. Steam engines were being developed as a means of replacing human labor and as a technique for moving vehicles.

By 1920 the development of the steam engine's successor, the internal combustion engine, had revolutionized transportation. The automobile was becoming available at affordable prices, airplanes were no longer a curiosity, and the Germans had already terrorized enemy forces with swarms of submarines. Household electricity was being taken for granted and information now traveled at the speed of light: the telegram was already giving way to the "wireless," or radio. The first television was less than a decade away, the first atomic bomb only two decades into the future.

The Civil War took place right in the middle of this incredible transformation from an ancient way of life to one not much different from that of today. As a result, the war became a laboratory for applying adolescent technologies to military situations. The results were mixed. Both sides used balloons for reconnaissance, but men found many obstacles to using what was largely a civilian amusement in battlefield situations. The first successful submarine attack occurred in the Civil War, but again the technology wasn't advanced enough to be a major factor. The torpedo would come less than five years after the end of the war, the internal combustion engine about twenty years later. The telegraph, in contrast, while very young, found widespread and important use in the war. Its effectiveness would produce significant changes in the way the military conducted operations.

During the 1800s, a by-product of the Industrial Revolution was the popularization of scientific knowledge. A technical society demanded that knowledge not be hoarded by a select fraternity of natural philosophers, but be delivered on a large scale to many men. By the time of the Civil War, many men who would not call themselves scientists had at least a passing knowledge of important scientific principles.

Predictably, most commanders in the war were conservative in their approach to technology, hesitant to break from tradition and, at least for the first year or two of the war, reluctant to try anything which might be construed as unfair. Still, certain men on each side stand out for their willingness to explore the possibilities new technologies could offer. In particular, as this book shows, George B. McClellan in the Union army and P.G.T. Beauregard in the Confederate army both appear ahead of their time in their grasp of the advantages inherent in harnessing technology.

The book is divided into two parts. Part 1, The Right Man for the Job, is a study of some notable consequences of the democratization of scientific knowledge mentioned above. Three creative colonels, each with a sound background in important fundamental science, found themselves in crisis situations in which their knowledge proved crucial. Chapters 1 and 2, describing the work of Henry Pleasants and Joseph Bailey, examine short-term crisis situations solved by science, while Chapter 3, a study of the work of George W. Rains, is a look at scientific creativity applied for the long haul and on a large scale.

Part 2 is a more general study of the intersection in time of the Civil War and three young technologies, now all-important in the military world. Chapters 4 and 5 examine submarine and air warfare, respectively, two methods of waging war which were still found wanting at the end of their Civil War trials. The final chapter of the book is a look at the development and use in the Civil War of the telegraph, and the effect, more generally, of instant communication on strategy and tactics.

The appendices provide the reader with a historical context for the Civil War status of submarines and ballooning, and also a primer on buoyancy. Strangely enough, this fundamental physics concept proves to be a common thread through much of the book. The same type of force that held Thaddeus Lowe's balloons aloft and the C.S.S. *Hunley* at the ocean's surface was also manipulated by Henry Pleasants to ventilate his mineshaft and by Joseph Bailey to save the Union fleet on the Red River.

I believe this book is unique in its perspective of the Civil War as seen by a scientist. Much of what is here is not new information, but is presented, arranged, and explained in a new way. I hope that each chapter will prove a self-contained resource for the topic involved. Some of the information in the book, particularly regarding the Augusta Powder Works, is truly new and seen here for the first time.

No book could thoroughly cover the influence of science and technology on the Civil War, and I have not tried to be encyclopedic in my coverage. I have picked what I felt to be the most important and fascinating cases, the kind of scenarios that leave educated readers of a general Civil War book saying "I wonder how they did that?" I hope it will prove useful and interesting to the educated layman interested in both the war and in science, and also to the scientist and engineer, with perhaps only a passing knowledge of the war.

I received help from many people in the course of writing this book. I would like to thank them here: Dr. Martin Gordon and Vicki Stouffer of White Mane Publishing and Beverly Kuhn of Beidel Printing House for their assistance and constructive criticism; the librarians at Longwood College and the University of Virginia and the staff members at the National Archives Still Prints Branch and the Library of Congress Prints and Photographs Division for their invaluable help in locating sources and images; Mrs. Lynn Gamma, archivist of the Air Force at the Air Force Historical Research Agency, for her help with documents related to Civil War ballooning; Gordon Blaker and Scott Loeur of the Augusta-Richmond County Museum and photographer Eric Olig for their help in reproducing the drawings of the Augusta Powder Works; Dan Dowdey and Dr. Ludwell

Johnson for permission to use their artwork; Jan Nielsen and Betty Woodie of the Department of Natural Sciences at Longwood College for general clerical assistance; Drew Lavan for supplying copies of George W. Rains's prewar patents and the Waltham Abbey gunpowder pamphlet and to the British Library for permission to use the latter; Dr. Maurice Maxwell for helpful chemistry discussions; Matt Smith for helpful discussions regarding the *Hunley*; Mark Kelly and Dr. Steve Arata for their writing advice and for taking time to review parts of the manuscript; and finally, my wife Paige for her love, help, and encouragement.

Part 1

The Right Man for the Job

Chapter 1

Henry Pleasants: The Mine at Petersburg

In late summer or early autumn of 1864, Confederate Brigadier General Archibald Gracie presented a gift to Mrs. William
Cameron of Petersburg, Virginia, in whose home he was a frequent
guest. The gift was a set of candlestick holders in the form of monu-
ments, made by an Alabama soldier and inscribed with these words:
"On the 30th of July the Yanks undermined our works at Petersburg, Va. At half-past four in the morning they put fire to the fuse,
and we went up. They charged our lines and kept them till evening,
when we drove them out with a loss to them of four thousand,
mostly Negroes." The candlestick holders were made from clay
thrown in the air by what was probably the most magnificent and
terrible explosion of the Civil War.[1]

The explosion arose from a bomb planted in an ingenious
method by members of the Forty-eighth Pennsylvania Infantry Regiment. The chaotic clash that followed is often called "The Battle of
the Crater" in reference to the massive hole left in the earth when
the bomb detonated. The decision to construct the bomb and its
method were functions of political pressures and the fortuitous
placement of men with the right skills at the right place and time.

The Civil War of 1864 found both Union and Confederate armies
in a different mode than in the chivalrous days of 1861 and 1862.
As forces under Major General William T. Sherman began to grind
their way from Chattanooga to Atlanta, the Army of the Potomac
began a similar dance of death with General Robert E. Lee's Army of
Northern Virginia. Beginning with the awful inferno known as the
Wilderness, sidestepping to Spotsylvania Court House and once more
to the butchery of Cold Harbor, the two armies pounded each other
with cruelty and savagery as they drifted slowly southward. Long
gone were cheers for gallantry shown by the enemy and magnificent flag-waving charges into the opposing lines. As May turned to

June, both sides (especially the Confederates) showed an increasing trend towards trench warfare, making mobile the tactics of the siege. Under the command of Major General George G. Meade and the watchful eye of overall Union general in chief Lieutenant General Ulysses S. Grant, the Union forces proceeded towards Richmond with a relentless determination to get the thing done. Across the trenches, the battle-hardened Confederates were just as resolute, keeping a tenacious survival grip on every mile of Virginia ground.

Though the overall effect of the spring campaign was to place the Northern troops increasingly closer to Richmond, things had not gone exactly according to Grant's master plan. As Grant saw it, what had kept the Confederate army alive to this point was the Union army's inability or refusal to coordinate efforts between its forces. Within any particular theatre or across the nation as a whole, when soldiers in blue attacked at one point it seemed that their comrades at some other crucial point were held back by politics or incompetence. This allowed the smaller and more poorly supplied Southern forces to constantly reinforce each other across interior lines of battle without fear of leaving a weak point.

Once in overall command, Grant decided to remedy this on a national scale and within his campaign against Lee's Army of Northern Virginia. Nationally, his descent into Virginia was timed to coincide with Sherman's drive to Atlanta and continued Union pressure in the Trans-Mississippi region. His Virginia plan also involved several components. First, he and Meade would pound Lee's troops, decimating their numbers and constantly shifting around the Confederate right flank toward Richmond. While this was happening, another Union force (under Major General Benjamin Butler) would put pressure on Richmond itself from the southeast. In addition, a third force would be sent to control the Shenandoah Valley. This would rob Lee of his major source of food and would also prevent him from diverting attention with a thrust towards Washington or other Northern cities.

Though Grant and Meade had held up their end of the deal, the other two sides of his three-sided vise had failed miserably. First, Butler, a political appointee known North and South for his military incompetence, had allowed his forces to be caught in a humiliating trap. Because of the treacherously mined waters and solid defenses of the James River, Butler's troops had disembarked from their ships about twenty miles short of Richmond. Their landing was on a peninsula called Bermuda Hundred between the James and the Appomattox Rivers, a peninsula with a neck only about four miles wide. After several unsuccessful thrusts at Petersburg and Richmond, Butler had retreated onto Bermuda Hundred to regroup. The

Confederates, under General P.G.T. Beauregard, took the opportunity to entrench across the neck, effectively taking Butler's forces out of the war altogether and at the expense of only a small Southern detachment. In the Shenandoah Valley, the news was no better. Union forces under Major General Franz Sigel had gotten only as far as Newmarket before a hodgepodge army consisting partly of teenage cadets from the Virginia Military Institute had routed them.

So now in the first week of June, Grant was closer to Richmond and had cut Lee's strength considerably, but was not nearly as close as he had hoped to be towards his real objective: Destroying the Army of Northern Virginia or forcing its surrender. A war of attrition was one the North would surely win, but time was a key element of the equation. In November, Abraham Lincoln would come up for re-election and the outlook was not favorable. Anti-war activists and Southern sympathizers were making great use of Grant's heavy losses in their effort to turn the public against continuation of the war. With little real progress apparently being made, and the youth of the nation falling in ever more bloody waves, it seemed hard to argue against the notion that the time had come for both sides to put up their guns. The once patriotic notion of preserving the Union at all costs had begun to seem a lot less important to many in the North as the reality of war hit home.

If Grant was going to make fighting look like the best solution, he had to make significant progress soon. As he studied the situation, another plan came to his mind. If he could not destroy Lee's sources of supply, he could still prevent the supplies from arriving.

A network of railroads fed Lee's army; it was a network that could be destroyed or controlled. From the Shenandoah Valley came the Central Virginia, by way of Charlottesville and Gordonsville. On 7 June, Grant dispatched a cavalry force under Major General Philip Sheridan to cut the Central Virginia and to team up with forces under Major General David Hunter, who had replaced Sigel in the Valley. Hunter, with those troops who had been under Sigel and some reinforcements, had already marched as far south as Staunton and was now turning towards the east. The rest of the railroads feeding Lee's troops came from Lynchburg, Danville and North Carolina, but all connected at Petersburg before continuing to Richmond. If Grant could take Petersburg and cut the Central Virginia, Lee's men would be quickly forced to starve, surrender, or fight.

To take Petersburg, Grant would somehow have to get more than one hundred thousand men moving away from the lines at Cold Harbor and marching fifty miles to the James River, half a mile wide and much deeper than the series of rivers both armies had been crossing from the Wilderness to Cold Harbor. If Lee sensed the movement, all evidence from the past indicated that he would be poised to pick the stretched-out army apart in detail. The path which Grant proposed was parallel to that followed by the Yankees under Major General George McClellan in his disastrous "change of base" retreat during the Seven Days' battles two years earlier.

On the night of 12 June, Grant put his forces in motion. By dawn of the next day, the Union trenches at Cold Harbor were empty and by evening the van of Grant's army was on the northern banks of the James. Union cavalry held all road crossings, leaving Lee (for once) blind to Grant's intentions. Lee suspected that Grant might move towards Petersburg, but Lee could hardly transport his army to the south of the James, leaving the back door to Richmond wide open. Lee moved his army south towards the river and waited.

As soon as possible, Grant was hurrying his forces across the James by steamship and across a twenty-one hundred-foot pontoon bridge.[2] Construction of the bridge was one of the war's most impressive engineering feats. The bridge was not only extraordinarily long, but was constructed to withstand the four-foot difference between high and low tides and was designed with a detachable center to allow the passage of gunboats and transports. It was completed in seven hours on the afternoon and evening of 14 June. At approximately 0200 on 15 June, Major General William Smith, with ten thousand troops, was ordered to rush down and establish a foothold in Petersburg, which was well fortified with trenches and breastworks, but held by very few Confederates.[3] As Smith's troops approached, the Petersburg lines (about seven and a half miles in length) were defended by only about twenty-two hundred men.[4]

Unfortunately for Grant, Smith seems to have been rendered overly cautious by the beating his troops had taken at Cold Harbor. Smith wanted to examine the enemy fortifications thoroughly and did not finish until almost 1600. Then it took Smith and his subordinates until 1900 to get the assault started. Late as it was, it was effective. Within two hours, Union troops had overwhelmed a large chunk of the thinly held Confederate line. Petersburg was wide open to attack when Smith's caution again got the best of him. Fearing Confederate reinforcements (which were coming, but slowly), Smith ordered his men to stop and solidify their gains. This just as two divisions under Major General Winfield Scott Hancock were arriving to aid Smith in his attack. The war in Virginia might well have been over in June 1864 if Smith had kept moving. As it happened, his weary troops and those of Hancock hunkered down for the night. The next strong Union attack would not come until 1800 on 16 June.

During the night, while the Union troops slept, the Confeder-ates were furiously rushing reinforcements to Beauregard as he had his men dig new lines closer to Petersburg. During the next two days, Beauregard did a masterful job of moving his undermanned troops to exactly the spots where the Union command had decided to test the lines. Troops continued to trickle in, until finally on the morning of 18 June, the Army of Northern Virginia and Lee himself arrived in Petersburg. After a series of disjointed attacks later that day, Grant glumly decided to give his men a rest and plan his next move. The Confederates had held. A month later Smith was relieved of field command.[5]

The other part of Grant's overall plan to destroy Lee's railroad supply network had not fared much better. Hunter had not turned east at Staunton, but had continued to move south up the Valley towards Lynchburg. At Lynchburg, he met forces dispatched by Lee and under the command of Major General Jubal Early. After a brief engagement, Hunter retreated completely out of Virginia, over the Allegheny Mountains and into West Virginia. Sheridan's men had performed some minor damage to the tracks of the Virginia Central northeast of Charlottesville but had been forced to withdraw after battling oppressive heat and rebel cavalry on 11 June and 12 June. Sheridan's forces returned to their base on the Pamunkey River on 21 June.

So, by the third week of June Grant was in a position both familiar and novel. Once again his forces stared across the trenches at their opposite numbers in gray and butternut. But now, there could be no more sidestepping towards Richmond. The battle be-tween Grant and Lee would have to be settled here. On 20 June Grant announced that "I have determined to envelop Petersburg."[6]

Grant had conducted a siege just the previous year at Vicksburg, Mississippi. It had taken forty-seven sultry days before the stubborn defenders had submitted. Petersburg, under Lee's eye, was going to prove a much harder nut to crack. Most impor-tantly, time was not on Grant's side. In addition to maintaining the morale of his troops during the tiresome sameness of the days in a siege, Grant was beginning to lose troops as their enlistment terms expired.

Grant's boss, President Abraham Lincoln, could not have been pleased with the prospects of a drawn-out siege. The people who had elected Lincoln with such optimism in 1860 were now weary of the war and everything associated with it. Many had grown to be outright hostile towards Lincoln and his administration. They rel-ished the thought of using their vote in the November election to put in his place someone who might allow the Union to gracefully pull itself out of what looked to be an interminable stalemate. Lincoln's best hopes of preserving the Union lay with Grant and Sherman and their attempts to take Petersburg and Atlanta. He needed success somewhere soon.

Nevertheless, on 9 July Grant had Meade order that the campaign would proceed by "regular approaches," meaning that the Union forces would now be spending their days moving at glacial speed in ever more complex trenches towards the Confederate lines. According to the traditional theories of war, the five formal stages of a siege consisted of: (1) investment, or surrounding the enemy; (2) artillery attack; (3) construction of parallels and approaches; (4) breaching of the enemy lines by artillery or mines; and (5) the final assault.[7] Stages 1 and 2 were already in progress (Union artillery had been pummeling Petersburg since 16 June) and the time had come for the men in blue to pick up their picks and shovels. The weather was unusually hot and dry and digging was not only difficult and slow, but dangerous. Confederate riflemen would shoot accurately at the slightest exposed movement. It seemed that taking Petersburg would certainly take too long to do Lincoln and the Union any good.

The land south of Petersburg, though largely flat, contains many small ridges, valleys, and knolls. Fortifications were built by both sides with the aim of taking advantage of these natural features whenever possible. At several places, this caused the opposing lines to be extremely close together. Near Blandford Church, the picket lines were less than four hundred feet apart. Just southeast of Blandford Cemetery Hill, the Confederates had placed a four-gun battery behind earthworks and flanked the artillery on either side with hardened infantry regiments from South Carolina. The ground here sloped gently down to the Union lines. At the bottom of the slope was a man who had an idea that might end the siege of Petersburg in days and not months. His name was Henry Pleasants.

Lieutenant Colonel Pleasants was in charge of the Forty-eighth Pennsylvania Infantry Regiment, part of the Union IX Corps. About a quarter of the four hundred men in the regiment had been anthracite coal miners in Schuylkill County before the war.[8] After the attack on 18 June, Pleasants's men had managed to end up entrenched closer to the enemy than did any other Federal troops.

Formed in the summer of 1861, the Forty-eighth was an experienced and unusually cohesive unit. Aside from seeing battle at Second Bull Run, Chantilly, South Mountain, and Fredericksburg, the regiment had performed well in other types of assignments. They had been highly commended by both citizens and military superiors for their firm but fair six-month occupation of Lexington, Kentucky, a border state city that was in a state of great tension due to political divisions.

They were also well experienced in military construction techniques. They had constructed a causeway at Hatteras Inlet, North Carolina, which had allowed Federal use of the two forts there. At Knoxville, they had constructed a devious defense consisting of water-filled moats and trip wires that had helped the Union forces repel Confederate Lieutenant General James Longstreet's forces in a stunning defeat. The four hundred and forty defenders suffered thirteen casualties while the three thousand Southern attackers had more than eight hundred. When the same trip-wire technique was used in Virginia the next year, Southern papers called it "a devilish contrivance none but a Yankee could devise."[9]

The Forty-eighth was a close knit regiment, with great rapport and respect between the officers and enlisted men. As a result, the Forty-eighth displayed an unusually high level of discipline and devotion to duty. They were also fond of their corps commander, Major General Ambrose Burnside, an affection that was returned by Burnside.

The Confederate position opposite of the Forty-eighth was necessarily a strong point, not only because of the close proximity of the enemy but because of what lay behind the position. A third of a mile west of the Confederates was the Jerusalem Plank Road running straight north into Petersburg. Blandford Cemetery Hill, just to the northwest, offered powerful control of the countryside to whatever troops might occupy it. Because of its importance, the Confederate position was given the name Pegram's Salient, though it was more commonly called Elliot's Salient. A breakthrough here might open the door for Union troops to rush into Petersburg, a breakthrough that might end the war. Such a breakthrough was exactly what Pleasants had in mind.

Pleasants, thirty-one years old, had been trained as a civil engineer. He had worked for the Pennsylvania Railroad, helping to drive a tunnel almost a mile long through the Allegheny Mountains. In the late 1850s, he had moved to Schuylkill County and had begun work as a mining engineer. A few days after the Forty-eighth settled into their trenches across from Elliot's Salient, Pleasants overheard one of his men say, "We could blow that damned fort out of existence if we could run a mineshaft under it." As Pleasants scanned his experienced eyes over the land between the lines, he began to realize that such a thought was not just an enlisted man's fantasy. It could be done.

It was going to be far from simple, however. Running a mineshaft was not easy work in peacetime. The conditions here made survival a game of chance even without the type of movement and exposure necessary to complete a major engineering endeavor. Sharpshooters were active and deadly at this short range. Both sides routinely lobbed mortar shells into the opponent's trenches at all hours. The positions on each side had quickly evolved into labyrinths of trenches and covered ways.

Aside from the treacherous nature of the environment, Pleasants had a second major hurdle. Though Pleasants was able to successfully get approval for his plan all the way through the chain of command from his immediate superior Brigadier General Robert Potter to Burnside to Meade and finally to Grant, he quickly found that he and his men were going to have to do the work without much assistance from above. Though Meade and Grant were anxious to find some way to break the rebel lines, it seems that they did not have much confidence in the potential success of this particular project other than as a means of keeping the enlisted men busy. Meade's engineering staff found the whole idea ludicrous. Though mining the enemy works was a normal part of siege warfare, it was done when the "regular approaches" had brought the opposing lines very close together.

Grant had authorized one of these "standard procedure" mines just a year ago in the Vicksburg campaign. After the regular approaches, the length of that mine had been only about sixty feet. The twenty-two hundred pounds of powder in the gallery had blown a decent size hole in the Confederate lines, killing six rebels, but the breach was quickly filled and the Federals repulsed.[10]

Nothing anywhere near the length of the tunnel Pleasants proposed had ever been constructed during a siege. How could Pleasants get the thing dug and keep it drained and ventilated all under the noses of the watchful Confederates? It seemed hopeless. Pleasants later said, "I found it impossible to get any assistance from anybody."[11]

The men of the Forty-eighth were excited by the idea, however, and Pleasants began to get them organized. He got a list of the men in each company who were miners and set them into round-the-clock three-hour shifts. Each man was to be awarded two drinks of whiskey when he finished his shift (this practice was stopped after about a week when several of the soldiers had saved up enough whiskey to get good and drunk). Picks and shovels were rounded up from surrounding troops, and though the picks were not the type used in mining (the push picks used in mining are straighter than those used for general purposes), Pleasants was able to get the blacksmiths of neighboring artillery units to modify them. Wheelbarrows would normally be used for moving excavated dirt out of the tunnel, but they could not be had, so hickory sticks were fastened to wooden cracker boxes (reinforced with iron hoops from pork and beef barrels) to make buckets.

To keep the tunnel from collapsing, it would have to be shored up with stout timbers. Pleasants's request to headquarters produced nothing, so he sent his men behind the lines to see what they could find. An old railroad bridge supplied part of what they would need and then his men found an abandoned sawmill five miles to the rear. He sent two of his companies back to operate the mill and cut the lumber they would need.[12]

The work began at 1200 on 25 June. The problem of drainage was not difficult to solve as the Confederate works were up a slight incline from the Federal lines. Making the tunnel at a slight upward angle allowed gravity to do the work of getting any water encountered out of the tunnel. When the digging began, the men were working through sand and after a day or so they got into a mixture of sand and clay. The experienced miners had little trouble keeping progress up to as much as forty feet a day (the average was about twenty-three feet per day). One man dug in the end of the cramped tunnel (the tunnel was about four and a half feet high and varied in width from about four feet at the bottom to about two feet at the top) while others carried the excavated debris out in their makeshift buckets. The contents of the buckets were then discreetly spread in the bottom of the ravine behind the Union works. Meanwhile others were coming in with timbers to shore up the ceiling, walls, and floor of the excavated portion. Lighting was accomplished by placing candles or lanterns along the walls at ten-foot intervals.

On 2 July progress stopped when the miners struck a layer of solid wet clay which made the ceiling begin to sag, causing it to almost reach the floor.[13] Re-timbering with stouter wood got the project back on track until a day or so later the miners hit a layer of marl, a putty-like mixture of clay and calcium carbonate which became rock hard not long after the air struck it. It was almost impossible to tunnel through and so Pleasants and his mine bosses decided to shift the tunnel upwards at an even greater angle to get back to the softer sand and clay (the tunnel rose about 13.5 feet in a horizontal distance of 100 feet, for an incline angle of about 7.7 degrees).[14] The men of the Forty-eighth managed to salvage some good from the marl, though, as they carved pipes from it and cut other pieces in the shape of badges with the IX Corps insignia and dried them in the sun to sell for twenty-five cents.[15]

After the tunnel had gotten about two hundred feet in length, Pleasants needed to deal with two more important problems. Where exactly was he going to place the powder magazine? If he fell short

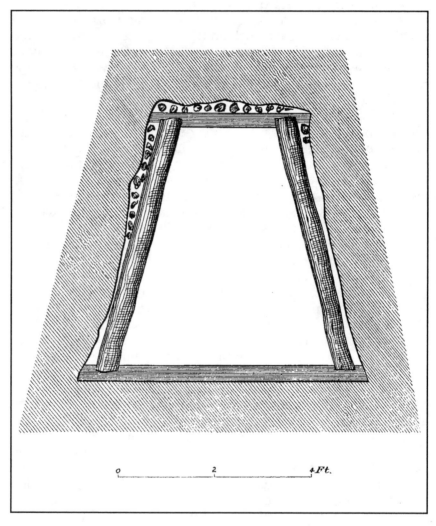

0   2   4 Ft.

Section of the Main Gallery

Official Records

of the Confederate forces or went too far, the effect of the explosion would be minimal. And how were his men going to be able to breathe when they got further and further under the hillside?

To calculate the exact length of the tunnel, Pleasants would require a theodolite, a surveying device usually used for measuring angles. A theodolite is a high precision transit, essentially a telescope mounted so that it can be rotated a measurable amount around both a horizontal and vertical axis. By measuring an angle and a length accurately, the surveyor can use trigonometry to accurately calculate the desired distance. Though Meade's engineers had a theodolite, it was not forthcoming. Pleasants finally obtained one after Burnside wired a friend in Washington, D.C. to send a theodolite down. In a letter Pleasants later wrote to his wife, he said, "If that thing had been made out of solid gold, and set with diamonds, it could not have been more precious to me."[16]

To make his measurements, Pleasants had to risk his life to Confederate snipers by peering over the front lines. To distract them, he had a group of soldiers place their caps on their ramrods and raise them slightly above the wall of the entrenchment. While the excited Confederates perforated the empty caps, Pleasants (with burlap over his head) was peering over the top recording the necessary data. In the course of the excavation, Pleasants was required to make five such triangulation measurements, risking his life each time.

Ventilation was to prove to be the most difficult problem to overcome and would require the most ingenious solution. As the men and lanterns and candles consumed oxygen and produced carbon dioxide, the air in the tunnel would become increasingly harder to breathe. The normal method of ventilating such a shaft was to use a sort of air pump called a miner's bellows or as an alternative, an innovative method devised by Pleasants himself. During the course of construction of the Sand Patch Tunnel in western Pennsylvania, beginning in 1854, Pleasants had solved the ventilation problem in a way that brought him some contemporary fame. From the surface of the mountain, four vertical shafts had been dug which intersected the tunnel shaft at regular intervals. At the base of each shaft, a fire was built which drew the fouled air out of the tunnel to be replaced by fresh air from the mouth of the tunnel.

Pleasants's request to Meade's chief engineer for a mining bellows met with no response, so he was going to be forced once again to improvise. The method that had gained him fame would not work here since the spots where the shafts would have to be dug were in the no-man's land between the lines.

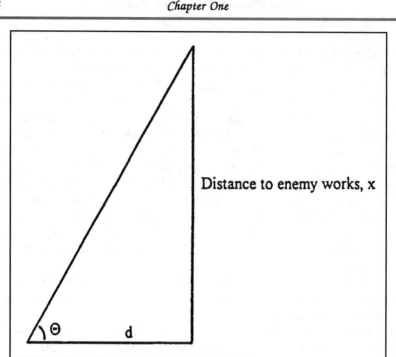

Distance to enemy works, x

Triangulation by Theodolite

By measuring the angle Θ with the theodolite and measuring the distance d, the unknown distance to the enemy works, x can be calculated from the trigonometric relation: tan Θ = x/d

Drawing by Author

It was this problem which was the main cause of the Union engineers on Meade's staff mocking the idea of the tunnel. According to Meade's chief engineer, Major James C. Duane, "such a length of mine had never been excavated in military operations, and could not be." On 6 July, Pleasants received a letter from Meade's headquarters:[17]

HEADQUARTERS ARMIES OF THE UNITED STATES
City Point, Va., July 3, 1864

(Lieut. Col. HENRY PLEASANTS)

In order to be enabled to have a clear judgment of the progress of the mining work in front of General Burnside's rifle pits, I would like to be furnished with—

I. A rough longitudinal section made after a certain scale and laid through our works neighboring the mine, the mine gallery, and through the enemy's works to be attacked by the mine. This section, with all important numbers inscribed, will show, besides the profile of our and the enemy's works, the location of the mine gallery entrance with reference to our own defense line; the arrangement of the entrance, whether by a shaft or by an inclined gallery, &c; the height of the gallery in both the places not framed and such as are supplied with frames; the length of the intended gallery; its depth under the natural horizon near the entrance and near the powder chamber, and finally the location, length, and height of the latter.

II. A profile of the gallery showing its width in framed and unframed places and the width of the powder chamber.

III. (a) When was the mining begun? (State day and hour.) (b) Has it been continued day and night without any interruption, and how many men were and are engaged on it at the same time? (c) When will the gallery be finished?

IV. What kind of soil is probably to be expected around the powder chamber?

V. What is the intended weight of the charge, and what is the expected diameter of the crater measured on its surface?

VI. By what means shall the mine be fired, supposed that it shall be fired as soon as possible and with the least loss of time?

VII. What means shall be used for tamping the mine, and at what length shall this be done?

VIII. Where shall be the stand-point of the miner firing the charge?

IX. At what time in the day shall the mine be fired?

X. What measures are premeditated by the engineer department in accordance with the commanding general to secure the possession of the crater effected by the mine and to facilitate its defense?

The questions above should be answered without delay and as shortly as possible only with reference to its numbers, *i.e.* answer to III, a, b, c, &c., IV, &c.

J.G. BARNARD
Brigadier General, Chief Engineer, U.S. Armies in the Field

For those who had given such little assistance in the enterprise and never taken the time to inspect it, the engineers seemed to be very interested in finding any possible flaws in the mine's construction. Angrily, Pleasants shot back a reply:

HDQRS. FORTY-EIGHTH PENNSYLVANIA VET. VOL. INFTY.,
Near Petersburg, Va., July 7, 1864.

Answer to question 2: The gallery or tunnel is supported by props along its whole course at a distance from each other ranging from three to thirty feet, according to the nature of the roof. When the tunnel reaches a point immediately underneath the enemy's breast works it is proposed to drive two galleries, each about 100 feet in length, whose position will be immediately underneath the enemy's fort and breastwork.

Answer to question 3: (a) At 12 m. on the 25th of June, 1864. (b) The mining has been carried on without interruption since it was begun. There are 210 men employed every twenty-four hours, but only two can mine at the extremity of the work. (c) The tunnel will reach the enemy's work in about seven or eight days.

Answer to question 4: Sandy soil.

Answers to questions 5, 6, 7, 8, 9 and 10 still under consideration. The mine is ventilated by means of an air-shaft, with a furnace to rarify the air and boxes to convey the gases from the interior of the gallery to the shaft.

HENRY PLEASANTS
Lieutenant-Colonel Forty-eighth Pennsylvania Regiment

In the last sentence of his letter, Pleasant was already anticipating the main question from Meade's engineers, a question he had answered in his typical ingenious fashion. The secret of his solution was the simple fact that warm air rises because it is less dense than cool air (or one might say that the warm air is more rarefied than the cool air), just as a cork rises through water because it is less dense than water. About a hundred feet from the tunnel entrance, just behind the Union picket line (and thus out of sight of the Confederates), Pleasants had his men dig a vertical shaft down to the tunnel. Between the position of the shaft and the tunnel entrance, the miners stretched an airtight canvas door. An eight-inch-square wooden air duct made of boards was then passed from the mine entrance, through an airtight opening in the canvas door and then along the tunnel floor to the mine face where the men were working.

On the far side of the partition from the tunnel entrance, Pleasants had his men set up a grate and build a fire. The effect of this was to turn his system into a giant air pump. As the tunnel air warmed, it rose out of the vertical shaft. This draft created a low pressure region at the mine face that was quickly filled by fresh air rushing through the ductwork protruding out of the canvas door. The solution was elegant in its simplicity.

When Potter informed Burnside of Pleasants's solution to the ventilation problem, Burnside was suitably impressed: "Good! That colonel of yours is a damned clever young man, Potter."[18]

Surprisingly, the Confederates seemed to have more faith in the whole idea than did Pleasants's superiors. Brigadier General E.

Porter Alexander had become convinced that something strange was happening near Elliot's Salient. Here, where the lines were so close together was exactly the point where Meade should be creeping up with his regular approaches. There was no sign of any activity, except for the constant sniper fire going both ways. According to Alexander, "Then suddenly a light broke in on me. They were coming, but it was not above ground...they were coming underground. They were mining us!"[19]

Excitedly running back to headquarters (so excitedly that he exposed himself and was shot in the hand), Alexander began to explain his idea to those present. A visiting reporter from the *London Times*, Francis Lawley, asked how long the tunnel would have to be. When Alexander answered that it would be in the neighborhood of five hundred feet, Lawley replied that the Confederates could not ventilate a tunnel of that length. The longest tunnel ever dug in military operations (and necessarily ventilated from the mouth of the tunnel) had been excavated by the British during siege operations in India and they had found that it was impossible to breathe once the tunnel exceeded four hundred feet. Alexander was convinced that the Federal troops contained enough clever coal miners to figure out some method of getting the tunnel to the necessary length. Lee also was concerned and ordered immediate countermeasures.

By the time Lee put the countermeasures into effect, the ventilation problem had been solved (as described earlier) and the tunnel was beneath the Confederate battery. Lee had his men begin digging vertical shafts, in order to detect or collapse the tunnel if it existed. Luckily for the Forty-eighth, all the shafts failed to hit the tunnel though two came very close on either side. Lee also placed observers in the trees on his side to search the Federal ground for evidence of fresh earth. Pleasants had his men scatter the excavated material thinly each night and then cover it with cut bushes.

According to Captain George B. Lake of the Twenty-second South Carolina, "The Federal troops had been mining for some time. We knew it and sunk a shaft on each side of the battery about 12 feet deep and then tunneled 20 feet or more to the front but the enemy's mine was under our tunnel. Our officers around the mine believed that we were going to be blown up."[20]

Lee, an experienced engineer himself, decided to check out the situation and almost lost his life doing so. Standing on the ledge of the parapet with General Gracie, both Lee and Gracie exposed their head and shoulders. An enlisted man, Smith Lipscomb of the Eighteenth South Carolina, quickly pulled both men down by their coats just before the parapet was swept by Federal rifle fire. "I thank you,

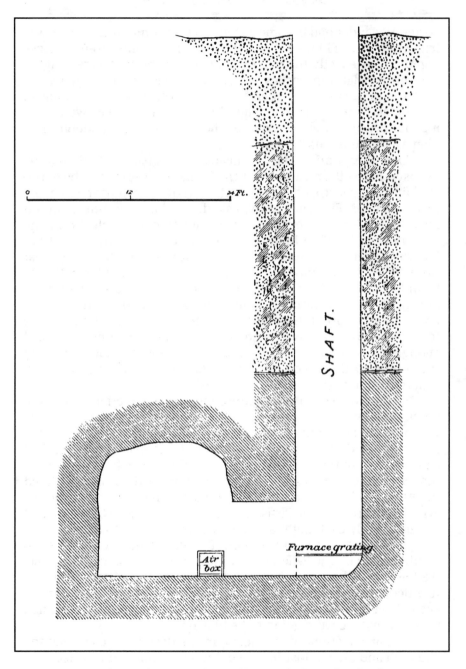

Section of the Main Gallery at the Air Shaft

sir", said Lee to Lipscomb, "I thank you."[21] In the end, though the possibility of a mine was much talked about in the Confederate lines, its presence was never detected.

Ironically, the Confederates just missed having readied the instrument they needed for detecting the mine. A private named Thomas Fowler, from the Forty-first Alabama, developed a borer that could excavate a ten-foot hole in fifteen minutes. It was not reported to his commanding officers until 3 August, a few days after the mine was sprung. And stranger still, though the Confederates complained for years after the Federal's mine exploded about the devious nature of the attack, they were apparently working on a much cruder version at the same time. It was exploded on 5 August, not far from the site of Pleasants's mine, but with very minimal damage.[22]

On 17 July, Pleasants's calculations and his men's hard work had placed the mine face directly under the Confederate battery. The end of the tunnel was about twenty-two feet below the surface of the ground and slightly more than five hundred and ten feet from the entrance. To maximize the explosive impact, Pleasants had his men dig two lateral galleries parallel to and just behind the Confederate trenches above. The gallery to the left was thirty-seven feet in length and that to the right was thirty-eight feet.[23] By 23 July this work was done and the mine was ready for its charge of powder. By Pleasants's estimate, about eighteen thousand cubic feet of material had been excavated.[24]

Eight wooden boxes, with tops open, were constructed in the lateral galleries to hold the powder. The powder was delivered to the mine entrance in twenty-five pound kegs, 320 kegs in all. Beginning at 1600 on 27 July, the kegs were carried in bags slung over the soldiers' shoulders to the galleries, and the powder dumped into the boxes. This work had to be done quickly so that a stray Confederate bullet did not ignite the powder as it lay waiting to be carried into the mine. The work also had to be done in the dark, since a lantern or torch could have spelled disaster. The wooden boxes were connected by wooden troughs filled halfway with powder, and the troughs from each side met at the end of the main tunnel. As the magazines were being filled, someone noticed that water was seeping into the lateral galleries. The loading of the charges had to be temporarily halted while wooden supports were constructed. The magazines had to be elevated to keep the powder dry. Finally, the loading was done. The total charge was about 8,000 pounds of blasting powder.

After the powder had been distributed throughout the wooden magazines, it was time to run a fuse. Meade's engineers

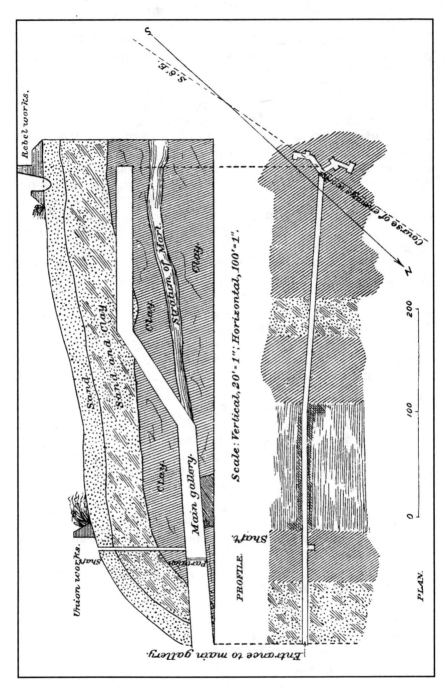

Profile and Plan of the Tunnel

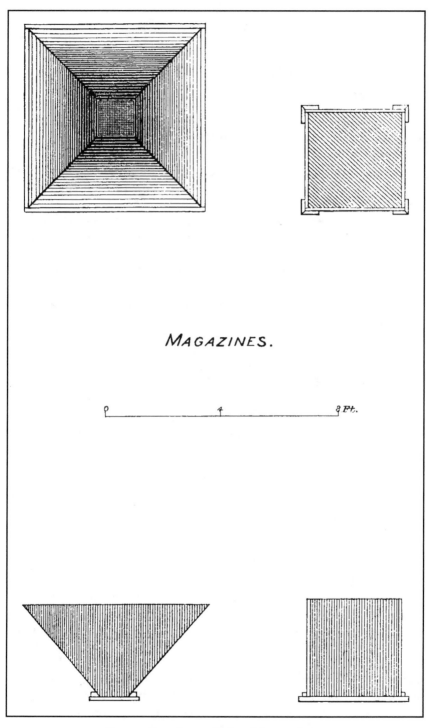

MAGAZINES.

Cross Section of the Magazines

had promised Pleasants a supply of wire and a galvanic battery (consisting of plates of two different types of metal connected in an electrically conducting solution) to detonate the powder electrically. As a backup, Pleasants wanted to also run a fuse, and requested three 500-foot sections of high-grade fuse. These promises, like the others, fell through. The wire and battery were never delivered and for fuse Pleasants was given ten-foot sections of low-grade common blasting fuse, which he spliced together to make an overall fuse 98 feet in length.[25] He wrapped the fuse in waterproof material throughout its length.

The final step in the construction of the mine was to block the far end of the main tunnel so that the explosion would be channeled upwards instead of back through the tunnel towards the Union side. One hundred and fifty men worked on the tamping, which consisted of sandbags stacked on top of each other and interspersed with logs set diagonally against the walls of the tunnel so as to be driven into the sides when the mine exploded.[26] The openings between the logs would also admit oxygen that could augment the explosion. This arrangement filled the last thirty-eight feet of the tunnel and was completed at 2300 on 28 July.

"All we need now is a match," said Pleasants.[27]

Because Burnside was worried that the Confederate countermines would detect or ruin the mine, he was able to get permission from Meade to set off the mine and attack the breach in the line as soon as possible. Meade set the time for the explosion as 0330 on 30 July.

By that hour, the trenches and covered ways were covered on the Union side with stillness and four divisions of the IX Corps ready to attack. Two additional corps were close by and the hillside behind the Union line was covered in artillery ready to pound the Confederate position and add to the mayhem.

Around 0315, Pleasants lit the fuse and crawled quickly out of the tunnel. At 0330 nothing happened. By 0400, still nothing. Pleasants, now greatly agitated, was sure of the problem. A month of backbreaking labor was going to be ruined because of cheap fuses. Sergeant Henry Reese (who had served as overall mine boss for the tunnel) courageously volunteered to go into the tunnel and check it out, not knowing whether the fuse had died out or was burning slowly for some reason. He found that the fuse had died out at the first splice and that he would need a knife and a new length of fuse to get the fuse back in order. On his way out, he met Lieutenant Jacob Douty coming in with the necessary materials. The two men relit the fuse at about 0430 and scrambled towards the tunnel entrance.

At their hillside command post behind the tunnel entrance, Grant, Meade, and even Burnside had become very agitated. The sky was getting light in the east and Grant ordered that if the explosion did not occur soon, the assault would take place anyway. Finally, at 0444 the ground began to rumble. For a brief instant the ground beneath the Confederate lines became rounded like a giant bubble and then exploded. Flame and smoke blew out of the ground, lifting up with it men and artillery and wagons and massive pieces of earth. The column reached hundreds of feet in the air, spreading out like a mushroom and raining down guns, stones, dirt, and human limbs all around.

Where a minute before Elliot's Salient had stood, there was now a massive hole in the earth, almost two hundred feet long, sixty to eighty feet wide and about thirty feet deep. Two hundred and seventy-eight Confederates had been killed or buried alive in the explosion and the screams of the wounded could now be heard. As the dust began to clear, the first Union soldiers on the scene were transfixed by the spectacle of the Crater, surrounded by chunks of earth as big as a house. Pleasants's "impossible" idea had opened up the Confederate lines with a gap big enough to drive a division through. Potter grabbed Pleasants's hand: "Colonel, you did it! You did it! It's perfect!"

Unfortunately for the Union, the great opportunity provided by the explosion was to go largely unexploited. The ultimate failure of the mine can be traced to politics and incompetence of the Union command. First, there was a controversial decision regarding which troops would lead the way into the breach caused by the explosion. Burnside logically had the freshest of his four divisions specially trained for the mission. The political problem was that the enlisted men in this division were all black. Meade objected to Burnside's plan, pointing out that if the attack was a disaster there would be an outcry across the North that the black troops had been led to the slaughter.

This meant that shortly before the day of the attack Burnside had to tap one of his other divisions to lead the charge. Inexplicably, Burnside allowed the choice to come down to drawing lots and the winner was the weakest of his divisions under the worst of his brigadiers, James Ledlie.

When the explosion occurred, and the time came for the charge it became obvious that somewhere in the command chain a crucial order had been lost. No one had made provision for getting the men over the parapet of the eight-foot high trench.[28] As orders came to advance, men furiously stacked sandbags or jabbed rifles into the trench wall to form makeshift ladders. What should have been a great wave of men became a disorganized trickle. As the men got to

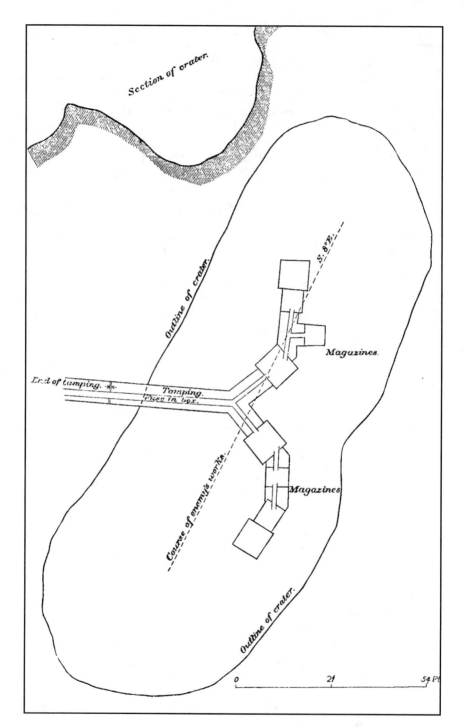

Section of crater.

Outline of crater.

S. 8°E.

Magazines.

End of tamping. Tamping. Fuse in box.

Course of enemy's works.

Magazines

Outline of crater.

0   21   54 Ft.

Overhead View of the Magazine Chamber

Official Records

the site of the explosion, most of them wandered aimlessly down into the smoking chasm, transfixed in awe by the magnificence of the Crater. The attack had become chaos. General Ledlie, who should have been commanding on the spot, was lying drunk in a shelter four hundred yards behind the Union lines.

As the other three Union divisions (including the black troops) streamed into the Crater and adjoining trenches, the Confederates were rushing in reinforcements and they were mad. The treachery of an underground attack was bad enough, but the sight of black troops seemed to fill the Southern troops with fury. What followed proved to be some of the most vicious fighting of the war. As the Union troops huddled in the Crater, they began to catch death from all sides. Confederate mortar fire rained down into the Crater and it was almost literally like shooting fish in a barrel. Confederate infantry jabbed bayonets over the rim of the Crater and fired into the blue troops from a range of only a few feet. Those who tried to flee back to the safety of the Union lines were mowed down. As the sun rose higher in the sky, the Crater and its surroundings began to appear as Hell raised to the Earth's surface.

Finally, a little after 1300 it was all over. Those who could make it back to the Union lines did, and the others died in the Crater or were carted off to Confederate prison camps. In the end, the ingenuity and hard work of the Forty-eighth Pennsylvania would not open the door that would end the war. In the words of Grant, after watching the debacle, "It was the saddest affair I have witnessed in the war. Such an opportunity for carrying fortifications I have never seen and do not expect again to have."

View of the Crater (1865)

Henry Pleasants

Inferno at Petersburg

Henry Pleasants

Henry Pleasants was born on 16 February 1833, in Buenos Aires, Argentina. His father had moved to Argentina to assist in the overthrow of a cruel dictator and assist in setting up a democracy. His mother was the daughter of a Spanish nobleman.

After his father died in 1846, Henry (who spoke only Spanish at the time) was sent to live with an uncle in Philadelphia. He learned English quickly enough to perform adequately in school. He was a shy child, but had a fiery temper that bespoke his Spanish ancestry.

Though he had shown little prowess in mathematics in school, Henry quickly became adept at engineering after his uncle helped him get a job with the Pennsylvania Railroad. By 1853, he had become senior assistant engineer of the railroad, and gained fame for his work on the forty-two hundred-foot long Sand Patch Tunnel through the Allegheny Mountains. When a favorite superior was dismissed from his position, Pleasants also quit, believing that his friend had been let go unjustly. He soon found work as a mining engineer in Pottsville, where he prospered and married.

Then tragedy struck. His wife, now pregnant, died unexpectedly and Pleasants become disconsolate, unable to function in his duties or everyday life. It was just at this time that the Civil War began and Pleasants joined up, if for no other reason (as he divulged years later) than that he might be killed in action.

But Pieasant seemed meant to live. He thrived in the harsh world of the war and rose to lieutenant colonel. He was well respected by those who served under him and those who commanded him, both for his military skills and discipline and for his engineering expertise. He and his regiment were commended for their conduct from 1861 to the end, especially for their work on the Petersburg mine. Pleasants himself mustered out of the service on 18 December 1864 and went back to Pottsville, eventually becoming the chief engineer of the Philadelphia and Reading Coal and Iron Company. He married and had three children. After a successful and happy postbellum life, he died of a brain tumor on 26 March 1880 at the age of forty-seven.

Chapter 2

Joseph Bailey: The Red River Dams

On War, the classic military text written by the Prussian general and military theorist Karl von Clausewitz in the 1820s, was well known in U.S. military circles at the time of the Civil War. The book was and is best known for one of its central concepts: "War is the continuation of politics by other means." All wars have political motivations, but rarely has a military operation had such blatant political overtones as the Union excursion up the Red River in the spring of 1864. Partially as a result of these political pressures, the Union leadership made some serious errors in judgment during the campaign, errors that nearly left a major part of a Federal gunboat fleet stranded. Just as with Henry Pleasants at Petersburg, Union hopes on the Red River ended up depending on the technical genius of a soldier in the ranks.

Though most of the significant military action during the first three years of the war took place in the mid-Atlantic corridor or along the Mississippi River, another region of the country remained of equal strategic importance in the minds of many in the Union command. Texas, and especially eastern Texas, was a prize worth winning for several reasons.

The most important reason was cotton. Mill operators in New England had their eyes on Texas as a source of cotton even before the war began. The idea of settling Texas with free men from New England became something of an obsession in Northern newspapers and political circles in the late 1850s. Part of the idea lay in simple economic need and part of it was philosophical. If Texas was settled by Northern free labor, so the reasoning went, the production of cotton there would be so efficient that the other states in the South would be forced to give up slavery to compete. In the words of one advocate, "The law of competition is inexorable."[1]

As the war began and turned from a short, sound whipping of the rebels to a real drawn-out conflict, the thinking in New England began to be predominated by economic survival. Textile mills needed cotton to operate, and with only small parts of the South in Union control the spindles began to slow and stop. By June 1862, only 25 percent of the available spindles in the Northeast were in operation.[2] Cotton was needed and soon. The only other significant producer of cotton outside of the Confederate states was India, but England was hoarding the cotton produced there. It appeared that the only realistic chance of obtaining large sources and supplies of cotton lay in the conquest of Texas.

Keeping Northern hands off the Texas cotton fields was of extreme importance to the Confederate cause. Not only would this hurt the North economically, but it would be of great help to the South. Cotton could be traded with European nations for arms, medicine, and food. It could also be used as a bargaining chip to persuade England, France or both to enter the war on the Confederate side.

By the early autumn of 1862, President Abraham Lincoln was feeling intense pressure from political heavyweights in New England and powerful figures in his cabinet (Postmaster General Montgomery Blair, Secretary of the Treasury Salmon Chase, and Secretary of State William Seward) to mount some sort of expedition into Texas. The problem was that Lincoln regarded the opening of the Mississippi River as a far more important military and economic objective in the West.

By mid-October, Lincoln had tentatively decided to try both operations simultaneously. Forces under Major General John A. McClernand, formerly an Illinois politician, would attempt to clear the Mississippi to New Orleans. Another force, recruited in New England and led by Major General Nathaniel P. Banks, would open up Texas. Banks was an ambitious career politician from Massachusetts, a former speaker of the house and governor, whose military experience had not been noteworthy. He had been soundly defeated the previous year by Confederate Major General Thomas J. "Stonewall" Jackson at Winchester and then beaten by Jackson again (though more credibly) at Cedar Mountain.

By early November, Lincoln had altered his plan. Political unrest in the northwestern states (including Democratic victories in the Republican Lincoln's home state of Illinois) had made him revert again to seeing the Mississippi as having paramount importance. As Banks and his men set to sea on 4 December, few aboard knew that their real objective had been changed to control of the lower Mississippi River. Many of the soldiers had volunteered in order to stake their claims in the fields of Texas, planning to call for their families as soon as they were settled. When the ships began to move up the Mississippi on 14 December, excitement among the men turned to disillusionment and anger. Their specific objective was now to be the river stronghold Port Hudson, Louisiana.

Perhaps to assuage the anger of his men and the angry politicians of the Northeast (including the newly appointed Northern "governor of Texas" Alexander Hamilton, who had accompanied Banks), Banks sent a Massachusetts regiment, along with cavalry and artillery detachments, to take and hold the Texas port of Galveston. If nothing else, Governor Hamilton would then have a piece of the Lone Star state on which to plant his flag.

The expedition was a disaster. After landing and establishing a beachhead barricade on 24 December with three advance companies, the Union forces found themselves under attack. On 31 December, about five hundred Confederates under Major General John Magruder attacked the barricade on land, and the five Union gunboats came under attack as well. The Confederate naval attack was made in ironic fashion, in light of the ultimate reasons for Union forces occupying Texas. Down the Buffalo Bayou and into the harbor came two Mississippi steamboats, padded from bow to stern in bales of cotton. These "cotton-clads" promptly captured one of the Union gunboats, forced the destruction of another, and drove the other three off. The three advance companies on the beach, now lacking the big guns on the boats for support, surrendered immediately. The Union occupation had lasted less than a week.

Banks now needed to turn his full attention to helping rid the Mississippi River of Confederates, a task that the Union forces found far more arduous than expected. As newspapers and politicians from the Northeast continued to hammer Lincoln for his failure to secure Texas cotton, Banks began to move upriver from New Orleans while other forces (now under Major General Ulysses S. Grant) moved south. Both forces got stuck trying to pry open Confederate strongholds perched on bluffs high above the river: Grant at Vicksburg, Mississippi and Banks at Port Hudson. By the time the weary and hungry Southern defenders finally hoisted the white flag of surrender, 1863 was more than half gone (Vicksburg was taken on 4 July, and Port Hudson's defenders surrendered four days later).

Finally, Banks could focus on Texas. The government in Washington was even more anxious than before to have Banks make progress in the Lone Star state. French forces had invaded Mexico and rumors were rampant regarding French aid to the Confederacy or even French annexation of Texas, Louisiana, and Arizona. In addition to that threat, large amounts of arms were being delivered by foreign ships just across the Mexican border and then brought across the Rio Grande into the Confederacy. Three reasons (cotton, the French, and the arms traffic) now compelled the North to take Texas or at least establish a presence there.

Lincoln's chief military advisor, Major General Henry Halleck, ordered Banks to move against Texas and suggested that Banks attack by way of the Red River. Banks protested for several reasons. He now believed that his forces would be better suited toward a move in the direction of Mobile, Alabama, in conjunction with other Union forces then preparing to move towards Atlanta and Charleston. To Banks, this option was not only superior in a military sense but in a political sense. Furthermore, moving against Texas via the Red River was sure to be an extremely hard task through a wretched landscape filled with poisonous snakes and scorpions. The barren country had no water in the summer and fall, and plenty of water but no roads in the winter and spring. For a man like Banks, who harbored presidential aspirations, military failure would mean the end of his dream of one day living in the White House.

When pressure from Halleck made it obvious that he was going to have to achieve a foothold in Texas, Banks decided to try a route that had more likelihood of success. Specifically, he planned to work his way down the Texas coast to Galveston and then move inland towards Houston. He was thus going to ignore Halleck's Red River suggestion. Throughout the war, Halleck often showed a propensity to suggest a plan rather than order it. This left him open for glory if the plan succeeded and left him a way out if the plan failed or if his subordinate chose another plan.

Banks issued his orders and five thousand men on twenty-two transports, escorted by four gunboats, arrived at Sabine Pass at the mouth of the Sabine River on 7 September 1863.[3] Waiting for the flotilla was a company of forty-seven Texans in Fort Griffin. On 8 September, the four Union gunboats approached the fort and came under heavy and accurate fire. Before long, two of the boats had been shot up and surrendered and the other two retreated back out of the bay. Major General William B. Franklin, in charge of the expedition, decided to head back to New Orleans rather than risk sending his men under such fire.

The next amphibious approach by Banks proved more successful, but still accomplished little. On 2 November, Federal troops landed at the mouth of the Rio Grande and planted the flag. The gain was merely symbolic, as wagons laden with cotton and guns merely made their exchanges further upstream. During the rest of the month, Union troops established beachheads on a few other barren sand dunes up and down the Gulf coast.

Halleck, however, was not impressed. He maintained that the best base of operations against Texas was in northern Texas, up the Red River. Halleck and Banks argued their relative positions by correspondence through the early winter. Finally, by late January, Banks had been persuaded to Halleck's position.[4] The reversal by Banks was not purely due to military arguments. Banks had received information that along the upper Red River there were thousands of bales of stored cotton, and several greedy Confederate officers who would, for a certain fee, arrange to make sure the bales were not burned when the Union forces approached.

These bales of cotton were too much of a lure for Banks to resist. Securing them would be a major coup, sure to put him in good stead with voters and political heavyweights in the Northeast. Moreover, someone was going to make large amounts of money with the cotton. Cotton had become one of the most valuable commodities in the country, with illicit trade across military lines and fortunes being made overnight. The vast quantities on the Red River would make someone wealthy, and it was up to Banks to see that the funds (the cotton was reputed to be worth more than one hundred million dollars in gold) got into the U.S. treasury.

Banks was to be given solid support for his expedition. Two veteran corps from Major General William T. Sherman's Army of the Tennessee (under the command of Brigadier General Andrew J. Smith) were to assist, as well as a powerful squadron of armored boats (clad in iron or tin) under Rear Admiral David D. Porter. The overall naval fleet consisted of sixty vessels (twenty-one of them transports for Sherman's men), mounting 210 guns. In addition, fifteen thousand men under Major General Frederick Steele would approach the Red River from Arkansas. In all, more than forty-five thousand Federal troops were to descend on the Red River and its cotton. A. J. Smith's men were to come up the river to Alexandria, where they would join up with Banks's troops, who would travel overland to that point.

The Confederate forces facing them were spread out and badly outnumbered. In overall command was the capable General Edmund Kirby Smith. Smith ordered forces under Major General Sterling Price to head off Steele and those under Major General Richard Taylor to hinder the movement up the Red River.

On 12 March, an infantry assault combined with the power of Porter's guns gave the Federals an easy victory over a small force of Confederates holding Fort De Russy, not far from the point where the Red River enters the Mississippi. The next objective was Alexandria, about thirty miles upriver. The fleet reached Alexandria on 15 March. Several days later, Banks had his forces there, also. The

Confederates promptly retreated to Natchitoches, forty miles farther up the river.

Banks was not yet able to take advantage of the opening. Just above Alexandria lay a set of rapids, passable only at certain times of the year. The depth of the Red River was very sensitive to precipitation received in the dry country to the north. With the coming of winter, the river normally began to rise, reaching an annual peak in the spring. This year the rise was not occurring, or was occurring to a very small extent. As a result, the water over the rapids was found to be too shallow to pass Porter's ironclads. Porter felt that even if he could somehow manhandle his boats up over the rapids, it would take a miracle to get them back down without destroying them on the rocks.

Pressured by Banks and the War Department, Porter decided to give the thing a try. In addition, Porter also had his eye on the cotton and the glory associated with its acquisition. At Alexandria, before the arrival of Banks's troops, his men had been furiously heading into the countryside and scavenging, in the name of the navy, any cotton they could find. There were certain to be larger "appropriations" upriver. After three days of struggling with heavy ropes, Porter and his men got his heaviest ironclad over the rapids. Shortly after, twelve more gunboats and the transports carrying A. J. Smith's men made it through and began the trip upstream. The rest of the fleet was left below the rapids to protect lines of supply and communication. Banks's men rode and walked up the trails following the river.

On 1 April, the expedition reached Natchitoches only to find that Taylor's men had abandoned the place and retreated again. It appeared that Kirby Smith was going to concentrate his forces at Shreveport. Banks now had to move quickly. He had received a telegram from Grant informing him that if it looked by 15 April that the capture of Shreveport was not imminent, he must return Smith's men for the spring operations in the Southeast. At Grand Ecore (just above Natchitoches), the stage road Banks's men had been following veered to the west before heading north to Shreveport. Was there a quicker way to Shreveport than the stage road? Another road on the east side of the river led to Minden and then southwest to Shreveport, but was much a longer route than the one Banks was already on. Unknown to Banks, the best choice was a small country road that paralleled the river on the west side. Not having the luxury of time to scout around, Banks stayed on the stage road and was forced to move away from the supply-laden boats and Porter's large guns. The small river road was not only a quicker path to Shreveport, but had ample forage. As it turned out, Banks had to accompany his

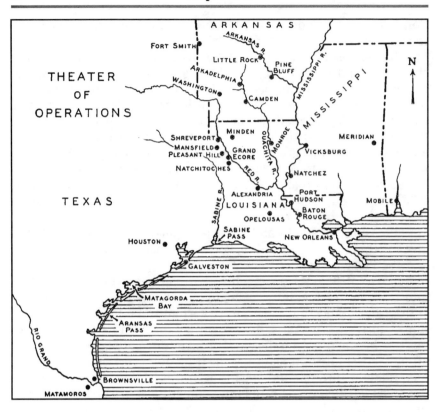

Red River Campaign: Theater of Operations

Red River Campaign: Politics and Cotton in the Civil War

troops with a monstrous supply train of more than one thousand wagons, struggling across bad roads in dry, desolate country.

The decision to move away from the river was the beginning of the end of the Red River expedition, for another important piece of information had eluded Banks. Taylor had had enough of retreating. On 8 April, Taylor's men surprised the Union troops by making a stand at Sabine Crossroads, just southeast of Mansfield. Shortly after 1600, Taylor ordered an assault. Initially, the Federals put up a strong defense, tearing holes in the Confederate lines. Taylor, however, had held a large reserve force back. Ordering them in just as all seemed lost, the Confederates suddenly turned the Union flank. Banks's men began to retreat and then, as Taylor's attack became more furious, to flee in a rout, tossing guns and equipment on the roadside. By the time the Union troops had regrouped and pushed back the now disorganized and exhausted Confederates, they were at Pleasant Grove, two miles away. Banks had lost twenty-two hundred men, twenty guns and more than two thousand supply wagons. During the night, Banks and his men retreated fourteen miles to Pleasant Hill, where they could find water and wait for Smith's men (who had left Grand Ecore a day later than Banks's troops) to reach him.

But Taylor was not resting. Marching through the night, early on 9 April his troops attacked the combined forces of Banks and Smith at Pleasant Hill. Now reinforced by Price's men (Kirby Smith had decide to concentrate on Banks and then turn later on Steele's descent from the north), Taylor displayed the strategic skills he had learned from Stonewall Jackson in the Shenandoah Valley, attacking simultaneously in the center and on both flanks. For awhile it appeared that the whole Federal force would collapse, but A. J. Smith's hardened veterans managed to outflank the Confederates, and suddenly the rout was headed the other way. The Federals, who had lost another fourteen hundred men, did not pursue.

It was time for Banks to give up his dreams of glory. His army had been shot to pieces by a smaller force; Sherman was demanding the return of Smith's troops; and Porter was anxious to get off the Red River before it got any shallower. By 11 April, Banks had his men back at Grand Ecore. Porter, who had been headed up the river for a planned rendezvous with the infantry closer to Shreveport, arrived back at Grand Ecore on 15 April. The trip back down the river had been tough, the water level now falling fast and Confederate snipers constantly harassing the boats and sailors.

Figuring that Banks had had enough, Kirby Smith now decided to turn most of his attention to Steele in Arkansas, and left Taylor with only about five thousand men to harass Banks's retreat. Harass he did, constantly pestering the Union forces on the water and on land as they began to move back towards Alexandria on 21 April. The bitter Union troops began to plunder and put the torch to every building they passed. This destruction of his native state greatly angered Taylor, who decided once more to attack (though now outnumbered five to one) at Monett's Ferry. The battle on 23 April ended in a draw, but Taylor continued his relentless pursuit. By the end of April, Banks had his men in Alexandria, where they were encircled by Taylor's troops.

Porter continued to move downstream, and with great difficulty. The waters were full of alligators and submerged stumps, and were growing shallower by the day. After being run aground in six feet of water, his largest and most powerful ironclad, the *Eastport*, had to be blown up to prevent its capture by the Confederates.[5] Two transports were sunk and the rest of his fleet had been badly shot up by the time they reached Alexandria. But Porter's real troubles were just beginning. The rapids above Alexandria were now far too shallow to pass his boats.

At least seven feet of water was required to get some of the boats over the rapids, and in some places the water was now only three or four inches deep. The Federals had a true predicament. The loss of most of the Mississippi river fleet to the Confederates would be both a military disaster and a humiliation. However, the Union could also not afford to keep such a large body of experienced infantry stuck at Alexandria and even if they could, forage for the horses and food for the men were sure to run out soon. Unless the river rose, which apparently it was not going to do in 1864, there appeared to be no way out other than to lose the boats. The river had also failed to rise in 1855 and in 1846, and the nine-year intervals made 1864 look to be part of a pattern which could wreck the western navy. Porter had long said that he could take his boats "wherever the sand is damp," and it appeared he would now have a chance to make good on his boast.

The rapids at Alexandria had been a navigation hazard for many years. The rapids were formed by two limestone reefs consisting of a mixture of sandstone, limestone, and clay and situated about a mile and a quarter apart.[6] Throughout the 1800s, there had often been talk of cutting channels through the reefs to make the passage safer and to provide more efficient transportation for the ever more important cotton crop upstream. No significant improvements had been made by 1864, however, and the rapids remained passable only for a short time during the spring rise. During the rest of the year, cargo had to be unloaded off one boat and carried around the rapids to a second boat in order to get to the Mississippi. The total drop over the passage was thirteen feet: seven feet at the upper rapids and six feet at the lower rapids.

A boat, or any object floating in water, can be said to "draw" a certain depth of water. Another way of stating this is that the boat has a "draft" of this amount of water. An object floats in water because of a balance between two forces, its own weight and the upward buoyant force created when water is pushed out of the way (this upward buoyant force is the same type of force responsible for lifting the warmer air out of Henry Pleasants's mine described in Chapter 1). The more water is pushed out of the way, the larger the buoyant force. Hence, a light boat has a shallow draft because it does not need to displace much water to balance its weight. A heavy boat sits lower in the water because it needs to push more water out of the way to balance its weight. Two boats of the same weight may have different drafts depending on how broad their bottom surface is. A boat with a broader bottom can displace more water without sinking to as low a depth as that required by a boat with a narrower bottom.

The gunboats stuck above the rapids were as a group, the finest military vessels in the west: the wooden *Lexington*, the tinclad *Fort Hindman*, and ironclads *Osage, Neosho, Mound City, Louisville, Pittsburg, Chillicothe, Carondelet*, and *Ozark*.[7] The lighter *Lexington* and *Fort Hindman* would have the smallest drafts, followed by the broad bottom ironclads *Osage* and *Neosho*. The drafts of the other ironclads were estimated by Porter to be: *Chillicothe*—five feet; *Ozark*—six feet; *Carondelet*—six feet, one inch; *Louisville, Mound City* and *Pittsburg*—six feet, six inches.[8] The problem faced by the navy was that the water over the rapids was shallower than the drafts of the boats. Through the jagged exposed rocks coming in from each shore, there snaked a channel through each set of rapids, shallow channels about twenty feet wide.

Just when all seemed lost, a solution was proposed. Strangely enough, the proposal came from a member of the army, not the navy. His name was Joseph Bailey, a lieutenant colonel from the Fourth Wisconsin Infantry and acting chief engineer of the XIX Corps. Bailey proposed raising the river to a depth that exceeded the drafts of the boats. Specifically, he proposed building a series of dams across the Red River to raise the water level.

Bailey had been thinking of such a scheme for several weeks. After the capture of Port Hudson, Bailey had used wing dams to float and release the Confederate transports *Starlight* and *Red Chief* from where they had been scuttled in a shallow creek, and he now wanted to try rescuing the fleet in the same way.[9] In these very different conditions, it would seem to be much more difficult, however. As Porter himself said later, "Under the best circumstances a private company would not have completed this work under one year, and to an ordinary mind the whole thing would have appeared an utter impossibility."

But Bailey's was not an ordinary mind. He was convinced that what he had planned could be done. A former lumberman, he had used these sorts of techniques many times to get logs down the Wisconsin waterways.[10] "I wish I was as sure of heaven as I am that I can save the fleet," said Bailey.[11] Captain John C. Palfrey made a careful survey of the rapids, and pronounced the idea practicable.[12] Bailey's superior, Major General William B. Franklin, a former engineer, saw the idea's merits, and convinced Banks. Banks took the proposal to the despondent Porter, who agreed, especially when Banks told him that the Army (who had gotten the fleet into this mess) would do all the work.

The site of the lower rapids, closest to Alexandria, was where Bailey planned to build his dams. The river here was a little more

The U.S.S. *Osage*

Photographic History of the Civil War

The U.S.S. *Louisville*

Photographic History of the Civil War

The U.S.S. *Pittsburg*

Photographic History of the Civil War

The Gunboat U.S.S. *Signal* Towing Materials for the Dam

Photographic History of the Civil War

than seven hundred and fifty feet wide. Bailey planned to build two wing dams, each about three hundred feet long, and one projecting from each shore. On the north bank, where large oak, pine, and elm trees were abundant, the wing dam would be made of large trees laid with their tops toward the current, their butt-ends held with logs laid perpendicular to the trees and interspersed among them, and with their branches interlocked and filled with chunks of limestone cut from the shore (this type of dam was usually called a rafter dam). For this work, Bailey had at his disposal a regiment of lumberjacks and loggers from Maine (the Twenty-ninth Maine).

On the south side of the river, the fields were cultivated and trees were scarce. Here Bailey proposed a different sort of dam. Huge "cribs" were to be constructed of logs and scavenged timbers, filled with a foundation layer of brush and then with all sorts of heavy items—stones from the river, bricks and stones acquired by demolishing nearby buildings, and machinery from neighboring sugar-houses and cotton gins. The cribs were probably fabricated on shore (where blacksmiths could make bolts to hold them together) and then floated into position with the help of steamers before being filled. The scavenging and construction on this side were done mostly by three New York regiments, the 116th, 161st, and the 133rd. The men on both sides worked, beginning on 1 May, in the hot sun during the day, by bonfires at night, and often up to their necks in the filthy water, with decomposing horse, mule, and human bodies floating by.[13] While this was going on, teams of wagons and flatboats were busy delivering the necessary materials. In all, Bailey had about three thousand men and up to three hundred wagons at his disposal.[14]

Bailey had much experience with both types of dams from his Wisconsin lumbering days, and he found a colleague (with almost as much experience) to help. Lieutenant Colonel Uri B. Pearsall, in charge of the Ninety-seventh Colored Infantry, was also a veteran dam builder. Pearsall supervised most of the work on the crib dams while Bailey (who rarely slept during this time and drove his men ruthlessly) looked over the tree dam coming in from the opposite shore.[15]

As the work progressed through the first week of May, the water slowly started to rise. Many aboard the boats and on shore had joked derisively about the project, but as the dams took shape, the jokes turned to admiration. "Before God, what won't the Yankees do next!" said one awe-struck contraband on the shore.[16]

Between the wing dams, Bailey had four naval coal barges scuttled to hurry along the rising of the water at the lower falls. The 24-foot by 170-foot barges were placed lengthwise parallel to the current and joined by long timbers so that they filled most of the

Union Soldiers Building One of Bailey's Dams

Another View of One of Bailey's Dams

space between the two wing dams, with gaps about twenty feet wide between them. The barges were loaded with sand, bricks, and iron rails and then held in place by wooden braces and long thick ropes from the shore.[17] The barge second in from the tree dam was loaded much more lightly than the other three.

Bailey's plan was to impound enough water so that Porter's boats could pass the upper falls. Once all the boats were over the upper falls, the lead gunboat would ram the lightly loaded barge out of the way and the boats could then ride the current over the second set of rapids.[18]

On 8 May, the three gunboats with shallowest drafts (*Fort Hindman, Osage,* and *Neosho*) were able to make it over the upper falls, and come to rest just above the dam. The others waited above the upper falls for the water to continue rising. That at least a few others did not cross at this time seems to be a product of Porter's lack of confidence in the project, which filtered down to the sailors lounging on the deck. When the naval men saw the first three boats actually cross the upper falls to the deeper water behind the dam, they seemed to realize that this thing could work after all.

To reduce the drafts of his vessels as much as possible, Porter ordered everything of great weight taken off. This included ammunition, guns, armor plating and, of course, bales of confiscated cotton. Most of this material was portaged by wagons to the lower side of the dam, but some of the armor and some of the guns were too heavy to cross several bridges spanning side streams entering the Red River.[19] The heavy guns were destroyed and the armor plating was dumped in a thirty-foot deep hole upstream to keep it out of Confederate hands. The now denuded ships were painted black in hopes of fooling the Confederates should the ships be able to continue downstream.[20] By reducing the weight of his ships, Porter was able to reduce their drafts by about a foot.[21]

But now, with three ships between the upper falls and the dam, and the rest still above the upper falls, Bailey's success began to work against him. At greater depths, water exerts more pressure and this extra pressure began to cause the dam to strain. In addition, when water is forced through a narrower channel, it picks up speed. This extra water velocity started to wear away at the edges of the barges where the gaps were. Banks and Bailey began to worry that the whole dam might be swept downriver before the depth would be sufficient to carry the rest of the boats over the upper falls and the whole fleet through the dam. Banks sent two urgent notes to Porter.[22] First, shortly after midnight,

The Union Fleet above the Falls in the Red River

HEADQUARTERS DEPARTMENT OF THE GULF
Alexandria, La., May 9, 1864—1 a.m.

Admiral PORTER:

Colonel Bailey informs me that the water has risen upon the dam 2 feet since sundown, and is still rising. It is impossible to say how long the dam may stand the effects of a continued rise. The pressure is terrific. The boats of the fleet ought to be put in readiness at once to take advantage of the high water. I have been up to the fleet this morning, and found everything so quiet and still that I feared that there might be unnecessary delay in the movements in the morning and I ask your attention to it.

N.P. BANKS
Major-General, Commanding

and then,

HEADQUARTERS DEPARTMENT OF THE GULF
Alexandria, La., May 9, 1864

Admiral PORTER:

Colonel Bailey informs me that the river is within 6 inches of its height of last evening, and is rising. There is a space of 20 feet or more between the tree-dam and the barge, which, when filled, will raise the water from 6 to 10 inches, giving, we think, sufficient depth for the passage of the boats. Every exertion ought to be made to get them ready to-night, so that they may pass the falls to-morrow. I regret to say that our forage is so reduced that it will be impossible for us to remain here without periling the safety of the animals attached to the trains and the artillery. We have exhausted the country, and with the march that is before us it will be perilous to remain more than another day. Colonel Bailey thinks that the water can be raised to the greatest height which it will attain any hour when the gun-boats may be ready for their passage. He does not want to accumulate the water until then, because a continued pressure is more dangerous to the safety of the dam than that of the weight of the water alone. I hope every exertion will be made to get the boats in readiness for passage to-morrow. Lieutenant Beebe informs me that his arrangements are complete for the removal of the heavy guns to the bridge and below as soon as they are placed on shore. The detail of teams has been changed, so that they will continue to work during the night.

N.P. BANKS
Major-General, Commanding

Union Fleet Coming through the Dam

The dam withheld the strain of the rushing water through the night but then, at around 0530 on 9 May, the pressure drove out the lightly loaded barge and the one between it and the tree dam. The barges then swung around against some rocks on the left, opening up an unfilled gap of sixty-six feet in the river. As the pressure was relieved, the accumulated water surged through the widened opening.

Porter had not taken the urgency of Banks's warnings during the night to heart. The boats above the upper falls were still unready for motion, with the exception of the timberclad *Lexington*. Finally realizing that his last hope for salvaging the fleet might be rushing away before his eyes, Porter, who had been down river observing the dam when it failed, jumped on a horse and rushed to the upper falls. If nothing else, he thought he might be able to save the *Lexington* and the three boats sitting in front of the dam before the water level decreased too far. He ordered the *Lexington* to make a run for it, over the upper falls and through the gap in the dam.

As the upper falls became shallower by the minute, the *Lexington* got under power and just scraped over the rapids. The captain then headed for the opening in the dam, fighting for control in the furious water. With a full head of steam, with thousands of soldiers lining the banks watching anxiously, she headed for the gap. In Porter's words: "She entered the gap with a full head of steam on, pitched down the roaring torrent, made two or three spasmodic rolls, hung for a moment on the rocks below, was then swept into deep water by the current and rounded to, safely into the bank. Thirty thousand voices rose in one deafening cheer..."[23]

Heartened by the *Lexington's* success, the *Neosho* was next to try the gap. Her captain called (against Porter's orders) for the steam engine to be stopped just as the boat neared the gap, a move that nearly cost him his ship. With a slower speed than the *Lexington*, the *Neosho* knocked hard off the rocks as she went over the lower falls almost vertically, her hull disappearing below the foam. A hole was knocked in the bottom, but the relentless current carried the *Neosho* too into the deeper waters below the dam. The hole was fixed within the hour.

Learning from the experiences of their comrades, the *Fort Hindman* and *Osage* came through without much trouble just as the water was getting too low for any further passage. Now four gunboats were safe, but six remained above the now exposed rocks of the upper falls.

Instead of feeling dejection and exasperation at the loss of much of their work, Bailey and his men felt confidence and pride in what they had done and felt determined to use their skills to save the rest of the fleet. And the collapse of the dam was not necessarily a disaster to Bailey's mind. The two barges that had been spun around produced a nice cushion against the rocks on the left side of the lower chute. Also, the sixty-six foot gap produced a much more manageable velocity of water than had the narrower gap, though with a reduced depth of water. What he would do is quickly erect another series of auxiliary dams at the upper falls. These dams would help raise the level of the water, but without the need for such a narrow gap that a dangerously high velocity of water would be produced.

On the south side of the upper rapids, he and his men constructed another stone crib dam and on the north side another tree dam. With renewed vigor of success and experience from the lower dam, the men worked quickly. By early afternoon on 10 May, the *Chillicothe* was able to barely scrape over the upper falls. At 1500, the *Carondelet* gave it a try and found that the water was still too shallow. It became wedged into the crooked channel with its bow close to the tree dam and its stern diagonally downstream. Surprisingly, before the *Carondelet* was freed, the *Mound City* was ordered to make its run and quickly became stuck next to the *Carondelet*, blocking the channel.

During this time, Banks's despair regarding the survival of his troops and horses continued to mount. Porter, however, having saved four of his boats, was now placing all his confidence and energy behind Bailey. After a note from Banks on 11 May which seemed to indicate that the Army was going to have to leave and also that those on board the ships were not matching the Army troops in terms of their exertions, Porter responded with a letter of his own which attempted to assuage Banks and assure him that they were all going to get out of this thing all right in the next two days. For military and political reasons, the fleet must be saved. According to Porter, "I hope, sir, you will not let anything divert you from the attempt to get these vessels all through safely, even if we have to stay here and eat mule meat."[24]

But mule meat was not to be on the menu, as Bailey and Pearsall were equal to the task before them. After the *Mound City* became stuck, Pearsall suggested the construction of another dam just below the rapids. This dam, constructed during the night of 10 May, was of a third type called a bracket dam. Two-legged trestles made out of logs were constructed using half-inch bolts. These trestles, which looked something like a sawhorse, had bolts driven partially into their bottom pieces. The whole arrangement was then pushed down onto the river bottom so that the bolts stuck into the soft

Sketch of the Gunboats Passing through the Dam

rock, and held the trestle in place. The trestles were then sheathed with planking.

The bracket dam was completed by 1000 on 11 May and by 1100 the water had risen another foot.[25] This was still not quite enough to free the two boats in the channel, but with the help of more lines from ashore, a winch (commonly called a windlass) on the *Chillicothe*, and the force of the water behind them, both boats were freed. The *Pittsburg* then followed more easily. Nature finally seemed to be cooperating with the Navy, also, as the river was finally starting to rise slightly from natural causes, most likely the backwater from the swollen Mississippi, one hundred and fifty miles distant.

The next day the *Pittsburg* and *Mound City* were positioned just below the wing dams in order to serve as auxiliary dams and also to use their wheels to throw more water on the rocks. The *Ozark* and *Louisville* succeeded in passing the upper falls with little trouble. The *Mound City* was the first to run the lower dam. The passage here was still not routine, as a steam pipe could easily be ruptured, scalding all below decks. But the *Mound City* made it through without incident and before dark on 12 May, the *Pittsburg* and *Carondelet* were through also. By the morning of 13 May, all six boats had joined the rest in the deeper, safer waters below the lower falls. Bailey and his men had saved the fleet.

The worst of the campaign was over for the Federals, though a few minor hurdles remained. After setting fire to Alexandria, Banks's troops moved south towards Simsport and the Atchafalaya River on 13 May. Once across, the Federals would be free of any threat from Taylor or Confederate reinforcements from Arkansas. There were minor skirmishes on the next three days, until finally Banks and his men came to the Atchafalaya. The backwash from the Mississippi had widened the Atchafalaya to more than six hundred yards across, a greater distance than could be spanned by all the pontoons available to the Federal force. If Banks chose to slowly move his men across by ferrying them in small boats, Taylor might wait until the force had become small enough to successfully attack and overwhelm.

Once again, it was Joseph Bailey to the rescue. Improvising as usual, he took every available boat, set them up side by side across the river, and then bolted them together with timbers laid parallel to the width of the river. He then covered these with timbers laid parallel to the flow of the river to serve as a bridge. Due to the different heights of the boats, the bridge was an undulating affair, but it served its purpose. By the morning of 20 May, the wagon trains and infantry had crossed and the bridge had been dismantled. Because of the serpentine, swaying nature of the bridge, the wagons

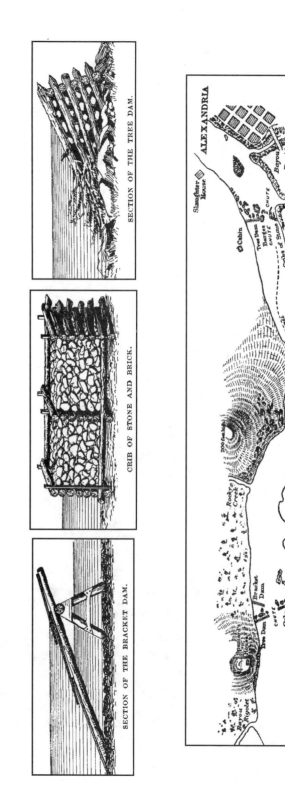

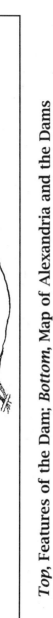

SECTION OF THE TREE DAM.

CRIB OF STONE AND BRICK.

SECTION OF THE BRACKET DAM.

SLAUGHTER HOUSE. ALEXANDRIA

Top, Features of the Dam; *Bottom,* Map of Alexandria and the Dams

Battles and Leaders of the Civil War

were pulled across by the men and the horses and mules led separately to avoid panic.[26] According to Banks: "This work was not of the same magnitude, but was as important to the army as the dam at Alexandria was to the navy."[27]

With the end of the Red River campaign, bitter recriminations began on both sides. Several of Banks's subordinates asked for reassignment or simply quit in anger. Banks himself was accused (probably falsely) of having been involved in cotton speculation from the start. Because of his political connections, Banks could not be removed from command, but Lincoln did the next best thing. He assigned the capable veteran Major General Edward R. S. Canby to the department as Banks's superior, a move that would keep Banks from having any further chances to cause military harm.

On the Confederate side, Taylor was furious at Kirby Smith for not using all available forces to destroy Banks and the fleet once they had them on the run. He wrote an angry letter to Smith, a letter which blamed the failure of the campaign on Smith's incompetence and asked for reassignment.[28] Smith had Taylor placed under arrest. The Confederate high command, realizing that Taylor was too good a fighter to be lost to the cause, solved the problem by promoting Taylor to lieutenant general and reassigning him to head Confederate forces in Alabama, Mississippi, and East Louisiana.[29]

As for Bailey, he received praise for his work from all quarters. He received the thanks of Congress and was promoted to the rank of brigadier general. The greatest testimonials to Bailey came from Porter and his naval colleagues. On 30 May, Porter asked his men to contribute money to a fund designed to buy a suitable token of appreciation.[30] In time, Bailey was presented with a $700 sword (a personal gift from Porter), a $1,600 silver vase from the navy (with a picture of the dam and the fleet engraved on the side), and $3,000 cash.[31]

Perhaps the greatest testimonial from Porter was his high praise of Bailey in his official report on the campaign. Some excerpts:

Joseph Bailey

National Archives, BA-188

"There seems to have been an especial Providence looking out for us, in providing a man equal to the emergency...This proposition looked like madness, and the best engineers ridiculed it but Colonel Bailey was so sanguine of success that I requested General Banks to have it done...every man seemed to be working with a vigor I have seldom seen equaled, while, perhaps not one in fifty believed in the success of the undertaking...Words are inadequate to express the admiration I feel for the abilities of Lieutenant-Colonel Bailey. This is without a doubt the best engineering feat ever performed...The highest honors the Government can bestow on Colonel Bailey can never repay him for the service he has rendered his country."[32]

Joseph Bailey

Joseph Bailey was born in Ohio on 6 May 1825.[33] His family moved to Illinois, where he spent most of his youth. He received a common school education, but eventually found his livelihood as a lumberman in Columbia County, Wisconsin. He married Mary Spaulding in 1846; five of their seven children survived. In the lumber industry, he gained experience driving logs down the river, a job that frequently required the construction of various dams and bridges. Not long after the beginning of the war, Bailey formed a company of lumbermen and the unit was assigned to the Fourth Wisconsin Infantry. Well respected, Bailey was commissioned a captain.

He served under both Major General Benjamin Butler and Major General Nathaniel Banks, rising to the rank of lieutenant colonel. He was in charge of an attempt to create an artificial cutoff of the Mississippi River at Vicksburg. After supervising the construction of government levees on the lower Mississippi, Bailey took part in the siege of Port Hudson. There (in unknowing kinship to Henry Pleasants!) he undermined one of the Confederate works with a 180-foot tunnel and loaded it with powder. The charge was ready to be detonated when the word of Port Hudson's surrender came on 8 July 1863. After his magnificent engineering feat on the Red River at Alexandria, he was promoted to full brigadier general of volunteers and brevet major general. In the latter part of the war, he took part in the reduction of Mobile, Alabama.

After the war, Bailey settled in Vernon County, Missouri. The newcomer was highly thought of and was elected sheriff in the fall of 1866. On 21 March 1867, he arrested two brothers named Pixley, who then got the upper hand on Bailey, shooting and killing him. He is buried at Evergreen Cemetery, Fort Scott, Kansas.

Chapter 3

George Washington Rains: Confederate Powder

By the end of the Civil War, only one major Southern city remained unoccupied by Union forces. Augusta, Georgia was too far south to be caught up in the fights between the Army of Northern Virginia and the Army of the Potomac and it was too far north to be crushed during Sherman's march to the sea. Somehow, crafty Confederate planners managed to foresee in 1861 that Augusta would be a sanctuary for the production of one of their most prized commodities: gunpowder.

The manufacture of gunpowder on a large scale is a demanding industrial task. How did the Confederacy, a nation mostly devoid of industry and increasingly cut off from the rest of the world by Union victories and the blockade, manage to supply gunpowder to its soldiers? The answer to the question lies mainly in the person of Colonel George Washington Rains, whose ingenious powder works at Augusta created what many at the time called the best quality gunpowder in the world. To understand the magnitude of Rains's accomplishment, one must know something about how gunpowder is made and also about Southern capabilities for doing so on the eve of the Civil War.

The gunpowder used in the Civil War was a mixture of three ingredients: sulfur, charcoal, and potassium nitrate (called "saltpeter" or "niter"). During the six or seven centuries prior to the war, men had empirically come to discover that the best proportion for the three constituents was 75 percent niter, 15 percent charcoal, and 10 percent sulfur. Charcoal and sulfur are relatively easy to acquire, but niter takes some work. It is found as a powdery crust on the walls of cellars and stables and also in some caves. It can also be made over time in "niter beds," used in America since at least the time of the Jamestown colony.

In a niter bed, vegetable and animal refuse (which contain significant amounts of nitrogen) are collected, mixed with limestone, old mortar and ashes and wet with urine and stable run-off. After decomposition (which usually takes about eighteen months[1]), the bed is leached with water, which is then allowed to evaporate leaving potassium nitrate crystals.[2]

The mixing of niter, sulfur, and charcoal was for many years accomplished by hand with a mortar and pestle. This resulted in gunpowder of widely varying quality and also required many man-hours to produce significant amounts of powder. By the 1400s, the job was automated with the invention of the stamp mill, which consisted of rows of bowls in which the ingredients were ground and mixed by means of heavy wooden beams (or "stamps") raised and dropped into the bowls. Gearing attached to waterwheels was normally used to raise the beams.

By the 1700s an improved device, the rolling mill, was in wide use. In a rolling mill, the gunpowder is crushed by means of two large iron wheels revolving around a central shaft. Along with the rolling mill, men eventually perfected techniques that produced gunpowder of much more consistent quality. By the time of the Civil War, the process had generally been refined to include five steps:

(1.) **Mixing:** The ingredients were first blended together, either by hand or mechanically.

(2.) **Milling (or Incorporating):** The ingredients were ground and pulverized (usually by a rolling mill, as described above). During this step and the previous step, it was crucial to keep the ingredients moist to prevent the formation of dust, which could explode.

(3.) **Pressing:** The crushed ingredients were pressed by hydraulic presses into dense "cakes."

(4.) **Corning (or Granulating):** The cakes were cracked, granulated, and sifted for grains of the right size, which depended on the purpose of the powder. This was the most dangerous step of the entire operation, and the corning building was generally located away from all other buildings and never approached while the machinery was in operation.

(5.) **Finishing:** The grains were tumbled in a revolving cylinder or barrel to round them and polish them. They were sometimes dried at the same time with hot air.[3]

When the Civil War began, there were many gunpowder mills in America and almost all of them were in the Northern states. The 1860 census showed only two significant Southern mills, and both were stamp mills.[4] One, run by J. M. Ostendorff in Walhalla, South

Carolina, was being used to make blasting powder for a railroad tunnel through the northwestern part of the state.[5] The mill employed only three men, and the powder made there was of inferior quality.[6] The Sycamore Stamping Mill, in Tennessee, about twenty miles northwest of Nashville, was larger, employing about ten men. Still, it was a stamp mill, which meant production was slower and the quality of the powder was not as good as that from a rolling mill. Also, Nashville was far enough north that Union occupation was a good possibility. There were other small mills in the South, but taken all together they would still be woefully inadequate for the job at hand.

There wasn't much finished powder on hand in the South. Confederate President Jefferson Davis had the foresight to send Raphael Semmes (later commander of the C.S.S. *Alabama*) north in February 1861 to procure powder from manufacturers eager to sell.[7] This brought in some powder, but the attack on Fort Sumter and the blockade quickly put a stop to such sources. Small amounts of powder were brought through neutral Kentucky until about September 1861.[8]

Federal powder (mostly old cannon powder) was seized from the Norfolk Arsenal when it was captured on 20 April 1861 and from other federal installations throughout the South.[9] Still, at the start of the war the Confederates probably had enough powder to supply only about fifty rounds per man in the armies they were forming.[10] Pre-war manuals specified 200 rounds per man going into battle, so the Southerners were hardly prepared for an extended conflict.[11]

The Confederates, without any significant powder mills and without much industry of any kind, were going to have to make enough powder to fight a large-scale war of unknown duration. In early April 1861, Davis appointed Josiah Gorgas as chief of ordnance of the Confederacy. Gorgas, an ordnance officer in the U.S. Army before his resignation on 3 April 1861, proved to be an excellent choice. He was industrious, resourceful, and reliable. A testament to his worth was the continued functioning of ordnance operations even after the fall of Richmond in April 1865.[12] According to Confederate General Joseph E. Johnston, Gorgas "created the ordnance department out of nothing."[13]

Davis and Gorgas together chose George Washington Rains as their man to take on the arduous task of providing Southern soldiers with gunpowder. Rains (whose brother Gabriel James Rains was superintendent of the Confederate Torpedo Bureau) had both military and industrial experience, and in retrospect it seems that Davis and Gorgas could not have chosen a better man for the job.

They instructed Rains to build an operation that would be centrally located and able to supply powder to the armies in the field and to the artillery of the forts, and essentially gave him *carte blanche* to accomplish it in whatever manner he could. It was crucial that the Confederates have their own powder supply. Though gunpowder would continue to be brought through the blockade to some extent, it was expensive and often of dubious quality. Powder that looked good would sometimes take on excessive moisture from the air, rendering it useless in battle.

The pressure on Rains to succeed was enormous. As Davis later wrote, "...it soon became evident to all that the South had gone to war without counting the cost. Our chief difficulty was the want of arms and munitions of war."[14]

On 10 July 1861, Rains left Richmond to begin his duties. He began a rapid railroad tour of the South, seeking the optimum site for the powder works. While performing this most essential function, Rains also had another, more urgent, task in front of him. Most of the little powder which was available to the Confederates had been sent to the troops in northern Virginia preparing to fight in what would be the Battle of First Manassas. Confederate forces under General Albert Sydney Johnston in Kentucky were in urgent need of ammunition.

Rains traveled to Nashville and with the help of a local man, S. D. Morgan, saw that the Sycamore Stamping Mill was improved with new stampers. Production of powder was still slowed by lack of niter. Governor Joseph E. Brown of Georgia had purchased a small shipment of niter from suppliers in Philadelphia shortly before Savannah was closed by the blockade and it was shipped to Nashville.[15] This helped the mill get started, but much more was needed. Rains directed that limestone caves in Tennessee, Alabama, Georgia, and Arkansas be worked for their niter and by October 1861 he and Morgan constructed a special refinery at Nashville for purifying the raw material into pure potassium nitrate. Using these methods, Rains was able to milk more than one hundred thousand pounds of powder out of the Sycamore mill (mostly for A. S. Johnston's use) before Nashville fell in February 1862.

In preparing for the war, the Tennessee government had contracted with a Mr. Whiteman of Manchester to construct another powder mill there. Rains advised Whiteman to construct a small rolling mill and by November 1861 fifteen hundred pounds of powder a day were being produced at Manchester.[16] Rains used the Manchester Mill as a training ground for men he would use at the much larger Confederate Powder Works, when finished, and at other points in the Confederacy. He sent trained powder makers to build mills in Texas and Arkansas, both with many caves rich in niter, and these mills helped keep the armies of the Trans-Mississippi supplied.[17]

In late November 1861, Rains also traveled to New Orleans to examine a small scale powder operation constructed there by the commander, Major General Mansfield Lovell. Lovell had set up two small mills capable of producing a total of two tons of powder per day.[18] Lovell also discussed with Rains his plans to procure niter from Europe (where the price was a quarter of the price in the U.S.) by chartering a cargo ship, the *Tennessee*, then at anchor in New Orleans. Unfortunately for Lovell, both his mills and his niter plan were doomed: New Orleans fell to Union forces in April of 1862.

While Rains helped his colleagues throughout the South, he continued to work on his primary mission. On 20 July 1861, during his tour of the Confederacy, he visited Augusta and found much to his liking.[19] By 25 July, he was able to tell Gorgas that he had made arrangements for construction or procurement of much of the necessary machinery, and that it would be at least three months before any powder would be made by the main works (it would actually take about eight months to get the operation going).[20] Construction of the plant at Augusta began on 13 September 1861.

Rains found Augusta to be favorable for a number of reasons:

A central location, with railroad access for easy distribution.

The Augusta Canal (built in 1845) could provide fairly pure water (free of lime and salts), water power, and barge access for shipment of supplies.

A substantial city, with access to skilled workmen and building supplies.

An available location close to the city, but not too close, due to the danger of explosion.

Rains bought enough land (starting about half a mile from the western city limits) of Augusta and encompassing about two hundred and forty acres so that the various buildings he had in mind could all be separated by at least one thousand feet from one another.[21] The plant was to be located in between the Augusta Canal and the Savannah River, which was a few hundred yards distant.[22] The Augusta Canal has three branches or "levels," and the plant was located on the first level, closest to the river. He enlisted a young civil engineer from Savannah to oversee the construction and local builders, Denning and Bowe, were contracted to do the work. According to Rains, the finished buildings, made of brick and granite from Stone Mountain, "could not be surpassed for excellence in workmanship."[23]

How did Rains come up with his plan and how did he obtain the necessary machinery in the rural South? Things fell into place through a mixture of ingenuity and good fortune. Though Rains was a skilled scientist and tradesman, he had no experience in making gunpowder. Near the beginning of his service, he somehow came into possession of a pamphlet written by Major Fraser Baddeley of the Royal Artillery, and an instructor at the Waltham Abbey Powder Works in England. This little book outlined the process necessary for making good gunpowder in large quantities, but unfortunately didn't include much in the way of details regarding the specific machinery or building design required. Though the pamphlet was a valuable reference, Rains would have to come up with the plans on his own.[24] Again, fortune smiled on Rains. A worker at the Manchester Mill in Tennessee, last name of Wright, turned out to have also worked at the Waltham Abbey Plant and was able to answer many of Rains's questions.

With the pamphlet and Wright as resources, Rains was able to spend his long hours on the trains in the summer of 1861 piecing together plans for the works. By 25 July he had worked out a general plan and made arrangements for much of the machinery required. He enlisted an architect, C. Shaler Smith, to draw up his plans and found an excellent machinist, William Pendleton, to oversee the fitting of the machinery into the buildings.[25]

The scheme created by Rains and brought to life by Smith was brilliant, and foreshadowed the sort of assembly line arrangement which would revolutionize twentieth-century America. The various buildings were to be laid out along a two-mile stretch of the Augusta Canal in order of their function, like a giant conveyor belt with receiving of supplies on one end and a magazine for storing finished powder on the other. Wooded growth was left between the buildings to isolate each from a possible explosion in one of its neighbors, so the product was worked down and across the canal by boats[26] and also on a special rail system designed by Rains on which the cars ran on tracks made of oak (to eliminate any chance of sparks).[27]

By looking at each of the main buildings in turn, one can get a sense of how the resourceful Rains gathered and pieced together parts from all over the South into a seamless operation, faster, safer, and better than any other in the world. He took the best of what high quality operations like Waltham Abbey had to offer and made improvements which made the Confederate Powder Works unique. He made full use of what little industry did exist in the South, and improvised when needed.

Refinery and Warehouse Building

The "assembly line" was laid out from east to west (actually, the canal runs on more of a southeast to northwest line). Shipments of raw materials were received on the far eastern end at the refinery and warehouse building. The building was a hollow rectangle, with the southern, eastern, and western sides under roof and the northern side without a roof. The southern side (facing the canal) was 250 feet long and the eastern and western sides extended back 275 feet. Square towers, which served as offices, were on each corner of the rectangle. The distance between the inside edges of the towers was 220 feet.[28] On Smith's original plans, drawn in 1861, two of the offices were designated as storerooms and one as a lab. According to later comments of Rains, they were all used as offices.

Two small warehouses for storage of sulfur and niter occupied the southeastern part of the structure and a larger niter storeroom (eighty feet by fifty-two feet) took up most of the northeastern section.[29] The western side was home to the boiler room used to operate the building's steam engines and to a machine shop. The northern side (the roofless one) consisted of two high brick walls used for storing wood. The extreme northeast portion of the building housed facilities for ballistic pendulums, used for constant testing of the explosive power of the powder. Rains had electro-ballistic pendulums built, similar to those he had used when teaching at West Point. The front (southern side) was the location of the refineries. Inside the hollow rectangle were a well, kilns for drying wood destined to become charcoal, equipment for extraction of niter from used powder, refuse from the powder works and most impressively, a huge chimney, into which ran all the flues from the numerous furnaces in the refinery building.[30]

Rains stated that he wanted to give the chimney "the appearance of a grand monumental structure" and in this he certainly succeeded. The five-foot square chimney flue was enclosed in a brick tower one hundred and fifty feet high with an ornate and large square base. The tower has the form of an obelisk, tapering toward the top. It still stands today as a testament to the workmanship involved.

The most important constituent of gunpowder is niter, and the more pure the better. The refinery for niter in this first building then may have been the most important component of the whole operation. Obtaining niter at all, no matter how pure, was no easy task. Most of the niter used at Augusta came from Europe on blockade-runners that brought their cargoes to Charleston, South Carolina or Wilmington, North Carolina. About thirteen hundred and fifty tons of the fifteen hundred tons of niter used at the works came in this fashion. The other one hundred and fifty tons were obtained from caves and other local sources.

Refinery Building and Laboratory, circa 1865

Rains did what he could to encourage the acquisition and production of more niter. He wrote a pamphlet, widely distributed in the South, called *Notes on Making Saltpetre from the Earth of the Caves*. On 11 April 1862, the Confederate government authorized the creation of a Nitre and Mining Bureau, under the direction of Isaac M. St. John.[31] St. John organized the collection of niter from caves, encouraged those too weak to fight to scour old cellars and tobacco barns and started huge niter beds in Columbia, S.C., Charleston, Savannah, Augusta, Mobile, Selma, and other spots throughout the South.[32] At the end of 1864, it was estimated that there was 2.8 million cubic feet of material in various stages of decomposition in these beds.[33] Unfortunately, the war ended before many of these beds were ready to be harvested. At the war's conclusion, it was estimated that these beds contained as much as four million pounds of niter.[34]

The niter refinery occupied the right central portion of the front wall of the powder works. The process by which Rains purified his niter is called fractional crystallization. The raw niter was placed into large pans of water that were heated to boiling by furnaces below the pans. The niter and impurities (mostly chloride salts) would then dissolve into the hot water. Upon cooling, crystals of niter would form at a different temperature than crystals of the impurities, and could be collected from the broth. This was traditionally done by hand, but Rains devised a method for doing this by machine, and this saved so much time that Rains was able to run his niter through the refining process two or three times to each time at any other powder works. As a consequence, his niter was of unequaled purity (Rains stated that the finished niter had less than one-hundred-thousandth part of chlorides left).

The device consisted of a bronze revolving wheel (to the edges of which a series of buckets were attached) which dipped down into a large (seven-foot diameter), shallow kettle. Hot niter solution was poured into the kettle, which was cooled by canal water that ran under it. This cooling began the formation of niter crystals in the liquid. As fast as the crystals formed, the sharp-edged buckets lifted them out and dumped them into a receiving vat, where any liquid was allowed to drain back to the kettle. When the operation was deemed complete, the liquid in the kettle was collected and taken to the facilities in the center of the building for continued treatment, as Rains tried not to waste even the smallest bit of the precious niter. The refined niter was stored in a small room just east of the refinery (in between the niter refinery and the niter warehouse).

At the northern end of the room there were also large evaporating and drying pans for purifying the niter by hand. The copper

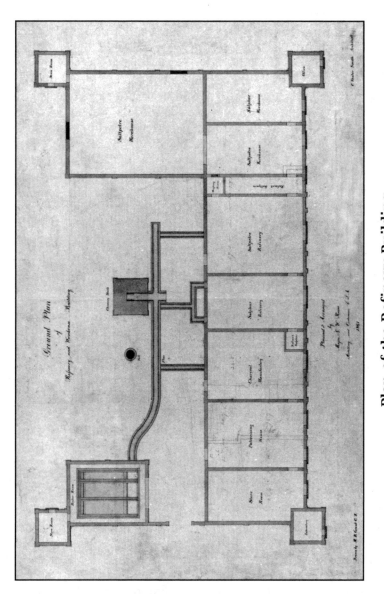

Plan of the Refinery Building

drying pans were made in Nashville, and the twelve iron evaporating pans (each with a capacity of five hundred gallons) were cast at the iron works on the Cumberland River in Tennessee. Four tanks for "mother liquor," from which the niter would be extracted, stood against the southern wall.

Next to the niter refinery in the front of the refinery building was the sulfur refinery. As with niter, sulfur of the highest purity is required for gunpowder of the highest quality. About one hundred and thirty tons of impure sulfur were received at the works from Louisiana, where it had been purchased before the war to be used in the process by which sugarcane juice is clarified.[35] After this stockpile was exhausted, Rains improvised by having men in various labs around the South "roast" sulfur out of iron pyrite (commonly called "fool's gold"). This was done so successfully that a steady supply of sulfur was not a problem.

Purifying the sulfur received to the quality that Rains desired required more improvisation. The raw sulfur was placed in kettles that were heated from below. As the sulfur turned to vapor (this process is called fractional distillation) it rose through an angled iron pipe to another kettle surrounded by cool canal water, where it condensed. The yellow solid collected in this vessel had to be pulverized and bolted (or sifted) before it could be used in gunpowder. For pulverizing the sulfur, Rains used rollers similar to those in the incorporating mills (though only about one-tenth the weight of those massive rollers).

Sifting the sulfur was a problem. This was normally done with silk, but when the original "bolters" had worn out, replacement silk was not to be found. Rains devised a different and, as it turned out, superior method. He had the pulverized sulfur placed in revolving barrels with hollow, perforated axles. The barrels had vanes around the circumference (similar to what one might see in a modern-day clothes dryer) to lift the sulfur and keep it from collecting on the bottom.[36] A light current of air was blown through the axle, depositing sulfur in a small adjoining room. The sulfur so deposited was much finer than that resulting from the normal bolting process.

Next to the sulfur refinery was the department for creating the third essential component of gunpowder, charcoal. Again, Rains had to improvise. Willow wood was generally preferred for gunpowder charcoal, but when this could no longer be obtained because of the war, Rains tried cottonwood, which was abundant locally. He found the wood to be at least the equal of willow and used it throughout the operation of the powder works.

To make charcoal, kiln-dried cottonwood (cut into sticks of about 1.5-inch diameter) was brought into the room on a spur of

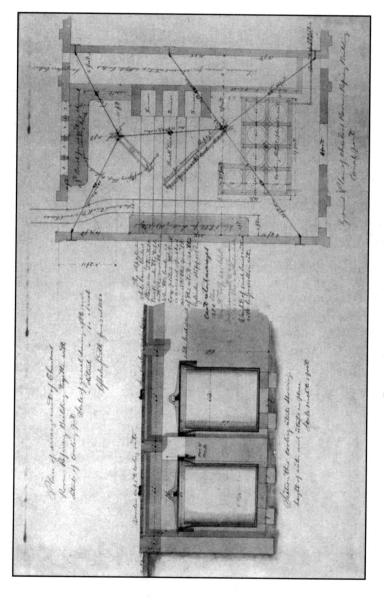

Plan of the Charcoal Refinery

the wooden-tracked railroad which ran from the woodhouse to the charcoal facility. From a wooden loading table (23.5 feet long and located against the northern wall of the room), the wood was placed into one of twelve sheet iron "slip" cylinders (about four feet long with a three-foot diameter) until the cylinder was full. This cylinder was closed and then moved by crane into one of four cast iron cylinders (of just slightly greater dimensions), whose top was then closed and then sealed with clay. The cast iron cylinders sat over furnaces. After being heated for about two hours, the slip cylinders were withdrawn from the cast iron cylinders and moved by crane to one of eight cast iron coolers beneath the floor, which had cool canal water circulating about them. This arrangement of cooling retorts was on the western side of the room, and measured 19.0 feet long by 14.5 feet wide. After cooling, the cylinders were moved again by crane to a broad L-shaped table in the southeastern corner of the room, onto which their contents were dumped.

The two cranes used in this phase of the operation consisted of vertical posts, about twelve inches square, with horizontal beams (about twelve inches by four inches) attached at the top. They stood in the center of the room, and were supported by an arrangement of overhead ropes that Smith referred to in his drawings as "spiders." The cranes were operated by a gearing mechanism on the vertical post that Smith called a "crab."

After imperfect sticks were removed, the remaining sticks of charcoal were placed into revolving barrels containing bronze balls that soon reduced it to a fine powder. The charcoal was then taken to a weighing center (located in a small room between the niter refinery and the niter warehouse), where nine pounds of charcoal, six pounds of sulfur, and forty-five pounds of niter were mixed to make sixty-pound charges.

It was in the mixing of the three ingredients that Rains might have made his most remarkable improvement on the standard methods for making powder. The combustion of the powder is most efficient when the particles of the constituents are in closest proximity to one another. Specifically, it is the combustion of the charcoal with the oxygen in the niter that provides the gases that cause the charge to explode. When Rains examined a grain of pulverized charcoal under a microscope, he noticed that it was extremely porous. In finished powder, these pores are filled to a great extent by niter. Making this happen in the incorporating mill is a slow process of continual grinding and pulverizing. Rains found a new method by which he could greatly speed up the entire process.

The sixty-pound charges were moistened and then placed into revolving copper barrels (eighteen inches in diameter) with three-inch, perforated brass axles. High-pressure steam was then blown through the axle. This melted the niter and allowed it to flow into and fill the pores in the charcoal. Upon cooling, the charcoal in the resulting damp solid had its pores completely filled with niter. The resulting mixture could be turned into finished mill cake in about an hour, as compared to four hours in a conventional powder works. Thus, this one innovation allowed the Confederate Powder Works to essentially quadruple production over other facilities.

The machinery in the refinery building was run by means of two eighty-horsepower steam engines brought from Atlanta.[37] The cast iron coolers, iron cylinders, and copper slip cylinders in the charcoal department were made by the Augusta Confederate Foundry and Machine Works. The iron and coal for these castings (and elsewhere at the works) came from northern Georgia and Alabama, and the copper (as with most copper used in the Confederacy) from Ducktown, Tennessee.

It should be noted that on Smith's earliest plans for the building, the arrangement of the refineries was as described above and as described by Rains later: niter, sulfur, and charcoal as one moved from east to west. A plan of the building drawn by Smith in 1863, however, shows the charcoal operation located between the refineries for niter and sulfur.

Laboratory

The laboratory building, a very attractive structure with a large clock tower, filled the ninety-foot interval between the refinery building and the incorporating mills. The building was never finished on the interior, and the work that was to be done there was performed at the Augusta Arsenal across town. The laboratory and the mill building on its western side were set further back from the canal than the refinery building, so that the fronts of the former were set even with the rear (northern side) of the latter.

Incorporating Mills

After leaving the refinery building, the charges now consisted of sixty pounds of thoroughly mixed, very fine sulfur, charcoal, and niter in the correct proportions. The charges were brought to the incorporating building, well designed by Rains and Smith for safety and efficiency. The building, with the laboratory on one side, presented a front of 291 feet, 6 inches feet to the canal. The building was divided into two sets of six mills, with a space between the two divisions. In this space there sat a 130-horsepower steam engine, which had been bought and brought to Augusta just before the war for use in a flour mill. It was perfectly suited to run the machinery in the incorporating mills. Each mill was about seventeen feet wide

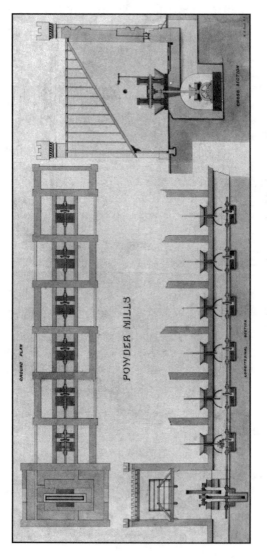

Plan and Section of the Incorporating Mills

(including the thickness of the walls) and about twenty-four feet deep, with walls about twenty-eight feet high.

The outer walls and the walls between the mills were massive, varying from four to ten feet thick. This design was intended to isolate an explosion in one mill from its neighbors. To encourage any explosive force to work away from the other mills, the front of each mill was made of light wood and glass which would give easily, and the roofs were made of lightweight zinc sheets (from Mobile). In addition, the mills were built so that they faced in alternate directions (i.e., the glass front of one sat next to the rear walls of its neighbors) and wing walls, about as high as the main walls, extended for about twenty feet from the back of each mill. The powder makers stood out among the wing walls, stopping and starting the various rollers by means of levers. As an additional precaution, a thirty-gallon barrel of water was positioned above each set of rollers. Each barrel was connected by an iron shaft to similar buckets in the other five mills of that division. Should an explosion occur in any of the six mills, all would simultaneously be doused.

The large steam engine operated the various mills by constantly turning an immense iron shaft, about a foot in diameter and nearly three hundred feet long. The shaft was in a long subterranean archway that ran the length of the entire incorporating building, and was connected to the rolling mills above by means of heavy gear wheels. An individual mill could be stopped or started by operation of the levers mentioned above, much as a modern automobile can be thrown in or out of gear by means of a clutch petal. The steam engine was connected to the shaft by an enormous (sixteen-foot diameter) gear wheel.

It should be mentioned here that Rains originally intended to operate machinery at the powder works with water power from the canal, but it became apparent very early on that the volume of water available was not adequate for the scale of operation he intended to construct. Hence, the Confederate Powder Works was probably the first such facility run by steam power.

Each incorporating mill consisted of a seven-foot diameter iron bed and two large iron rollers. Through the center of the bed rose a large vertical shaft, which revolved when connected to the main shaft below. A five-inch wrought iron axle ran horizontally through the vertical shaft and a roller (each was six feet in diameter, fifteen inches thick and weighed five tons) was attached on each side so that it stood vertically and rode around the circular bed like a wheel.

The rollers were at different distances from the center vertical shaft, so that the path of one would partially overlap that of the other. This increased the grinding effect on the charge placed on the bed. A two-foot high wooden curb lined the outside of the bed to keep the powder from falling off and a metal sleeve was placed around the vertical axle to prevent powder from falling through the center of the bed. A scraper followed behind each roller, breaking up the compressed powder, mixing it and keeping it in the path of the roller.

After the sixty-pound charge had been on the bed for about an hour (with the rollers revolving about ten times per minute), it had been milled into a blackish gray cake about $5/8$ of an inch thick. It was now ready to be cooled.

The machinery of the incorporating mills required Rains to stretch the South's industrial base to its limits. The large iron shaft and the gearing for it were cast at the Webster Foundry and Machine Works in Chattanooga. The iron beds and most of the rollers were cast at the extremely busy Tredegar Iron and Machine Works in Richmond, Virginia. As the Tredegar facility was overloaded with orders for heavy artillery and other government needs, two of the rollers were cast in Macon and two in Chattanooga. The giant gear wheel connecting the steam engine with the main shaft was cast and finished in Atlanta.

Cooling Magazines

The finished cake was then transported across the canal to the cooling magazine building. The building was 130 feet, 9 inches long and 24 feet, 6 inches wide. Inside were four magazine chambers, each ten feet square, excavated into the cool Georgia clay. After the cake had cooled and hardened, it was ready to be granulated. Rains found that due to the efficiency of his new mixing technique and to the weight of his rollers, compression of the cake by hydraulic presses was unnecessary, saving even more time. He had originally provided for a press house in his plan, and one was constructed on the same side of the canal as the cooling magazines but a bit further down. It housed two hydraulic presses from Richmond operated by a water wheel (water was piped in from the canal for this purpose). After discovering that this pressing step was not needed, the press house was only used for production of very fine grain powder.

Granulating Building

After cooling, the mill cake was brought back across the canal to the granulating building. This facility was about fifteen hundred feet down the canal from the incorporating building (which, by connection through the empty laboratory, was essentially one facility with the refinery). In the granulating building, the cold mill cake was broken into grains of different sizes, which were then sorted into receptacles. This was accomplished by passing the cake through

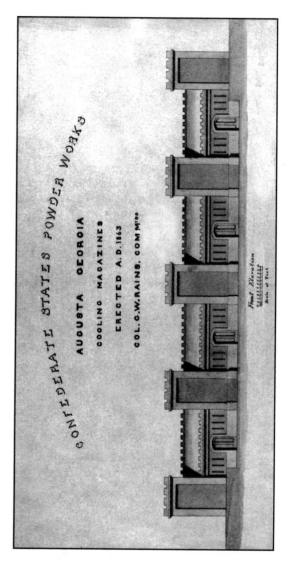

CONFEDERATE STATES POWDER WORKS

AUGUSTA GEORGIA

COOLING MAGAZINES

ERECTED A.D. 1863

COL. G. W. RAINS, COM Mᵈ⁰

Front Elevation

Scale of Feet

Elevation of the Cooling Magazine Building

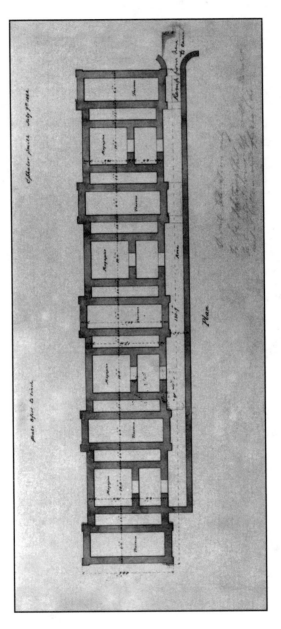

Plan of the Cooling Magazine Building

a machine which had small rotating bronze cylinders, the first set with teeth and the second set smooth. The powder then passed over screens and sieves, grains of the same size falling into the same receptacle. Usually the grains were on the order of $^1/_{25}$ of an inch in diameter for smoothbore powder and about $^1/_{20}$ of an inch for rifle powder.[38] For very large grain powder (in which the grains had dimensions on the order of an inch), used in the largest artillery guns, the cakes were broken up outside of this machinery.

Drying, Dusting, and Glazing Building

Next stop on the "assembly line" was the drying, dusting, and glazing building, twenty-five hundred feet farther down the canal from the granulating building. The building had dimensions of 95 feet long by 79 feet, 2 inches wide. Again, Rains created a system that saved considerable amounts of time and labor over conventional methods. At places like Waltham Abbey, powder was dried slowly in trays over steam pipes and then dusted and glazed in a separate process. Rains combined all three steps into one by placing the powder into a revolving cylinder (each was four feet long, with a two-foot diameter) with a perforated hollow axle. Air heated by having passed through an arrangement of steam pipes passed through the axle, drying the grains and carrying off the powder dust. The agitation of the grains in the revolving cylinder provided the necessary smoothing and glazing. The gunpowder was now finished and ready for packing and shipping.

Packing House

The powder was taken fifteen hundred feet farther down the canal to the packing house, where it was weighed out and placed into wooden boxes designed by Rains. Rains found that these boxes, about one foot square and two and a half feet long, were stronger and packed more tightly than the barrels typically used for powder. The packing house was 35 feet long and 27 feet wide.

Magazine

Full powder boxes were brought to the magazine building, three-quarters of a mile farther down the canal. The magazine, set back about one hundred yards from the canal and surrounded by a high fence, had a capacity of about one hundred tons of gunpowder. A railroad spur line was built from the magazine across the canal to the Georgia Railroad as it fed into Augusta.

Rains gave ample attention to both safety within the plant and to security from external attack. As often as possible, copper or copper alloys (i.e., bronze) were used when metal was called for in the plans as copper is the only common metal that will not spark.

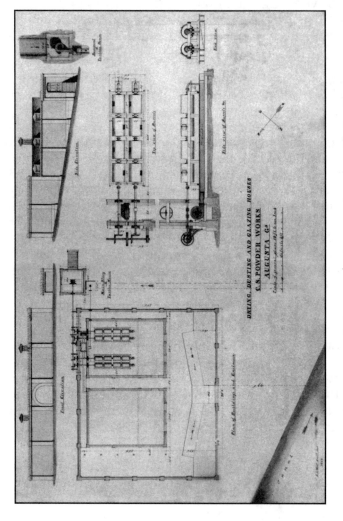

Plan and Elevation of the Drying, Dusting, and Glazing Houses

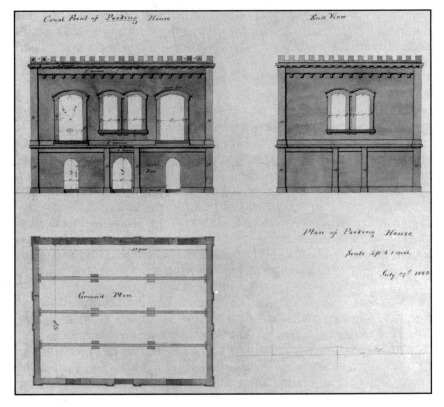

Plan and Elevation of the Packing House

Courtesy Augusta-Richmond County Museum

The incorporating building as a whole was a masterpiece of efficiency combined with safety. The steam used in the drying building was created in boilers located in a boiler house two hundred yards farther down the canal. The chimney for these boilers was a hundred yards further down the canal, and connected to the boilers by a subterranean flue. A spark would have to drift over three hundred yards to land on the metal roof of the drying building. Rains attention to detail extended to his workers, who were required to wear rubber-soled shoes (to lessen the chance for creating a spark).[39] All walkways from the canal into the various buildings were made from compressed sawdust.[40]

Once Rains had completed the works and perfected his powder-making process, there were no serious accidents at the plant, a remarkable feat in light of the enormous amount of explosive material that was handled. The only fatalities occurred at an explosion at a temporary wooden granulating building shortly after the works began operation. This building was on the same side of the canal as the cooling magazines, but about one hundred yards farther down the canal. About three tons of gunpowder were in the building, but the granulating equipment was not in use; the seven workers there were waiting for a boat with mill cake to arrive from the incorporating house. A sentinel stood guard outside and a boy with a mule was in an adjoining shed. The foreman had been called away and the resulting explosion probably occurred from an inadvertent match thrown on the floor by a smoking workman.

A dense growth of pines around the building funneled debris from the explosion upward to a height estimated by Rains to be around five hundred feet. Everything within a radius of about fifty feet of the building was destroyed, and all nine people near the facility killed. The only damage elsewhere in the works was in the form of broken windows and a slight movement of the roof in the permanent granulating building just across the canal, which was soon to be ready for use.

There were three explosions at the incorporating building, all before Rains turned to his revolutionary method of steam-treating the charges before milling. Two were insignificant, and the third caused two slight injuries. This last did serve as a good test for the safety design of the facility: the roof was blown off, the glass front blown off the exploding mill, and all the adjoining mills were drenched with water. This damage was quickly repaired.

Rains took every possible precaution to prevent outside attack or sabotage. The loss of the powder works would have been a disaster for the Confederacy. A sentinel (usually a sixteen to eighteen-year-old boy) was posted outside of each building, twenty-four hours a day.[41] High brick walls surrounded each building and each building had but one entrance.

The main threat was from a naval force coming up the Savannah River, especially after Fort Pulaski at the mouth of the river was taken in April 1862 (just as Rains started operations). Five miles below the works, an eight-inch Columbiad cannon and a garrison from the Georgia Light Guards were stationed on Shell Bluff. Between this point and the works, the river was obstructed with sunken trees, boxes of rocks, submarine torpedoes, and chains supported by rafts. Even if a force was able to bypass these obstacles, the Savannah River was notoriously difficult to navigate without an experienced pilot. Rains posted trained sharpshooters on the banks of the river below the city to pick off the pilot of any boat which was fortunate enough to have made it that far. As a last line of defense, Rains (who had the rank of lieutenant colonel) trained many of his powder workers, many of them disabled veterans, into a military unit under the direction of C. Shaler Smith, who had a captain's rank in the Confederate army. Also at Rains's direction, earthworks and small forts were constructed around Augusta and manned by home defense forces by early 1862.

Union land forces did not threaten the powder works until Sherman's army turned northward from Savannah. Strangely, Sherman and his sixty thousand troops bypassed Augusta and struck instead at Columbia, South Carolina. Some residents of Augusta seem to have actually considered this to be an insult to their city, and for years afterwards there was a rumor that Sherman had left Augusta alone because of his affection for a woman there with whom he had a romance years before the war. This was, of course, nonsense. Another story, slightly more plausible (and described in more detail in Chapter 6), proposed that a Southern telegraph operator had duped Sherman into avoiding Augusta. The reality, as Sherman himself explained later, was that Sherman had no need to burn Augusta: "The moment I passed Columbia, S.C., your factories, powder mills and the old stuff accumulated at Augusta was lost to the only two Confederate armies left—Lee's and Hood's...I used Augusta as a buffer."[42]

During its three years of steady operations, the Confederate Powder Works was an unqualified success. The powder works began to crank out gunpowder on 10 April 1862 (though many of the buildings were not completely finished until the next year) and continued until 18 April 1865, when Rains called a halt to operations.[43] During this time, the works produced 2,750,000 pounds of gunpowder. The plant was never worked to full capacity, according to Rains, but still produced about five thousand pounds of gunpowder each day, working daylight hours Monday through Saturday.[44] The plant was fully capable of increasing production for emergencies: an order for twenty-two thousand pounds of powder during the siege of Charleston was met in two days. The Confederates were quite fortunate, however, that no major land battles occurred between First Manassas in July 1861 and the opening of the powder works in April 1862.

On 18 April 1865, Rains brought down the Stars and Bars and the garrison flag of the powder work's defense forces for the last time. "Sadly I took down the last beloved flag and folded it away," he wrote later.[45] "The fires went out in the furnaces; the noise of the mills ceased; one by one the workmen slowly went away, and once more I stood on the banks of the canal alone."

After the works were closed, more than seventy thousand pounds of powder remained in the magazine facility. This powder was later used by the U.S. Army for its School of Artillery Practice at Fort Monroe "on account of its superiority." Rains states that Charleston would have fallen to assault by Union ironclads had his powder not been capable of propelling shells through their armor.[46] Jefferson Davis, who called the facilities built by Rains "the best in the world," was of the opinion that the C.S.S. *Alabama* would have been victorious in the famous naval battle with the U.S.S. *Kearsarge* if supplied with Augusta powder.[47] The *Alabama's* powder had deteriorated after two years at sea, and was ineffective against the *Kearsarge*, clothed in iron chains.

The powder works was host to many distinguished military and civilian visitors. According to the usually modest Rains, "The great extent of the Powder Works and their immense capabilities were the admiration of all visitors."[48] A glowing article about the works was printed in the *London Times* and reprinted throughout the European continent. Josiah Gorgas said the powder works was "a superb mill" and "wonderfully successful." Major General Benjamin Huger of the Department of the Trans-Mississippi said the powder works were "equal to two generals." Lieutenant Colonel James Arthur Lyon Fremantle of Her Majesty's Coldstream Guards, visiting the Confederacy in 1863, noted "the wonderful speed with which these works have been constructed, their great success, and their immense national value."[49]

Rains estimated the cost of production of his powder during the first year (in which the works produced about one million pounds of powder) as $1.08 per pound, as compared to about $3.00 per pound as received from Europe, a savings to the Confederates of about two million dollars.[50]

In 1880, the Sibley Cotton Factory was erected where the refinery, laboratory, and incorporating buildings had once stood. The bricks and stone that had once made up the world's best gunpowder works were used to create drains and culverts in Augusta. Only the great chimney of the refinery was left to stand, as it still stands today (reportedly, one or more of the original grinding wheels may be located today in Centennial Park in Nashville).

In 1878, the chimney was deeded to the Confederate Survivors Association as a monument and was dedicated on 26 April 1882. Testimonial tablets, one in honor of Rains and one in honor of the powder works, were embedded in the chimney about twenty feet off the ground. The keynote speaker, fittingly enough, was George Washington Rains. When he died in 1898, one of the provisions in his will was that the garrison flag he had hauled down that April day in 1865 be buried for eternity underneath the massive obelisk which stands as a monument to his greatest achievement.[51]

George Washington Rains

George Washington Rains was born in Craven County, North Carolina in 1817, the eighth child of Gabriel and Hester Rains. After receiving his education at New Bern Academy, he received an appointment to West Point in 1838 from the state of Alabama. Rains graduated in 1842 as first captain of cadets, first in his class in scientific studies and third in his class overall (the fifty-six graduates included such men as James Longstreet, John Pope, and William Rosecrans).

His excellent record brought him a commission as second lieutenant in the Engineer Corps. After helping in the construction of Fort Warren in Boston Harbor, Rains (apparently yearning for more action) asked for and received a transfer to the Fourth Artillery on 7 July 1843. After a year of duty at Fortress Monroe, he was employed as assistant professor of chemistry, mineralogy, and geology at his alma mater.

Rains resigned his teaching post in 1846 as the Mexican War erupted, and rejoined his artillery regiment. Rains was the first American officer to enter Vera Cruz, and was breveted twice for bravery: to captain for conduct at Contreras and Cherubusco, and to major for his service at Chapultepec.

He resigned from the army in 1856 and went into business as one of the proprietors of the Washington Iron Works in Newburgh, New York. It was here that he gained industrial knowledge, which combined with his scientific knowledge, would be extremely useful to him in Augusta. He received several patents while working in Newburgh.

When the Civil War erupted, Rains traveled to Richmond, where he was commissioned as a major of artillery. During the war, Rains was superintendent of both the Confederate Powder Works and the Augusta Arsenal. The Augusta Arsenal was the main supplier of field artillery ordnance to the Army of Tennessee and to troops in the south and west.

After the war, he returned to education, accepting a position as professor of chemistry and pharmacy in the medical department of the University of Georgia in November 1866. He served as dean of the medical faculty until 1883, and continued on the faculty until his retirement in 1894 at age 77. He died in Newburgh on 21 March 1898.

George W. Rains
Courtesy Augusta-Richmond County Museum

Part 2

Technology Meets the Civil War

Chapter 4

War under the Sea: Submarines

In early 1864, as Henry Pleasants and his Forty-eighth Pennsylvania Infantry made their successful subterranean attack at Petersburg, the Confederates were also working on a plan to attack Union forces from underneath. In this case, the attack would be even more unconventional—it came not from underground, but from under the ocean.

The idea of using submarine vessels in war was not new (see Appendix 2), but the Confederates were to open a new era in naval warfare. Without much industry and without much of a navy to speak of, the Confederacy was to become the first nation to use a submarine to successfully attack and sink an enemy vessel.

This event which came to pass in Charleston, South Carolina on 17 February 1864 was due to the confluence of a number of factors. The phrase "necessity is the mother of invention" was never more appropriately applied than in the case of the submarine C.S.S. *H. L. Hunley*. The right political and military situation brought the right men with the right skills to Charleston, and together they produced a result that would not be duplicated for another fifty years.

Before examining the progression of work that led to the *Hunley*, it is interesting to ponder what was happening on the Union side during the same time frame. If a successful submarine attack were to be made during the Civil War, why would it not come from the industrial juggernaut of the North? Apparently for the same reasons that led the British to reject Robert Fulton's submarine *Nautilus* earlier in the century. The U.S. Navy controlled the seas to a large extent, and controlled them completely around the coast of the United States. Their warships overmatched whatever the puny Confederate navy might put on the water. They had little need for a submarine vessel, for such a vessel would have few targets. And the capture of such a vessel could only help their enemy. Thus, the development of submarines was not a high priority in the U.S. Navy.

Still, a few forays into the field were made. Brutus de Villeroy, a French inventor and professor of mathematics and design, moved to Philadelphia in 1859.[1] He had built and successfully tested a small submarine in his hometown of Nantes as early as 1832. He had proposed a submarine to the French Ministry of Marine during the Crimean War, but his plan was not accepted.[2] By early 1861, he was working on a new submarine in his adopted country. After he tested the craft in the Delaware River, suspicious police arrested de Villeroy as a possible spy.[3] That day's issue of the *Philadelphia Evening Bulletin* stated that the "mysterious machine...was to be used for all sorts of treasonable purposes, including the trifling pastime of scuttling and blowing up government men-of-war."[4]

Although de Villeroy had been considering military applications (as well as salvage operations) for his craft, he was not a Confederate agent. After his arrest, the commandant of the Philadelphia Navy Yard, Captain Samuel F. DuPont, ordered three officers (Commander Henry Hoff, Commander Charles Steedman, and Engineer Robert Danby) to examine the craft and interview its inventor. Once convinced of de Villeroy's patriotic intentions, the trio then examined the submarine in detail. Their report to DuPont, dated 7 July 1861, showed that they were favorably impressed.[5] The boat was a thirty-three-foot-long screw-propelled iron tube, which had the following attributes: (1) The boat could stay submerged for a "length of time"; (2) The boat could be submerged and raised at will; (3) Diver's hatches allowed men to leave and return to the boat while it was submerged; and (4) Divers could work outside the boat while breathing through an air hose connected to the boat.

Encouraged by the report, de Villeroy sent letters to Secretary of the Navy Gideon Welles and to President Abraham Lincoln, encouraging the U.S. Navy to buy his submarine. His letter to Lincoln, dated 4 September 1861, states:

> I wish to propose to you a new arm of war, as formidable as it is economical...with a submarine boat like mine...it becomes an easy matter to reconnaissance the enemy's coast, to land men, ammunition, etc., at any given point, to enter harbors, to keep up intelligence, and to carry explosive bombs under the very keels of vessels and that without being seen.[6]

Welles forwarded the letter to Commodore Joseph Smith, chief of the Bureau of Yards and Docks, and asked for a recommendation. Smith recommended that a larger version of the present craft be built on a "no pay for failure" basis. On 1 November 1861, a contract was let to Mr. Martin Thomas of Philadelphia who had been funding much of de Villeroy's work. The contract specified a craft forty-five feet in length, five and a half feet from the keel to the deck, and four feet, eight inches across the beam.[7] It was to be completed in forty days, with de Villeroy as superintendent of construction. Four men, Henry Lambert, John Lambert, John France, and Rode Alexander, were to be listed as operatives on the craft, with $10 added to their wages for the perilous service.

Construction on the submarine began in the Philadelphia shipyard of Neafie and Levy. A formed iron skin was riveted to an iron framework, and then filed down for streamlining purposes. The propulsion system was quite unusual. Eight oars were located on each side and fitted into the hull through watertight fittings. The oars were hinged on a metal rod and folded like books on the forward stroke and opened on the backstroke.[8] De Villeroy may have adopted this idea from a design (apparently never built) of Armand-Maziere in France in 1795, whose submarine was meant to work by "a number of oars vibrating on the principle of a bird's wing."[9] The crew was to consist of one officer, two helmsmen, two divers, and sixteen seamen.

By the deadline of 10 December, the submarine was far from finished and it had become apparent that Thomas and de Villeroy did not work well together.[10] The navy granted an extension, but progress was still slow. By 22 January, Commodore Smith threatened to not accept the vessel if it was not ready to be shipped in four days. Apparently, the navy had selected the submarine to be tested in a contest with the Confederate navy's first ironclad, the C.S.S. *Virginia* (formerly the *Merrimack*), which was expected to be ready in Norfolk, Virginia at any time.

Finally, on 1 May 1862, the submarine, painted dark green and christened the *Alligator*, was lowered to the water in Philadelphia.[11] On 14 May, Samuel Eakin was assigned as acting master of the boat (the navy and de Villeroy had grown disenchanted with each other by this time and he had no further connection with the *Alligator*). The original task of the *Alligator* was no longer necessary, however. The *Virginia* had been effectively stalemated by the *Monitor* in March, and had been destroyed by the Confederates on 11 May as the Union forces took control of the Norfolk Navy Yard.[12]

Without a definite plan for the boat, the U.S. Navy officially took it into service on 13 June, and on 19 June the tug *Fred Kopp* began to tow the *Alligator* down the Delaware River and through the Delaware and Chesapeake Canal, finally reaching Hampton Roads on 23 June.[13] Smith instructed Flag Officer Louis M. Goldsborough, who commanded the North Atlantic Blockading Squadron, to use the *Alligator* to whatever purpose he saw fit. After some thought, Goldsborough decided that the submarine might be useful in solving some problems up the James River.

Union gunboats were unable to get near Richmond (and thus help Major General George B. McClellan's land forces exert pressure on the city) because of the situation at Drewry's Bluff, just seven miles downstream from Richmond. There the Confederates had placed Fort Darling atop the bluff, too high for naval guns to strike, and had placed wooden cribs filled with stones (similar to those used by Joseph Bailey on the Red River) across the river as obstructions. Goldsborough thought the submarine might be useful in cleaning out the channel, allowing the boats (under the command of Commander John Rogers) to clear the fort and attack Richmond.

Another possible use for the submarine was in destroying the railroad bridge which passed over the Appomattox River at Petersburg: supplies for General Robert E. Lee's forces defending Richmond came across there. Destroying the bridge might disrupt Lee's operations long enough to give McClellan the upper hand.

Goldsborough immediately had the boat sent up the James River to Rogers, but he seemed to not believe that the submarine would do much good. He wrote to Welles that the *Alligator* was "next to a very useless concern."[14] Rogers received the boat at City Point on 25 June.[15] After examining the boat and talking with the crew, Rogers was impressed with the *Alligator* in general, but saw little potential for success with it in his situation. On 29 June, he ordered the boat sent back to Hampton Roads and in his letter to Goldsborough he states:

> I send back to Fortress Monroe for further orders the machine for blowing up obstructions in the James River...Pickets observe every movement...In going up the Appomattox to Petersburg the machine will show above water, since on the bars there is not depth to submerge her...She is, in the present posture of affairs here, and from physical causes, utterly powerless to help our cause, but in the hands of our enemies, destruction to us...This machine is so terrible an engine, if employed against us, that if I retain her I must keep a strong force to guard her. It is simpler to send her back for further orders. I have no use for her.[16]

In the letter, Rogers also expresses the opinion that the submarine could not be of much use in removing the cribs of stones at Drewry's Bluff, which would be best removed whole by tugboats. The *Alligator* drew six feet of water and required another foot and a half for a diver to clear the hatch at the bottom, or seven and a half feet in all. The Appomattox River was not that deep, meaning that the *Alligator* would approach the railroad bridge not as an unseen commando ship, but as a floating unarmed target.

Goldsborough immediately sent a letter to Rogers concurring with his opinion:

> You did right in returning the submarine propeller to Hampton Roads. I never thought that it could be of the slightest service to you, and so, in effect, informed the Department. I always thought, indeed, that it would prove, as it has done, only a source of expense and embarrassment. But where are the two principal persons, Messrs. Eakin and Thomas? Under no circumstances should they have been allowed to separate themselves from it...These are not times to permit people to indulge idle curiosity to the prejudice of the public interests.[17]

On that same day, Goldsborough wrote to Welles again and asked permission to have the *Alligator* sent to Washington for safekeeping, stating that "at best it can operate successfully in clear and tolerably deep water."[18] The *Alligator* was sent to Washington, where it remained until early August. At that time, Assistant Secretary of the Navy Gustavus Fox wrote to Lieutenant Thomas O. Selfridge: "Mr. Selfridge, if you will take the *Alligator* up the James River and destroy the *Virginia II*, I will make you a captain."[19] Selfridge took command of the boat and began to test it. He had trouble controlling the craft and his report dated 8 August 1862 did not give a favorable view of the *Alligator's* potential usefulness.

Still, some in authority wanted to see the boat put to use. In late 1862, the oars were removed and replaced with a screw propeller. President Lincoln witnessed a test of the *Alligator* on 18 March 1863, and the boat apparently performed well.[20]

Samuel DuPont, now an admiral and in control of the South Atlantic Blockading Squadron, requested that the boat be sent to him to help attack the defenses of Charleston. On 30 March 1863, the boat, being towed by the U.S.S. *Sumpter*, left the Washington Navy Yard and headed towards Port Royal, South Carolina (held by the U.S. Navy since November of 1861).[21] Two nights later, in heavy seas off Cape Hatteras, one of the two towlines broke, causing the *Alligator* to swing out of control and threaten the *Sumpter*.[22] Since the *Alligator's* crew was aboard the *Sumpter*, acting master of the *Sumpter* J. D. Winchester decided to cut the *Alligator* loose, hoping that if she stayed afloat she could be recovered when the weather cleared. The next day, 2 April, the other towline was cut loose but Winchester's hopes were not fulfilled. The U.S. Navy's first submarine submerged for the final time.

Around this same time, Lincoln tried to interest the navy in plans that had come to him from Pascal Plant, plans for a rocket-propelled submarine. Naval experts scoffed at the plan as impractical. Later in the war, Plant did run tests for the navy on a rocket-propelled torpedo. The navy apparently did not like this invention any better as it traveled erratically.[23]

The U.S. Navy began work on another submarine later in 1863.[24] Designed by Scovel S. Merriam and built by O. S. Halstead of Newark, New Jersey, the *Intelligent Whale* was thirty feet long and hand-propelled by a crew of six.[25] Like the *Alligator*, the *Intelligent Whale* had hatches for divers to exit and enter the submarine. The *Intelligent Whale*, which reportedly took the lives of thirty-nine men during testing, was not completed until the war had ended. It can be seen today in the Washington Navy Yard.

In 1864, the Navy received plans for a submarine from Lodner D. Phillips of Michigan City, Indiana. Phillips had been working on submarines since 1845, and had successfully built one in 1851 in which he had reportedly stayed all day on the bottom of Lake Michigan. He had been proposing the construction of one of his submarines to the navy since 1852.[26] His 1851 submarine (called the *Marine Cigar*), forty feet long and four feet in diameter,[27] supposedly had many advanced features, such as an air purification system and an electric motor.[28] His design for a military submarine was similar to the 1851 submarine, but was plated with cast iron on the top deck to withstand small-arms fire and reportedly was armed with a torpedo which was to be launched by means of a rocket fired along the water's surface.[29] The Permanent Commission of the Navy Department recommended that "an appropriation sufficient for the construction of one of the smaller vessels" be made, but there is no record that such a submarine was ever constructed.

Again, without the need for a submarine fleet, the Union navy never did much more than dabble with the idea. In the South, however, the idea of attacking from under the waves became an obsession for a small group of men. Their resolve, in combination with the political and military need for such a vessel, brought history's first successful attack by a submarine vessel.

At the beginning of the war, the Confederate navy consisted of little more than the 237 former U.S. Navy officers who had sworn allegiance to the Confederacy and a few revenue cutters captured at Southern ports.[30] Abraham Lincoln proclaimed a blockade of all Southern ports, a move that turned out to be a political error on several counts. According to international law, a country dealing with internal insurrection simply closed its ports to foreign commerce until the insurrection had been subdued. By announcing a blockade, Lincoln accorded the Confederacy the status of a belligerent nation. In addition, international law stated that the blockade did not need to be respected unless it was truly effective. In April

1861, the Union navy had ninety warships with which it was to patrol thirty-five hundred miles of Confederate coastline.[31] As the war progressed and Union industrial might began to show, the blockade naturally became more effective. Though never a perfect seal, by the last year of the war the blockade had forced Southerners to do without many goods (the South's foreign trade was eventually reduced by more than two-thirds).[32]

The role of the Confederate navy was really two-fold. First, the task of trying to lessen the increasing Union stranglehold where possible and prevent ports from being captured. Secondly (and probably more importantly) was to protect the backdoor of the outmanned Confederate armies from attack. As lacking in ships as the Confederates were, it made sense to rely on ingenuity where possible. Submarine attack vessels and submarine torpedoes seemed to be a fruitful avenue to explore. A letter to the *Columbia* (Tennessee) *Herald* from an inventor named Frances Smith and dated 10 June 1861 states the case succinctly:

> From the Chesapeake to the mouth of the Rio Grande, our coast is better fitted for submarine warfare than any other in the world. I would have every hostile keel chased from our coast by submarine propellers...[33]

The Federal naval officers were well aware of the likelihood of the Confederates trying to attack either by submarine vessels or by submerged mines. A letter (dated 27 October 1861) from Flag Officer Goldsborough (mentioned earlier) to Commander William Smith of the frigate *Congress* offered words of caution:

> Be on the alert for submarine infernal machines. The insurgents at Norfolk are said to possess one calculated to be used under water, and thus to attach a torpedo with a time fuse to a ship's bottom. It is, I understand, to be first towed tolerably near a ship by means of a tug, or else by boats with muffled oars, then to be submerged and so navigated to the vessel against which it is to operate...[34]

A week before Goldsborough had written to Secretary of the Navy Welles nervously informing him of a suspicious craft towed to Hampton Roads from Baltimore by the steam tug *Ajax*. The craft had been designed and built by Ross Winans of Baltimore, an inventor who had been imprisoned for being a secessionist before the war. Before the war, he had also worked on a semi-submerged iron vessel designed for transatlantic service.[35] The craft being towed into Hampton Roads on 19 October 1861 consisted of the two tapered ends of this prior vessel, connected to form what looked very much like a small submarine. Goldsborough had his chief engineer Charles Loring examine the boat on 20 October and make a sketch of it.

According to the engineer in charge of the craft, its purpose was to serve as a water tank to convey seawater to Baltimore where the Winans Steamboat Company could conduct experiments on scale deposits in marine boilers. Loring saw nothing in the boat that seemed to contradict this account.[36]

Still, Goldsborough saw the water tank as a potential weapon against his fleet. His initial letter to Welles on 20 October states that the Confederates might "use it against us as an infernal machine...In my judgment it would not be prudent to allow this tank to go elsewhere than back to Baltimore."[37]

Major General John Dix at Fort McHenry in Baltimore learned that Goldsborough had detained the craft and immediately telegrammed Secretary Welles, affirming that they were well aware of Winans's experiments: "We know all about it, and if you will order it released and allow it to come back you will aid the cause of science."[38]

Welles then ordered Goldsborough (through a letter from Dix) to let the tank be filled with seawater and be towed back to Baltimore before he received Goldsborough's letter relating his misgivings about the craft.[39] As a result, Goldsborough sent a confidential letter to Dix on 26 October, restating for Dix his concerns:

> GENERAL: May I take the liberty of enquiring of you whether the tank, about which you wrote me on the 21st instant, has returned to Baltimore? In my judgment, that affair ought to be very closely watched and not permitted to leave Baltimore again. Surely the experiments...can be conveniently deferred to a more propitious time...Were the tank to get adrift from a tug, and thus fall into the hands of the insurgents, disastrous consequences might ensue, as from the nature of its construction it could very readily be converted into an engine of destruction.[40]

There is no record of this craft traveling from Baltimore again. Up the James River at this same time, however, there was apparently a submarine boat that was reason for real concern on Goldsborough's part. Allan Pinkerton, head of George McClellan's intelligence group, testified after the war that one of his agents had been present at trials of a submarine boat on the James River at Richmond. The boat was apparently built at the Tredegar Iron Works there at a cost of about $6,000, and was designed by James Jones.[41] In November 1861, a Mrs. E. H. Baker (Pinkerton's agent) joined a group of officers and civilians ten miles down the James from Richmond to witness the test of a weapon designed "to break up the blockading fleet at the mouth of the James."[42]

A barge was anchored midstream as a target. The submarine approached from a distance of about half a mile, descending to

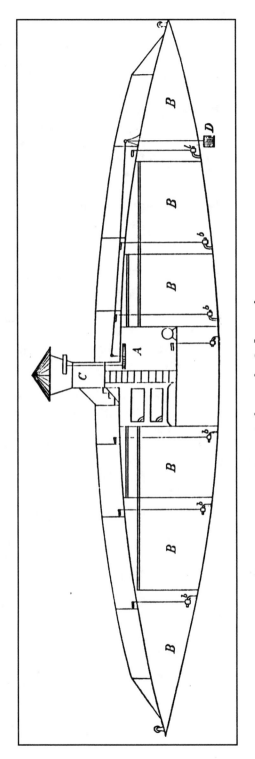

Ross Winans's Submarine

leave only a green float on the surface (the float apparently held up an air hose connected to the submarine). Nearing the target, the submarine attached itself to the target with a suction cup and two or three men in rubber diving suits then worked to screw in a torpedo. After releasing the suction cup and retreating to a safe distance, a lanyard was pulled to trigger the explosion.

The demonstration worked perfectly and Mrs. Baker was alarmed to learn that what she had seen was just a working model of a much larger craft then under construction at Tredegar. She sent her report to Pinkerton who in turn notified Welles to have ships in the Hampton Roads area put on alert.[43] History, however, notes nothing further of these James River submarines.

While some writers doubt the existence of these Richmond submarines, there seems little doubt that Jones existed and was a capable inventor of underwater weapons. A batch of Confederate mail was intercepted while being carried across the Mississippi River in November 1863. It contained a letter from Jones dated 13 October 1863, informing his correspondent that the previous week he had set ten torpedoes in the Pamunkey River, planned to set fourteen more in the following week, and had seventy-four more nearing completion.[44] Another letter contained plans for building submarine vessels west of the Mississippi. Later in the war, Jones seems to have relocated to the Trans-Mississippi region. Union intelligence officers learned in March 1865 that Jones (apparently now residing in Lavaca, Texas) had been busy building more submarines, one at Houston and four at Shreveport, Louisiana.[45] The boats were reported to be forty feet long, four feet deep, and forty inches wide, built of iron and pointed on the ends. The submarines were hand cranked by two men and carried torpedoes (attached to wooden members on each end) which detonated on contact. If these submarines saw action, reports have not survived.

The story of the world's first submarine to see successful action (i.e., sinking an enemy vessel) began in New Orleans in 1861. James R. McClintock and Baxter Watson, machinists and marine engineers, began to combine their talents in designing and constructing a submarine vessel to use as a privateer.[46] With a letter of marque from the Confederate government, private ship owners could prowl the seas in search of enemy vessels. Captured ships and cargo became the property of the privateers. Lacking a substantial navy, the Confederate government also offered a bounty for the destruction of enemy warships.

Watson and McClintock's vessel was launched in early 1862 at the Government Yard on the New Basin.[47] The vessel, under the command of John K. Scott, began trials on Lake Pontchartrain, destroying at least one target barge in the process. The torpedo, detonated by a clockwork mechanism,[48] was screwed into the bottom of the target by means of a crank within the submarine (several accounts state that the explosive was mounted on the end of a wooden spar and detonated with a lanyard).[49] The main problem with the vessel seemed to be in difficulty of navigation. Without a periscope, the crew relied on a compass, which behaved erratically inside the iron vessel. As a result, the crew needed to surface fairly often to check their heading. (This type of problem was not remedied until after the Civil War—first with the addition of compensating magnets to the compass and in modern times with the gyroscopic compass.)

John Scott was granted a commission for the vessel, dubbed the *Pioneer*, on 31 March 1862. The boat is described in Scott's application as a "propeller," thirty-four feet in length, four feet deep, and four feet across through the middle section (the end sections were tapered to conical points), manned by two men and carrying a magazine of explosive matter.[50] The boat was made from $1/4$-inch iron plate bolted to an iron frame with $5/8$-inch rivets, countersunk for streamlining purposes.[51] There was an eighteen-inch diameter round hatchway located amidships and horizontal iron fins (thirty-five inches long and sixteen inches wide) for depth control.[52] The vessel apparently had no air supply (though some accounts credit the vessel with a snorkel consisting of a rubber hose connected to a float) or ballast tank, and the only safety measure was a detachable iron keel which could be released to increase buoyancy.[53] The commission was granted upon a $5,000 bond, the sureties being Horace L. Hunley and Henry J. Leovy.

How Hunley became involved with the project is unknown. He worked at the Customs House in New Orleans with Scott and his brother-in-law Robert R. Barrow and was listed in the application as part owner along with McClintock and Watson, so he certainly knew of the project early on.[54] No more is heard from Barrow or Leovy in connection with submarines.

Within weeks of its commission, however, the *Pioneer* was to meet its end. When the Federal Blockading Squadron, under Captain David G. Farragut, entered New Orleans in late April 1862, the *Pioneer* was sunk to prevent its capture. After the war, McClintock stated: "This boat demonstrated to us the fact that we could construct a boat that would move at will in any direction desired, and at any distance from the surface. The evacuation of New Orleans lost this boat before our experiments were completed."[55]

Since the time of the Civil War, an interesting controversy has developed over the ultimate fate of the *Pioneer*. In 1878, a relic that looked like a small submarine vessel was discovered by workers on a dredgeboat on Lake Pontchartrain and laid on the shore. In 1895, four boys stumbled across the relic, now lying hidden in tall weeds, and notified a group of men working nearby. The relic was soon put on display at Spanish Fort, but was again forgotten. Finally, in 1909 it was moved to the Louisiana State Home for Confederate Soldiers where it remained for many years.

In 1957, the relic was moved to the arcade of the Presbytere, outside Jackson Square in New Orleans where it remains today. James Kloeppel makes a convincing argument that the relic today, known as the *Pioneer,* is actually another submarine vessel.[56] A more recent study indicates that the relic may be the *Pioneer* after all.[57] There is evidence that there was at least one other submarine craft built in New Orleans before the *Pioneer.*[58]

In any case, after sinking their fledgling submarine, McClintock, Watson, and Hunley fled to Mobile, Alabama. The general in command at Mobile, Major General Dabney H. Maury, was receptive to their plans to construct another version of their submarine attack craft.

There had apparently already been some efforts made in Mobile towards the construction of a submarine. Frances Smith, author of the letter to the editor advocating submarine warfare quoted earlier, has been given credit with having built a submarine early in the war at Mobile.[59] His letter (which was apparently distributed widely through the South) had an obvious influence on the design of the *H. L. Hunley,* as will be seen presently. In his letter, he called for the construction of submarines about thirty feet long, shaped like cigars, with a central section of dimensions roughly four feet by three feet.

Other reports credit a man named Alstitt with attempting the construction of a submarine at Mobile, but without success.[60] Supposedly designed to be sixty-five feet long and powered by steam on the surface and by electric motors and batteries when submerged, their is no record of the boat being successfully constructed and tested. (The first confirmed dual-propulsion submarine would not be built for several more decades.) The armament was to be a group of watertight powder cases located along the side of the boat. These were to be released under an enemy vessel and then detonated electrically by attached wires. The design certainly seems more sophisticated than any other submarines of the era. The story may be apocryphal. Alstitt may have been involved in the attempts to use an electric motor in the next venture by Watson, McClintock, and Hunley and not actually involved in building a boat of his own design.[61]

Watson, McClintock, and Hunley soon found the atmosphere in Mobile to be to their liking. They found the Park and Lyons machine shop to be an excellent place for the construction of their next submarine. As well as having all necessary facilities and equipment, the shop also had as temporary employees two men who would figure greatly in the history of the *H. L. Hunley*. Lieutenants William Alexander and George E. Dixon of the Twenty-first Alabama Infantry had been assigned to the shop after their unit took heavy losses at the Battle of Shiloh.[62]

Alexander was a twenty-five-year-old mechanical engineer by trade who had arrived in Mobile from England in 1859.[63] Dixon, a Kentucky native, was also a mechanical engineer.[64] Their superiors ordered them to stop their other work at the shop and devote their attention to the plans of the three men from New Orleans. Some sources have called the submarine they began to work on the *American Diver* while others have named it the *Pioneer II*.

The boat (according to a letter of McClintock's) was thirty-six feet long, three feet wide, and four feet high, with tapered ends (the similarity to the design proposed a year earlier by Frances Smith is obvious).[65] The resourceful Mobile crew apparently spent several months in 1862 trying to formulate some means of propulsion other than human labor. They attempted to propel the boat with an electromagnetic motor, a device that was still in its infancy even for small-scale applications. The motor must have not been able to generate sufficient power to propel the submarine, as they soon tried to install a steam engine. By 1862, the steam engine was a widely used device, but never before had anyone attempted to use it in an environment of limited oxygen (oxygen would be required for combustion of the fuel used to heat the water). McClintock and Watson (who had been involved in the manufacture of steam gauges before the war) may have considered running the boat on the surface, building up pressure in the boiler and then submerging, running the submarine's propeller off the built-up pressure.[66] Though this technique was used successfully in some submarines later in the 1800s, the attempt in Mobile to run the *American Diver* on steam was a failure.

Finally the designers decided to use a propeller shaft, fitted so that four men could turn it. In early 1863, the *American Diver* was ready to be tested. After several test runs in the Mobile River, it was obvious that the boat was not living up to expectations.[67] It was slow (with a top speed of about two miles per hour) and cramped.[68] Nevertheless, it was decided that if the boat was towed through Mobile Bay to a point near Fort Morgan, it might be possible to make an attack on one of the boats of the growing Federal fleet there. In

Alstitt's Submarine

This sketch by a French artist appeared in *Harper's Weekly* in 1864.

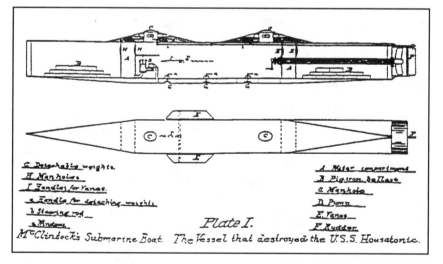

The *American Diver*

This is not, as the caption would indicate, the *Hunley*. The legend reads: A, Water compartment; B, Pig-iron ballast; C, Manhole; D, Pump; E, Vanes; F, Rudder; G, Detachable weights; H, Manholes; I, Handles for Vanes; a, handle for detaching weights; b, steering rod; c, windows.

the first week of February, the boat was towed out of Mobile in rough seas. Waves began to break over the open hatchways of the submarine (left open for ventilation purposes) and the *American Diver* was soon swamped. The boat sank (without loss of life) and remains on the bottom of Mobile Bay today.[69]

Undaunted, the persistent Confederates decided to apply their hard-won knowledge to a third submarine vessel. They estimated their potential cost for the next boat to be about $15,000 and began to seek financial help from others in the Mobile community. E. C. Singer (a mechanical engineer of some renown, and at that time manufacturing most of the underwater mines in the Confederacy) bought a one-third share for $5,000, Hunley bought another $5,000, and the remaining shares went to R. W. Dunn, Gus Whitney, and J. D. Breaman.[70] The bounty offer by the Confederate government entitled the owners to fifty percent of the value of any Union shipping sunk by the submarine.

The third submarine was begun at the Park and Lyons shop. An article by William Alexander, written in 1902 and widely published in newspapers in the South, describes the construction of the submarine in detail.[71] The main part of the boat was formed from a cylindrical boiler about twenty-five feet long, which was cut in half lengthwise and then joined by two twelve-inch wide iron strips. Tapering sections of iron were joined for and aft to this cylinder, to make a vessel about thirty feet long and about four feet in diameter in the center.

To adjust buoyancy, bulkheads were constructed between the end sections and the center section, thus turning the ends into ballast tanks. Water could be let into the tanks through valves and ejected by manual pumps. A mercury gauge open to the water on one end (as outside water pressure rose, so did the column of mercury in the gauge) allowed those in the boat to monitor their depth. In addition, cast iron sheets were fastened to the bottom of the vessel. These sheets could be released by turning T-bolts, which ran out of the hull through water-tight fittings.

Fine tuning of depth was achieved by manipulation of horizontal fins (five feet long and eight inches wide and located on either side of the submarine near the rear) by control shafts which ran through water-tight fittings into the ship. The boat was steered by a wheel (in the forward section of the main compartment) connected to a shaft which ran to the rudder.

The crew of nine entered through two oval hatchways, sixteen inches by twelve inches and eight inches high. The hatchways bolted on the inside and were sealed with rubber gaskets. Glass ports were spaced in the vertical part of the hatches to allow for sighting a

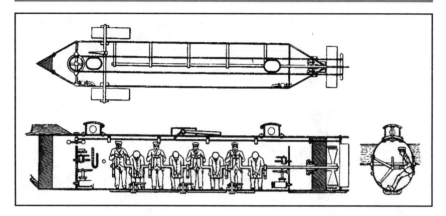

Sketch of the C.S.S. *Hunley* by W. A. Alexander

Official Records

course from inside the submarine. A shaft, which could be open and closed by a stopcock, ran through the top of the boat in order to admit and expel air.

Eight of the men took their places at a crankshaft connected to a propeller. The men sat on the port side, with the shaft being supported by brackets on the starboard side. The three-bladed propeller itself was placed in a wrought iron band to prevent it from being tangled by a line thrown into it.[72] The skipper stood with his head in the forward hatch, sighting through the glass ports. He simultaneously controlled the diving fins and the rudder and monitored the depth gauge and compass (adjusted with magnets to offset the iron hull) by candlelight. He also was responsible for opening and pumping out the forward ballast tank. The crewman in the rear controlled the rear ballast tank. (The author notes that the attachment of a flywheel to the propeller shaft would have certainly eased the burden on the crew of continuous cranking of the shaft.)

On 31 July 1863, the owners arranged to demonstrate their craft. A barge was placed in the middle of the Mobile River. The submarine approached, towing a rope connected to a contact mine. The sub dove under the barge and dragged the mine against it. The mine exploded, destroying the barge, and the submarine soon reappeared, the crew opening the hatches to hear the sounds of a cheering crowd.[73] The operation of the boat was much smoother and faster than that of the *American Diver.*

Impressed Confederate authorities decided that the submarine would have more potential use in Charleston, South Carolina. Charleston (one of only two Confederate ports left open on the Atlantic) had been under bombardment for over a month and a growing Union fleet was cutting off all commerce into and out of the port. In addition, the water at Charleston was deeper than that at Mobile, making it easier to get the submarine under the target.

Baxter Watson and Gus Whitney traveled to Charleston where they met with the military commander, General Pierre Gustave Toutant Beauregard. After hearing them out, Beauregard immediately sent a telegram to stations between Charleston and Mobile:

CHARLESTON, S.C., August 7, 1863

Quartermasters and Railroad Agents on Lines from Charleston, S.C. to Mobile, Ala:

Please expedite transportation of Whitney's submarine boat from Mobile here. It is much needed.

G.T. BEAUREGARD[74]

The submarine was hoisted from the harbor at Mobile and placed across two railroad flatcars (the typical flatcar was only about two-thirds the length of the submarine), secured, and covered with canvas. By 15 August, it had arrived in Charleston and by 20 August all the owners except for R. W. Dunn were also there.[75]

The situation in Charleston was much more desperate than that in Mobile. On 22 August the Federals began to lob shells all day and night on the citizens of the defiant city. To prevent a complete collapse of morale, the Confederate command needed to strike back quickly. Around this time, the submarine was being taken out on at least three nights to the mouth of the harbor where the Federal ironclads were anchored.[76] Each time it returned without attacking. During this period, the crew apparently consisted of McClintock (as captain) and Whitney (manning the rear ballast tank) and seven other men, probably workers under Singer or from the Park and Lyons shop.[77]

The hardened military commanders at Charleston quickly became disgusted with what they perceived as timidity on the part of the civilians in the submarine. On 23 August, the military seized command of the submarine. By 26 August, the submarine was being taken on test dives under the command of Lieutenant John Payne and eight Confederate sailors. Their inexperience was soon to lead to catastrophe.

On 29 August, after diving in the harbor for several hours, Payne ordered the crew to dock at Fort Johnson to prepare the boat for making an attack that night. It was then that disaster struck, though the exact circumstances are unclear. In one version, the submarine docked next to a small steamer. As the crew was beginning to exit the submarine, the steamer began to leave the dock. The submarine became entangled in the ropes of the steamer and was pulled over on its side with the hatches open. Payne was able to leap to the steamer, while two other crewmembers were able to get free of the hatches.[78] A fourth crewmember, Charles Hasker, went to the bottom (thirty to forty feet down) with his foot caught in the hatch. As the submarine filled with water and the pressure equalized, Hasker was able to pull free and rose gasping to the surface. The other five crew members (Michael Cane, Nicholas Davis, Frank Doyle, John Kelly and Absolum Williams) perished.[79] An alternative version of the accident is that the inexperienced Payne accidentally set the horizontal fins in diving position as the submarine moved forward with hatches open, quickly causing it to be swamped.

By 14 September, two civilian divers had managed to locate, secure, and raise the submarine. On 19 September, General Beauregard received a letter from Horace Hunley offering to take over the control of the submarine with a new crew. In his letter he states "...I propose if you will place the boat in my hands to furnish a crew (in whole or in part) from Mobile who are well acquainted with its management and make the attempt to destroy a vessel of the enemy as early as practicable..." Beauregard agreed.

It was apparently around this time that the submarine started to be known as the *H. L. Hunley* (it had been called, among other things, the fish boat and Whitney's submarine boat). Though Hunley had overall control of the boat's operations, it appears that he was not planning to be part of the crew. Instead, Lieutenant George Dixon and Thomas Park (son of the co-owner of the Park and Lyons shop) were to command the front and rear of the ship, respectively. The remainder of the crew came from Mobile, with the exception of Charles Sprague, who had escaped through the rear hatch during the accident that occurred on 29 August. Sprague was an underwater demolition expert, probably responsible for maintaining the explosive torpedo of the *Hunley*. All the men involved had experience with operating the boat.

After arriving in the first week of October, the crew began to sharpen their skills by staging mock attacks on the C.S.S. *Indian Chief*, which was anchored in the Cooper River. They quickly began to gain confidence in their abilities as they submerged time and again, dragging a dummy torpedo or barrel against the hull of the *Indian Chief*.

On the morning of 15 October 1863, for reasons that remain unclear, Hunley himself was at the forward command position instead of Dixon, who was not on the submarine that day. This time, after submerging under the *Indian Chief*, the *Hunley* did not reappear within several minutes as it normally did. Soon it became apparent that another tragedy had occurred and that there were no survivors.

Since the submarine had proven itself to be a dangerous weapon under Dixon's competent command, the authorities lost no time in beginning a search to recover the wreckage. On 18 October, divers located the submarine.[80] Salvage operations showed the sub to be buried bow-first in the mud at an angle of about thirty degrees. The boat was pulled once again to the surface on 7 November.[81]

William Alexander's 1902 article explains in great detail his hypothesis on the cause of the accident. After giving the order to dive, Hunley would have adjusted the horizontal fins to diving position and opened the valve to the front ballast tank. As the glass holes in the hatches submerged, the submarine plunged into darkness. Apparently Hunley had not yet lit his candle (he was found still clutching the unlighted candle), and as he fumbled in the darkness to light it he forgot to close the valve on the ballast tank. As the *H. L. Hunley* plunged to the bottom, both Hunley and Park furiously tried to pump out their ballast tanks. Park was successful, but in the confusion Hunley apparently forgot that his valve was still open.

As water began to rise in the craft (one flaw in the design was that the bulkheads did not rise to the top, allowing water to spill over from the ballast tanks into the crew compartment), the men tried to release the iron castings on the bottom, but were unsuccessful. As the water rose, it forced the air in the submarine into the hatchways where Hunley and Park were found asphyxiated. The rest of the crew (Henry Beard, Robert Brockbank, John Marshall, Charles McHugh, Joseph Patterson, and Charles Sprague) drowned.[82] Why the crew consisted of only eight men that day is unknown. The crew sent from Mobile also contained a man named White, but he was not aboard when the submarine sank on 15 October.

While Beauregard no doubt admired Dixon's courage in volunteering to continue on with a new crew, he consented only on the basis that the craft be used on the surface and not submerged.[83] This would make it similar in effect to the *David* class of steam-propelled, low profile crafts, one of which had been used in Charleston with some success against the Federal warship *New Ironsides* in October. Dixon apparently had other ideas, however, and was to continue training his crew with the *Hunley* in a submerged mode.

Dixon returned to Mobile, where he told Alexander of the recent events in Charleston and convinced him to return there with him. Dixon was convinced that under competent command, the boat could be operated safely. Once in Charleston, Dixon and Alexander recruited a crew from the men of the *Indian Chief*, who had seen the *Hunley* in operation many times.[84] During the late fall and early winter of 1863, Dixon and Alexander trained the men thoroughly in the operation of the boat.

Training an average of four nights a week, the men built up their endurance and their experience by working up to practice runs as long as fourteen miles.[85] During this time period, a man named Belton deserted from the Confederate navy and divulged the existence of the *Hunley* to the Union naval command.[86] By the next day, Union engineers were at work building up rope and metal mesh riggings around the ironclads at the mouth of the harbor.[87]

In the face of these developments, it was decided that the *Hunley* should target the wooden ships of the fleet anchored well outside the harbor. To this end, the crew moved their base of operations to Battery Marshall, on the northern tip of Sullivan's Island, north of the harbor. At about this same time, Dixon and Alexander also changed the method by which the *Hunley* would deliver its explosive charge to the target. During the first months in Charleston, the mode of attack had been to drag the torpedo by a rope behind the submarine. The submarine would then dive under the target, causing the torpedo to hit the target ship and explode.

With the prospect of having to travel a number of miles (the nearest wooden ship of the blockading fleet at this time was believed to be twelve miles from the harbor) in rough seas, it was believed that this mode of delivery might be too dangerous to the *Hunley*. The alternative was to fasten the torpedo to a spar on the front of the ship. The *Hunley* would drive the sharpened tip of the spar (a steel point with saw-tooth edges) into the wooden sides of the target and would then back away.[88] Once at a safe distance, a lanyard (a strong rope attached to a reel on top of the sub) would be pulled, igniting the charge.[89] There is some evidence that the spar arrangement had been considered as early as the days of testing in Mobile, due to the shallow water there.[90]

On 5 February 1864, Alexander received orders to report back to Mobile to use his skills in building a breech-loading repeating gun. "This was a terrible blow both to Dixon and myself, after we had gone through so much together," Alexander later wrote.[91] Alexander's spot was filled by a volunteer (C. F. Carlson of F. W. Wagener's artillery company).[92]

About a week later, fortune finally smiled on the *Hunley* and its crew. A new Union warship, the *Housatonic*, was seen to be anchoring about three miles from the mouth of the harbor. To avoid any potential threats from the *Hunley* or a *David* class torpedo boat, the Union command ordered the *Housatonic* to keep up a full head of steam and post six lookouts, ready to spot any threat or blockade runner.

On the clear night of 17 February, the paths of the *Hunley* and the *Housatonic* crossed in a manner that would leave their names inevitably linked. On that afternoon, Dixon made some repairs to

U.S.S. *Housatonic*

Official Records

the torpedo mechanism, and then around 1900 (about an hour after sundown) gave the order to proceed into the Atlantic.[93] At about 2045, a lookout on the *Housatonic* saw a shape moving through the water about one hundred yards off the starboard beam, a shape he at first mistook for a porpoise. When the Union sailors finally realized the threat, the *Hunley* was already too close for the *Housatonic* to aim its large guns at it, and the Confederate sub began to run a gauntlet of small-arms fire from the men on board the warship. Fixing the torpedo to the hull of the *Housatonic* and then withdrawing, the men of the *Hunley* were soon rocked by a tremendous underwater explosion.

A gaping hole was opened in the *Housatonic*, which immediately sank, listing to port in fairly shallow water. Five men of the 155 on board the *Housatonic* perished in the attack, while the other 150 managed to survive by climbing into the rigging, which remained out of the twenty-seven-feet deep water.[94] The *Hunley* had managed history's first successful submarine attack.

The story of the *Hunley* to this point is fairly well documented. Now begins the part of the saga that has been shrouded in mystery for well over a century. After the attack, the *Hunley* never returned to its base. For many years, it was assumed that the *Hunley* went down with the *Housatonic*, either pulled down with it or destroyed in the explosion. This belief persisted in spite of a Union examination of the wreck of the *Housatonic* in November of 1864. The Union sailors searched the area immediately around the *Housatonic* and dragged

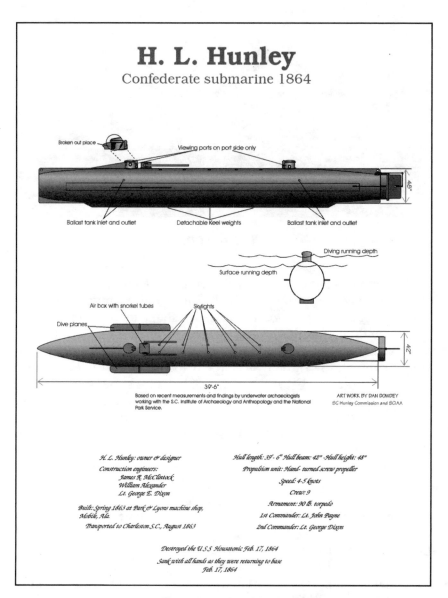

Modern Drawing of C.S.S. *H. L. Hunley*

Based on measurements and findings by underwater archaeologists.

Drawing by Dan Dowdey, and used with permission of artist

the ocean floor at a radius of five hundred yards around the wreck and found nothing.[95]

Many subsequent articles about the *Hunley* insisted that the submarine had been located near the *Housatonic*, some even claiming that the bodies of Dixon and his crew had been located within. In fact, it is now certain that the *Hunley* was well on its way back to its base before it met its demise. Conjecture about its fate ended when the wreck of the *Hunley* was finally discovered in 1994, only about one mile from its home base. The discovery was based on evidence from the Court of Inquiry into the sinking of the *Housatonic*. Seaman Robert Flemming (one of the *Housatonic's* lookouts that night) testified that a full forty-five minutes after the *Housatonic* sank, he observed a blue light in the water. This was apparently a signal, using a calcium light covered with a blue lens, from Dixon to his home base informing them that they were on the way back. (The bright calcium lights used in Civil War days relied on mixing calcium carbide [from limestone] with water to make acetylene, which burns brightly). The signal was to be answered with a similar light to enable the *Hunley* to locate the base. A report filed by Lieutenant Colonel O. M. Dantzler, Battery Marshall's commanding officer, stated:

> The signals agreed upon to be given in case the boat wished a light to be exposed at this post as a guide for its return were observed and answered.

So the *Hunley* almost completed its historic mission, but sank within site of shore. Perhaps the small-arms fire had penetrated the glass portholes of the hatches, allowing water to enter, or maybe the boat was swamped when Dixon opened the hatch to signal the shore. In any case, the wreckage is at this date being carefully examined in the hopes of possibly raising it to the surface for display. Interested readers can follow the progress of the effort on the World Wide Web.[96] Accurate measurements of the wreckage have turned up some discrepancies with the standard measurements from Alexander's 1902 article (which he came up with from memory, almost forty years after he had worked on the submarine). The *Hunley* is actually 39 feet, 5 inches in length and 3 feet, 10 inches in diameter. A $4^3/_4$-inch keel runs outside the bottom of the hull. The dive planes are 6 feet, 10 inches long, not the 5 feet, 8 inches noted by Alexander.[97]

The *Hunley* was not the last Confederate submarine. There is record of at least two more submarines constructed later at Mobile. A thirty-eight-foot wooden submarine, sheathed in ¼-inch iron, was apparently built but sank during testing in Mobile Bay.[98] Better known was the *Saint Patrick*, built by John P. Halligan in Selma during 1864.

It was propelled on the surface by a steam engine and underwater by hand.[99] The submarine was sailed down the Alabama River to Mobile in November 1864.[100]

By December, General Maury had decided that Halligan was not going to be a sufficiently aggressive commander and replaced him with Lieutenant John T. Walker (in a scenario reminiscent of Beauregard's replacement of McClintock with Payne at Charleston). On the morning of 27 January 1865, Walker and his crew attacked the U.S.S. *Octorora* in Mobile Bay. The submarine's copper torpedo (on a twelve-foot spar extending from her bow) made contact with the Union ship but failed to detonate.[101] A sailor on board the *Octorora* grabbed the *Saint Patrick's* smokestack and held tight until forced to relinquish his grip when a crewman on the submarine fired at him. As the submarine retreated, heavy small-arms fire from the Federal ship failed to damage it. The *Saint Patrick* saw no further offensive action.[102]

The efforts on both sides, especially those of the Confederates, went a long way towards aiding the development of the submarine as an offensive naval weapon. Union Admiral John A. Dahlgren's reaction to the sinking of the *Housatonic* typifies the wave of alarm which followed the events of 17 February 1864: "The Department will readily perceive the consequences likely to result from this event; the whole line of blockade will be infested with these cheap, convenient, and formidable defenses and we must guard every point. The measures for prevention may not be so obvious."[103] Dahlgren's fears were not realized, as Charleston fell by land exactly a year after the sinking of the *Housatonic*.[104] It was not until the autumn of 1914 when the British submarine *E-9* sank the German cruiser *Hela* that another successful submarine attack occurred.[105] One can not help but admire the courage of the men of the *Hunley* and other Civil War submarines who placed their lives in peril for their cause aboard these primitive crafts.

Chapter 5

War in the Sky: Balloons

On 18 June 1861, President Abraham Lincoln received the following telegram at the White House:

> To the President of the United States
> Sir: This point of observation commands an area nearly 50 miles in diameter. The city, with its girdle of encampments, presents a superb scene. I have pleasure in sending you this first dispatch ever telegraphed from an aerial station, and in acknowledging indebtedness for your encouragement for the opportunity of demonstrating the availability of the science of aeronautics in the military service of the country.
>
> T.S.C. Lowe[1]

Thaddeus Sobieski Constantine Lowe sent the telegram by a novel method and from a novel location: Lowe was in a balloon tethered five hundred feet above the Columbian Armory several blocks from the White House.

Three years before the men of the *Hunley* manipulated the buoyancy of an iron craft in water, men on both sides of the Civil War were working to investigate the military possibilities of buoyancy in a more ethereal fluid: the air around us. The story of military aeronautics in the Civil War is a mixed story of bravery, petty rivalries, and lost chances.

As described in detail in Appendix 3, ballooning was already in its seventh decade by the time the Civil War began. Aeronauts (as balloonists were called) had already made trips hundreds of miles in length and the sight of humans ascending in balloons had become relatively common at fairs and demonstrations by 1861. America had a number of well-known aeronauts: James Allen, John LaMountain, Thaddeus Lowe, John Steiner, and John Wise were the most prominent. This group occasionally collaborated in their ventures, but more often bickered and cast aspersions at one another as each sought to become pre-eminent in the field. These rivalries had become especially intense just before the war because several in the group were competing to become the first man to cross the Atlantic Ocean by balloon.

The French had used balloons for military observation not long after the first humans ascended. Still, in the years between the French Revolution and the Civil War, the use of aerial observation had been very limited and of questionable success. Though the use of balloons had been suggested to the U.S. military on several occasions, they had never been used in battle in this country. One great drawback was that true navigation of balloons was still unknown: aeronauts worked either with balloons tethered to the ground or took their chances with the vagaries of the winds aloft. As with submarines, there was a great reluctance by most military leaders to exploit unproven technologies.

On 15 April 1861, Lincoln issued his proclamation calling for seventy-five thousand volunteers for ninety-day terms. As the Union forces prepared for war, there was a frenzy of activity in Washington, including efforts by the most prominent aeronauts to capture the attention of the military and the administration. As both sides fumbled their way through the first few months of the war, the military ballooning that occurred was mostly an uncontrolled sideshow. Not until the Union and Confederate armies got down to more serious business in 1862 did authorities take a closer look at what the aeronauts were doing and how they were doing it. The chaotic nature of ballooning on the Union side in the period from March 1861 to February 1862 can probably best be understood by looking at a chronology of the interplay among the various aeronauts.

April–May 1861

James Allen

One of the first volunteers to enlist in Providence, Rhode Island was thirty-six-year-old James Allen, already famous as the "New England Aeronaut," though he had made his first solo flight less than four years earlier.[2] In response to Lincoln's proclamation, Allen volunteered his services as an aeronaut to the First Regiment, Rhode Island State Militia, commanded by Colonel Ambrose Burnside. Allen and his townsman, William H. Helme, were "authorized to act at aeronauts in connexion [sic] with the movements of the regiment."[3] On orders of Governor William Sprague, Allen left Providence for Washington, D.C., where he arrived with two balloons by the end of May.

John Wise

At about the same time that James Allen was volunteering with the Rhode Island militia, an even more famous aeronaut was volunteering for service in Lancaster, Pennsylvania. John Wise, fifty-three years old, had made his first ascension in 1835 and was well known not only for his balloon exhibitions, but also for his many scientific experiments conducted aloft. Though Wise had offered his services as a balloonist in the Mexican War, when Lincoln's call for men came he volunteered as a captain of an infantry company from his hometown.[4]

John LaMountain

John LaMountain of Troy, New York, was especially well known for his long-distance free ascensions, including one he made with Wise from St. Louis to upstate New York. Twice during the spring of 1861, LaMountain wrote to Secretary of War Simon Cameron offering his services as a balloonist and both times he was met with silence.

Thaddeus Lowe

Though far less experienced than several of his competitors, Lowe came to Washington in 1861 with a widespread reputation and more importantly, with powerful connections to the administration. Before the war, Lowe had been among those attempting to be the first to navigate the Atlantic through the air. In 1860, he had tested an immense craft called the *City of New York* (later renamed the *Great Western*), with which he hoped to make the ocean crossing. On both occasions in September 1860 that he actually tried to begin the voyage, however, the balloon's envelope had sprung a leak.[5]

His attempts had not escaped the notice of Professor Joseph Henry, secretary of the Smithsonian Institution, who became an ardent supporter of Lowe. (We will hear more of Henry, whose experiments with electricity and magnetism had placed him among the nation's most prominent physicists, in Chapter 6 on telegraphy in the war.) Henry suggested that Lowe test the theory that strong high altitude winds blowing eastward (recall LaMountain's free ascensions) would make the trans-Atlantic trip possible by first riding those winds from an inland city to the East Coast. Accordingly, on 20 April 1861, Lowe ascended from Cincinnati (where the editor of the *Daily Commercial*, Mural Halstead, had also become a Lowe supporter) with the intent of landing somewhere in the Chesapeake Bay region. Midway through the voyage, Lowe descended to check his location and got caught in a southerly stream of air. To rise back to the easterly current would have meant the removal of all ballast, so Lowe decided to ride it out, eventually coming to earth in Unionville, South Carolina.[6] The trip of about one thousand miles had taken nine hours.

Sketch of Allen's Balloon in Camp, June 1861
Library of Congress, LC-USZ62-40041

Lowe's rough reception from the locals was not surprising in light of the attack on Fort Sumter the previous week. Assailed by some as a Yankee spy or propagandist (Lowe was carrying copies of the Cincinnati paper to prove the location and time of his ascent) and by others as a devil, he was thrown in jail briefly in Columbia, South Carolina. Eventually, several prominent citizens were able to vouch for him and obtain his release.

June 1–June 15, 1861

James Allen

On 9 June, Allen inflated the larger of his balloons with coal gas at a gas main located at Third Street and Massachussetts Avenue and had the balloon (ballasted with sandbags) towed to the Rhode Island regiment's camp a mile north of the Capitol.[7] There he ascended in the balloon (fifty feet tall, thirty-six feet in diameter and tied to a mooring rope) to a height of five thousand feet. The next day, the regiment was ordered to Harper's Ferry, where the men stayed for about a week before returning to Washington. It is possible that Allen and his balloons accompanied the regiment, but there is no record of an ascension during this period.

John Wise

While Wise waited for formal recognition of his company by the governor of Pennsylvania, he received a telegram from Major Hartman Brache of the Bureau of Topographical Engineers asking the cost of construction of a balloon of 500 pounds lifting power and also for Wise's pay requirements if he was to serve as balloonist.[8] Wise replied that the balloon could be made for $300 and that his services to the government would be free. Brache's telegram was sent on 10 June, the day after Allen's first balloon inflation in Washington.

John LaMountain

On 5 June LaMountain, after waiting in vain for several months to hear some word from Washington, received an unsolicited offer to serve as aerial observer from Major General Benjamin Butler. Butler was in charge of the Department of Virginia and stationed at Fortress Monroe at the tip of the James River peninsula. As mentioned in Chapter 1, Butler was a politically appointed general, not a career military man, and this may account for his being open to the idea of using balloons. Butler was also in a tough military situation, one in which he needed all the help he could get, no matter how unconventional. Fortress Monroe was surrounded on all sides by hostile forces, and Butler needed to have a clear idea of what he was up against. LaMountain agreed to Butler's offer, though he would not arrive at Fortress Monroe until 23 July.[9]

Thaddeus Lowe

Lowe's train trip from South Carolina back to Ohio had a deep effect on him. Seeing the massive war preparations throughout the South made him realize that service to his country would for now be more important than thoughts of crossing to Europe. By 6 June, Lowe had arrived in Washington, and had gotten an audience with Secretary of the Treasury Salmon P. Chase, a good friend of Mural Halstead. Impressed, Chase mentioned Lowe to Secretary of War Cameron. Cameron in turn interviewed Joseph Henry, and they agreed that Lowe would make a demonstration of the military value of aerial reconnaissance.[10] On 11 June, Lowe met with Lincoln, who seemed quite interested in the balloon's possibilities.[11]

June 16–June 30, 1861

John Wise

On 26 June, Brache telegraphed Wise again, and asked the cost of a more substantial balloon. At this time, Thaddeus Lowe had made the impressive demonstration alluded to at the beginning of this chapter and perhaps Brache had a better idea of what he wanted. In any event, Wise said the cost for the more sophisticated balloon described by Brache would be $850 and could be made in two weeks. Wise was given instructions to begin his work, and on 1 July, a public announcement was made of Wise's attachment to the Army as a civilian balloonist.[12]

Thaddeus Lowe

Lowe's demonstration took place on the grounds of the Columbian Armory on 18 June. Lowe made a tethered ascent to about five hundred feet and then sent Lincoln the telegraph message mentioned at the beginning of this chapter. The message was sent by telegraph operator Herbert Robinson,[13] who ascended with Lowe (along with George McDowell, of the American Telegraph Company).[14] A telegraph wire hung down from Robinson's telegraph key in the balloon to a reel on the ground. The other end of the wire was connected to a line that ran between the War Department and the office of the telegraph company in Arlington, with an extension to the White House. Lowe also sent messages to the War Department and to Philadelphia, and Lincoln may also have sent a reply to Lowe.[15]

After the demonstration, the balloon was towed to the White House lawn where it was moored for the night. The next day, Lowe ascended again and repeated his telegraph demonstrations. By this time there was great excitement in the press regarding the possibilities of combining aerial observations with telegraphic communications. It is interesting to note, in light of the resultant fame that came to Lowe because of his demonstrations, that his very first ascension in 1858 had been at a celebration in honor of Cyrus Field's trans-Atlantic telegraph cable.[16]

As word spread of the demonstrations, General Irwin McDowell, in command of the Union forces at Washington, sent word from his Arlington headquarters that he would like Lowe to report to him. Lowe arrived on 22 June, and immediately made an ascension, though his observations were apparently of little value. The next day, Lowe and his equipment were moved forward to Falls Church, where he made two ascents. Though he saw little because of the wooded terrain, Lowe was able to establish a telegraph connection with McDowell's headquarters in Arlington.[17] Up again on 24 June, an officer in the basket with Lowe was able to make a detailed map of the surrounding area. Satisfied with the results to this point, McDowell had Lowe return to Washington on 25 June.

In spite of his connections, when he returned to Washington, Lowe found that the government had hired Wise to build the first U.S. military balloon, as he had underbid Lowe by $200. Wise offered to let Lowe operate the balloon, but Lowe, with characteristic lack of tact, declined: "I would not be willing to expose my life and reputation by using so delicate a machine...made by a person in whom I had no confidence."[18]

July 1–July 15, 1861

James Allen

In early July, it had become obvious that a major clash was likely to occur between Union and Confederate forces near the railroad junction at Manassas. On 8 July, Allen received instructions to ascend with Lieutenant Henry Abbot, a thirty-year-old West Point graduate, and make observations of Confederate outposts near Washington.[19] Allen spent all night trying to fill his balloon (using a crude hydrogen generator), but by daybreak he had only managed to fill the top half. Allen knew that this was an unstable situation, but Abbot insisted on making an ascent. By the time Abbot had gotten to five hundred feet, he knew Allen had been right. The deflated bottom half of the balloon acted like a sail, twisting the balloon so violently that Abbot could not count Confederate troops and guns, though he could see them.

General McDowell had ordered the test. Abbot reported to him that he thought the balloon might be of use if properly filled. In light of Allen's ineffective hydrogen generator, this meant filling with coal gas from the city gas line. McDowell approved and on 14 July Allen began filling both his balloons with coal gas at Alexandria. The older of his two balloons burst before it could be totally filled. The other was filled properly, and sixty men from the Eleventh New York Zouaves were assigned the task of towing the balloon to Falls Church, in preparation for the Union movement on Manassas. Before they had gotten far, a strong gust blew the balloon into a telegraph pole and the envelope burst.[20]

The accident was the first example of the problems suffered by Civil War balloonists when inexperienced ground crews moved their balloons. This, among other things, eventually led to the establishment of a balloon corps under Thaddeus Lowe. After the accident, Allen returned to Providence, where he remained until the spring of 1862 when he was called to join Lowe's corps. He and his brother Ezra served well under Lowe, and James Allen briefly took command of the corps when Lowe fell sick after the Battle of Malvern Hill.

July 16–July 21, 1861

John Wise

Wise completed his balloon on 16 July (two days after Allen's fiasco with the telegraph pole) and arrived in Washington on 18 July. On 19 July, Wise received orders to inflate his balloon and report immediately to Centreville, near Manassas. Wise took his balloon to the Columbian Armory for inflation from the gas main there. As described below, he found Lowe inflating his balloon, but military officials ordered Lowe to take his balloon off the main and Wise to put his on. The inflation was not completed until 0200 on 21 July.

Twenty men from the Twenty-sixth Pennsylvania Infantry were ordered to transport the balloon by moonlight to Manassas. The balloon, with a capacity of twenty thousand cubic feet, had a basket of willow and cane, covered on the bottom with sheet iron to protect the occupants.[21] Wise also planned to carry percussion grenades, pistols, and a rifle in the basket.[22]

By 1200 on the twenty-first, the balloon had been carried about halfway to Manassas. Already the men could hear guns from the war's first large battle, which had begun that morning. Major Albert J. Myer, chief signal officer of the army, and in charge of the balloon detail, became anxious that the balloon would arrive too late to take part in the battle. Myer, over objections from Wise, ordered the balloon tied to a horse-drawn wagon. Before long, the balloon had become wedged in a tree and was ripped as the men tried to free it. Myer ordered the dejected Wise to take the balloon back to Washington for repairs.

Thaddeus Lowe

Despite his initial rejection by the army, Lowe continued to make demonstrations at the Smithsonian and by mid-July his persistence began to pay off. Worried that Wise might not have his balloon completed in time for the impending battle at Manassas, officers at the Bureau of Topographical Engineers asked Lowe to join the Union advance. As Lowe was beginning the inflation of his balloon at the city gas main, Wise showed up with his balloon, and officers ordered Lowe to step aside.

When word of Wise's failure reached Lowe the next day, he determined to join the advance anyway. By 21 July he had reached Falls Church but found the routed Union army headed back to Washington. Lowe returned to Fort Corcoran, just across the Potomac from Washington, the next day.

July 23–August 31, 1861

John Wise

Wise managed to repair the damage to his balloon by 23 July, but by then McDowell's beleaguered army was back in Washington. The next day, Wise was ordered to make ascensions in Arlington (by this time, Lowe had begun making ascensions from Fort Corcoran at the Virginia end of the bridge over the Potomac River).

Wise went up on the afternoon of 24 July and observed Confederate advance forces.

The next day, Wise was ordered to take the balloon to Ball's Crossroads for more observations. At sunrise on 26 July, Wise and his men had begun to cross the bridge across the Potomac when bad luck struck again. Wind tangled the balloon's mooring ropes with telegraph wires lining the bridge. Before the men could untangle the ropes, the wires had sawn through them, setting the balloon free. Alert troops in Arlington saw the escaped balloon and downed it with several volleys of musket fire.[23] This was the only time during the Civil War that a balloon was brought down by fire (the first American balloon to be shot down by enemy fire fell during the Spanish-American War in 1898).[24]

Captain A. W. Whipple, who had ordered Wise to bring the balloon to Ball's Crossroads (and who had also given the orders for Wise to bring the balloon to Centreville), was now disgusted with balloons in general and with Wise in particular. He met Wise and berated him severely for his failures. Wise, also a bit disgusted, answered that "the balloon part of the disastrous affair" at Bull Run "was just about as good as the fighting part."[25]

Wise, who had received no food or lodging, and had to pay for balloon repairs himself, now waited in vain for further orders. On 10 August, he received a request from a civil engineer in the West to come out and build a balloon. Wise left Washington on 13 August. By October he had returned to Pennsylvania and, ever the patriot, raised a cavalry company there. He served for several months before poor health forced his retirement.

Thaddeus Lowe

By 23 July, rumors abounded that the Confederate army was going to sweep in and take Washington; citizens and soldiers alike were in a state of panic. Consequently, Lowe decided to check out the situation. On 24 July, he made a free ascension to about three miles in height from which he was able to see that the great majority of Confederate troops were still camped near Manassas. He was not able to relay this information until the next day, however. A strong gust of wind blew him into Alexandria, where Union pickets, thinking him a spy, began to shoot at him. Releasing ballast, Lowe was blown still farther out, two miles past the Union lines before descending. Severely injuring his ankle in the landing, Lowe had to hide until darkness while Confederates searched for him. That night a search party from the Union side, made up of volunteers from the Thirty-first New York and including Lowe's wife, found him and salvaged the balloon.

LaMountain Ascending near Fort Monroe
Library of Congress, LC-USZ62-5653

The next day, Lincoln called for Lowe, and on the following day both men went to see General of the Army Winfield Scott. This meeting led to Lowe's appointment on 2 August 1861 as the U.S. military's first aeronaut. Lowe was to construct a sturdy new balloon for military operations (during the construction of which he would be paid $5 a day) and would then be paid $10 a day for service as an aeronaut. Lowe proceeded to Philadelphia, where he built the balloon, and was back in Washington by 28 August.[26]

John LaMountain

Meanwhile, LaMountain had arrived at Fortress Monroe. LaMountain began to inflate his balloon on 24 July, using sulfuric acid and iron scraps to generate hydrogen. He ascended the next day, but there was too much wind for him to make good observations. After several days of poor weather, LaMountain ascended again on 31 July and made what was probably the first effective use of aerial reconnaissance by the United States military. From an altitude of fourteen hundred feet, he could see for about thirty miles in all directions. Among his observations, he noted a force at Sewell's Point of several hundred men. This encampment, hidden from Fortress Monroe by trees, had been rumored to hold several thousand men. The Confederates noted LaMountain's ascent.[27]

On 3 August, LaMountain ascended from the deck of the armed transport U.S.S. *Fanny*, which docked near Sewell's Point. From this vantage point, LaMountain could see Confederate troops digging gun pits for artillery that could be aimed at Fortress Monroe and nearby shipping. Some of the Confederates tried to hide from the balloon, while others were enraged and shouted profanity at LaMountain.[28]

LaMountain continued to make ascensions through 10 August. He was able to estimate troop strengths by counting tents or at night, by counting campfires. In response, the Confederates instituted what were probably history's first "blackouts."[29] But by 10 August, LaMountain had run out of supplies for generating hydrogen. LaMountain asked and was granted Butler's permission to return home to retrieve a larger balloon and a more efficient hydrogen generator. Butler seemed pleased with LaMountain's work, describing his observations as "very successful" and the information obtained "of great advantage."[30]

Fall–Winter 1861

Thaddeus Lowe

The fall of 1861 around Washington was in some ways the calm before the storm of battles which 1862 would bring to the region. Except for the relatively minor Union debacle at Ball's Bluff near Leesburg in October, the armies mainly stared at each other across the Potomac, waiting for spring to bring new action. During this time, Lowe was extremely active, ascending on more than twenty days between late August and the end of September. The relative lull in military activity gave Lowe and the ground crew appointed to him a chance to hone their skills, and his observations of Confederate camps were useful if not of paramount military importance in the long run. Lowe also was able to take up important military leaders, including Irwin McDowell, Fitz-John Porter and George McClellan, who seemed impressed with the balloon's vantage point.[31] On 24 September, Lowe performed for the first time a now common military feat: directing artillery fire from above. Using telegraph and flag signals, Lowe was able to direct artillery fire at Confederate positions around Falls Church.

Sensing the military's growing confidence in his methods, Lowe proposed to McClellan that a balloon corps be formed. McClellan approved, and by early fall Lowe had been directed to construct six more balloons, along with twelve portable gas generators. Lowe also began to recruit aeronauts for his corps, and eventually used nine other men besides himself: William Paullin (dismissed in January 1862), John Starkweather, Ebenezer Locke Mason (dismissed in

Lowe's Balloon, Fall 1861

Harper's Weekly, 26 October 1861

spring 1862 over a pay dispute), Ebenezer Seaver, James Allen, Ezra Allen, John Steiner, Jacob Freno (dismissed in March 1862 for disciplinary reasons), and John Dickinson (reported to be in command of a flight in October 1861).[32] Lowe's father, Clovis Lowe, was also hired as a general repairman and assistant.

John LaMountain

LaMountain left Virginia on 16 August and returned on 12 September. During this time, Butler was transferred and replaced by Major General John Wool. To LaMountain's consternation, Butler had apparently told Wool nothing about LaMountain. Wool wrote a letter to Secretary of War Cameron asking for instructions in putting LaMountain to use and sent LaMountain to Washington to hand-deliver it.[33]

By this time, Lowe had made many balloon demonstrations in and around Washington and the authorities had begun to once again look favorably on the possibilities of aerial reconnaissance. In particular, McClellan (who would soon lead the Army of the Potomac) and Brigadier General Porter were quite interested in Lowe's activities and must have looked upon LaMountain's arrival as being helpful to the cause.

The pre-war rivalry between Lowe and LaMountain was probably unknown to McClellan, but he must have sensed tension between them immediately. He instructed Porter to interview the two of them together to get a better idea of how they might work together. During the interview, both men agreed that they would cooperate fully with the other for the good of the Union cause,[34] though Porter must not have been totally comfortable with this as he later told McClellan that "both are jealous."[35] On 27 September, LaMountain was officially assigned as a civilian aeronaut with the Army of the Potomac.

During the next several months, LaMountain was to successfully employ a technique he had mastered to some extent before the war: the free ascension. The military situation around Washington was perfect for this type of ballooning, because the Confederate forces in Virginia were located mainly to the west of the Union forces around Washington. LaMountain could let low altitude winds blow him westwards above the Confederate camps and then ascend to high altitudes. At these greater heights the winds normally blow from west to east and would allow him to return to base. (The core of the jet stream, which blows from west to east over the United States, is normally located at an elevation of about thirty-five thousand to forty thousand feet, but its effects can be felt down to altitudes as low as five thousand feet. Outside of the jet stream, the prevailing wind patterns at high altitude are also from west to east).

LaMountain gave his first demonstration of the technique over Washington on 1 October, and then made his first reconnaissance of the Confederate camps on 18 October. Ascending to fourteen hundred feet, he was able to make accurate troop counts as he sailed from camp near Washington all the way out past Manassas. Then, ascending still higher to a point where he encountered the persistent west-to-east winds, he made his return. He descended into a camp of soldiers of German descent under Brigadier General Louis Blenker. Thinking LaMountain to be a Confederate spy, the soldiers savagely attacked both him and the balloon, and he barely escaped serious injury before he reached the safety of Blenker's tent.[36]

Throughout the next month, LaMountain continued to make useful observations and his superiors appear to have been pleased, enough so that the army purchased LaMountain's two balloons for permanent use. Then, on 16 November, disaster struck. A heavy wind blew LaMountain's larger and higher quality balloon off its moorings and into the sky. It was never recovered.

LaMountain had become aware that Lowe had two balloons in storage in Washington, and requested that he be allowed to use one of them. In his request, he sowed the seeds of his own demise as he began to tear apart the fragile alliance he had promised with Lowe. He accused Lowe of hoarding the balloons because Lowe was jealous of LaMountain's aeronautical skills. He also speculated that Lowe was keeping the balloons (whose construction had been funded by the government) in storage so that he could buy them back at low cost when the war had ended.

While he waited for his request to be processed, LaMountain continued to perform ascensions with his smaller (and poorer quality) balloon. On 10 December, he spent several hours over the Confederate camps, making very accurate reports, before ascending to seventeen thousand feet and riding the high altitude winds home. This sort of surveillance had an effect on the Confederates. General Joseph Johnston refers in his reports to "the infernal balloon" and Major General James Longstreet proposed camouflaging all guns with sheds covered with leaves and brushwood.[37] Longstreet also stated that the Confederate's Quaker guns (logs painted to look like cannons) would not be of much use if the Union continued to probe their positions in this manner.

As a result of his continued ascensions, the press began to hail LaMountain's exploits. This attention irked Lowe, especially an article in the *New York Herald* entitled "The New Aeronautic Department under Professor LaMountain" in which Lowe was not even mentioned.[38] Lowe protested to McClellan, saying that LaMountain was nothing but a showman who was giving serious aeronautics a bad name. He further told McClellan that LaMountain had been ridiculing him in the press for years, which was true. By this time, McClellan had taken a liking to Lowe and promptly informed LaMountain that all balloons would now be under Lowe's supervision, and that LaMountain needed to come to an understanding with Lowe if he wished to continue in service.

The rivalry had become too heated for such an understanding to occur. LaMountain continued to make ascensions in his old balloon, but also continued to request access to Lowe's balloons and to accuse Lowe of devious behavior in keeping the balloons to himself. By February 1862, the dissension between the aeronauts had worn out the military commanders and on 19 February, McClellan dismissed LaMountain from service with the Army of the Potomac. In his half of year of service, LaMountain had made a number of ascensions of military value, but his long rivalry with Lowe was too strong to keep both in the employ of the army.

LaMountain's dismissal left Lowe in control of Union military aeronautics, at least to the extent that any civilian had control of the enterprise. Like many other facets of the Union war machine, bureaucracy and administrative incompetence were to take a heavy toll in the U.S. Balloon Corps.

By early 1862, Lowe had six of his portable generators. He had also supervised the modification of a naval coal barge, the *George Washington Parke Custis*, into the world's first aircraft carrier. Navy carpenters decked the hull over, built a small shack for the aeronaut, and fitted the deck with one of the portable generators.[39] This was a true balloon boat, unlike the *Fanny*, which had towed LaMountain's balloon.[40] The boat, towed by a steam tug, was used to transport balloons quickly to various points on the Potomac for observation during the late fall and winter of 1861.

In early 1862, Lowe was ordered to send two aeronauts with equipment to other theatres of the war: John Steiner was sent to the upper Mississippi and John Starkweather to South Carolina. In March, Lowe himself was uprooted. On 23 March, Lowe and the Balloon Corps were ordered to prepare to move to Fortress Monroe to take part in McClellan's Peninsula campaign.[41] Instead of the relatively placid observations along the Potomac, the corps was now to be the eyes of an advancing army.

The corps arrived on 5 April, and Lowe made his first ascension later that day. During the next few days, Lowe made more tethered ascensions, sometimes taking officers, including Fitz-John Porter along. Porter, it seems, was becoming comfortable enough with being aloft that he was also ascending on occasion by himself. On 11 April at 0500, Porter had arrived at the balloon camp and ordered James Allen to prepare the balloon for flight. Rushing, Allen attached only one tether line. To everyone's horror, when Porter had barely gotten off the ground, the line, rotted by an earlier acid spill, snapped with an explosive sound.[42]

To add to his problems, Porter noted that the line to the balloon's valve was tangled. Unable to release gas, he ascended rapidly. Maintaining his presence of mind, after the balloon began to reach an equilibrium altitude Porter started to make careful observations of the Confederate positions. Porter finally climbed carefully up the balloon's netting and untangled the valve line, beginning his descent to earth.

As Porter landed with a thud on an unoccupied tent, cavalry and soldiers rushed to him from all directions, giving a loud cheer when they saw he was all right. One in the crowd, however, was a Confederate saboteur who tried unsuccessfully to get close enough to the balloon to light it on fire. This would-be saboteur escaped, but several other Confederates sent to damage the balloon on other occasions were caught and shot.[43]

Lowe was aloft often during April, mapping out targets for the artillery barrage which was planned to open the way for the attack on Yorktown. Lowe was in the balloon and detected the

Lowe in the *Intrepid*

Thaddeus Lowe

National Archives, BA 1973

Confederate evacuation of Yorktown just before the planned at-tack on 4 May. As described later, Confederate John Bryan's bal-loon observations of the Yankee preparations had been instrumental in leading to the evacuation.

As McClellan's forces began to push up the peninsula, the Bal-loon Corps traveled on their balloon boat up the York and Pamunkey Rivers to White House and had joined the infantry at Seven Pines by 20 May. During the next few days, Lowe made several important ascensions with Union Brigadier General George Stoneman, who said "he had seen enough to be worth a million dollars to the govern-ment."[44] Lowe's very presence was demoralizing to the Confeder-ates, as he always made sure that the name of his craft, *Constitution*, faced towards the streets of Richmond, which he could see clearly with field glasses.[45]

In late May Lowe had three balloons in operation near the Virginia capital, and he made what may have been his most impor-tant observations of the war. McClellan's forces were split across the rain-swollen Chickahominy River, and on 31 May Confederate

Using the *Constitution* to inflate the *Intrepid*

Lowe Observing the Battle of Fair Oaks from the *Intrepid*

Courtesy of Library of Congress, LC-B811-2348

General Joseph Johnston began an attack on the forces south of the river near Seven Pines. Aloft in the balloon *Washington* near Mechanicsville (about six miles from Seven Pines), Lowe saw the Confederate advance. With the telegraph lines down, Lowe descended and rode by horseback to his camp near Seven Pines, warning McClellan of the impending attack. This warning allowed McClellan to order forces north of the river across as reinforcements. These forces arrived just in time to prevent what might have been a Confederate rout.

Lowe and James Allen were able to observe the Battle of Seven Pines (or Fair Oaks) aloft, sending many accurate reports of troop movements. When Lowe had arrived at his camp, he had seen that his large balloon *Intrepid* (with which he could rise to greater heights and carry a telegraph operator) was only partially inflated. Realizing that inflating the balloon from his generators would require valuable time, Lowe improvised. He had a tinsmith turn a teakettle into a funnel and transferred hydrogen from the smaller *Constitution* to the *Intrepid*. In the words of one of McClellan's officers: "It may be safely claimed that the Union Army was saved from destruction at the Battle of Fair Oaks...by the frequent and accurate reports of Professor Lowe."[46]

Lowe and his men continued to make observations throughout the Union disaster known as the Seven Days' battles in late June and early July, though both Lowe and James Allen were sick with fever. Allen briefly took charge of the corps at Harrison's Landing when Lowe was too ill to lead.

By August the Confederates were taking the war northwards, the Army of the Potomac was withdrawing back to northern Virginia, and two of Lowe's biggest supporters were in political trouble. Losing confidence in McClellan, Lincoln decided to keep him in command of the Army of the Potomac, but replaced him as general in chief of the U.S. Army with Henry Halleck. Porter fared even worse, being cashiered from the army after charges (from which he was not exonerated until 1886) that he had failed to obey orders at Second Manassas.

By the time of the Battle of Antietam in mid-September, McClellan had come back (temporarily) into favor with the administration, but he was not able to call for Lowe until 17 September, the day after the battle. The drawn battle of Antietam, which should have been a Union victory, turned instead into a series of repulsed, disjointed Union attacks. McClellan was sorry that the balloon corps had not been present "as the balloon would have been invaluable to me during that engagement."[47]

Sketch Made in 1863 of Lowe, Aloft

National Archives, BA-2116

Lowe made ascensions in the vicinity of Sharpsburg and Harper's Ferry for McClellan early in the fall of 1862, but as the armies again moved south into Virginia, McClellan ordered the Balloon Corps back to Washington for the winter. In November, McClellan was removed from command permanently by Lincoln, who was fed up with the general's cautious nature, and replaced with Major General Ambrose Burnside, who had used both James Allen and John LaMountain with some success earlier in the war.

Burnside sent for Lowe and his men in late November as the Union army prepared to force a crossing of the Rappahannock River at Fredericksburg. On 13 December, Lowe ascended for the first time, but because of fog was not able to see much until about 1000. He shouted his observations to Burnside's men and took officers aloft with him, but no one noticed the strong Confederate position behind a stone wall on Marye's Heights.[48] Union troops were decimated as they made several futile attempts to take the position that afternoon.

After the Union defeat, Lowe and his men continued to make observations from winter quarters in Falmouth, across the river from Fredericksburg.[49] Burnside had been replaced by Major General Joe Hooker, whose appointment would signal the beginning of the end of the use of balloons in the Civil War. Through his assistant adjutant general, Hooker ordered Captain Cyrus Comstock to take charge of the Balloon Corps. Until this time, Lowe had received orders from a number of officers, but was given virtual autonomy in exercising his missions. Comstock intended to manage every aspect of the corps.

Comstock and Lowe did not get along, and Comstock viewed the balloon enterprise as inefficient and, for the most part, useless. He cut everyone from the payroll except Lowe and the Allen brothers, and cut Lowe's pay to $6 per day. He also took exception to Lowe's bookkeeping, which had been poor. As a result, Lowe tendered his resignation on 12 April 1863.[50] In his letter he offered to serve free of pay, perhaps hoping to shame the officers into returning to him some of his old authority. In this, he was disappointed: the offer to fly without pay was accepted, but he was to remain relatively powerless. When a request came from Washington for an aeronaut to go to Charleston, Lowe volunteered James Allen. Comstock derided Lowe for not going through proper channels and reversed his decision.[51]

In late April, troop movements started that would lead to the Battle of Chancellorsville. Lowe and the Allens were aloft often during the days preceding the battle and during the battle itself, floating a thousand feet above the left bank of the Rapphahanock.[52]

Inflating the *Intrepid*

National Archives, B680

During the battle, the Confederate position at Marye's Heights in Fredericksburg was taken, and the Union commander, John Sedgwick, gave the balloonists much credit for their observations leading up to the attack.

Leaving a small force at Fredericksburg to face Sedgwick, Confederate commander General Robert E. Lee withdrew the majority of his troops to the west towards Chancellorsville to meet Hooker's main force, attacking from that direction. Lowe reported this movement, which Hooker elatedly misinterpreted as a retreat by Lee.[53] When the Confederates ran head-on into Hooker's forces (who outnumbered the Confederates by two to one), Hooker seemed stunned and had his men dig in around Chancellorsville.

After stopping Hooker's initial momentum, Lee gambled again on 2 May and sent Lieutenant General Stonewall Jackson's forces on their famous flank march around the Union army, culminating in a devastating surprise attack on the Federal XI Corps. The men in Jackson's column reported seeing a Union balloon, but there are no indications that Lowe or the Allens were able to see the Confederates.[54] The first balloon report from Lowe was given at 0615 and he continued throughout the day to attempt to get some grasp of the confusing situation below him. His reports mention high wind that made observation difficult. Combining these conditions with the thick forest in the area, it is probably not surprising that Jackson's men remained invisible to him.

Lowe's Portable Gas Generators

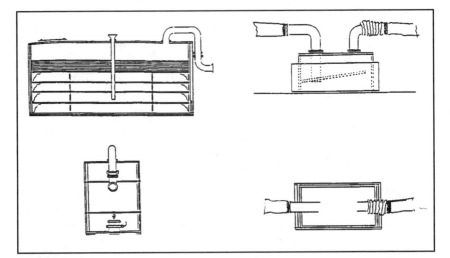

Lowe's Gas Purifier

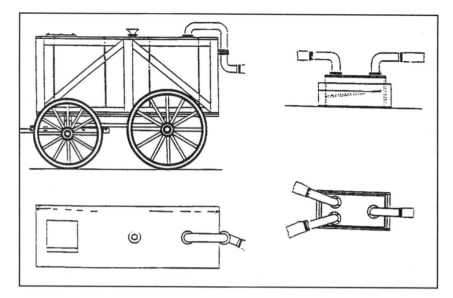

Lowe's Gas Cooler

Lowe's Gas Generators

U.S. Capitol in background, Washington, D.C., circa 1861

On 6 May, Lowe approached Comstock with hopes that, in spite of the Union defeat, his useful observations at Marye's Heights may have made Comstock think more positively about the Balloon Corps and perhaps consider restoring his salary. Again he was disappointed and Lowe immediately asked to be relieved. Comstock assented, and thus ended Lowe's connection with the U.S. Army.

The Allens continued to work with Hooker's army for another month, and made observations in early June of the Confederate movement westward that would eventually lead to the Battle of Gettysburg.[55] As the Union army moved northwards towards the clash with Lee's Confederates, the Allens and their balloons were left behind. This seems to have been a mistake in that the balloons would probably have been useful in observing Confederate movements around Gettysburg, particularly the attack on the Round Tops on 2 July which nearly destroyed the Union position. In the troop movements preceding the attack, Colonel E. Porter Alexander was careful to keep his artillery out of sight of the Union signal station on the larger of the two hills. It would certainly have been more difficult for Porter to hide the movement from a balloon. According to Porter (who, as described later, had made balloon ascents for the Confederates during the Seven Days' battles): "...I have never understood why the enemy abandoned the use of military balloons early in 1863, after having used them extensively up to that time. Even if the observers never saw anything, they would have been worth all the cost for the annoyance and delays they caused us in trying to keep our movements out of their sights. That wretched little signal-station upon Round Top that day caused one of our divisions to lose over two hours, and probably delayed our assault nearly that long."[56]

Even after the dissolution of the Balloon Corps, Lowe continued to press for its re-establishment in some form. As late as 1864, he was still giving demonstrations for the navy in Washington. But it was not to be, and it would be thirty years before the United States military would once again use balloons.

Though the Balloon Corps under Lowe had performed some useful service, it is really surprising that they did so well. Lowe hurt himself with his ego and resulting clashes with other aeronauts. The corps was probably hurt more, though, by the lack of support and confidence in the endeavor by the military community as a whole. When Lowe had support, as in the Peninsula campaign, he did well. Otherwise, the results were as marginal and inconsistent as the battlefield results of the string of commanders under which he served.

Though Lowe was successful in attaching his enterprise to the military, neither he nor his men had true military status. Their families received no pensions, and if captured the men would probably have been executed by the Confederates as spies.[57] Though Lowe never wore a uniform, several of his men wore unofficial insignia on their headgear for a short time (B.C. for Balloon Corps or A.D. for Aeronautic Department).[58] The insignias were discarded as they brought ridicule from the "real" soldiers nearby.[59]

Since Lowe's balloons were the first aircraft built expressly for the United States military, it is worth taking some time to look at his equipment and methods of operations. The envelopes of Lowe's military balloons were constructed of sections of fawn-colored India silk sewn together by seamstresses. The envelopes were colored and decorated in unique fashion by the men who flew in each of them, a tradition that continues on military aircraft to this day.[60]

Each balloon was fitted with a mahogany valve on top of the envelope in order to vent hydrogen and decrease altitude. The valves had brass fittings and were operated by India rubber springs by means of a rope that hung down through the envelope to the passenger basket.[61] The envelope was treated with varnish to make it as impervious as possible to leakage of hydrogen.

The envelope was connected through a network of linen cords to a wooden "concentration ring." The wicker basket was attached to the concentration ring by more cords from below, and a second wooden ring was placed between the concentration ring and basket to spread the lower ropes away from the passengers. The wicker baskets varied in size from a small one-man version to a larger basket that could accommodate up to five men. The baskets were painted red, white, and blue and carried 100-pound bags of sand for ballast. Once reaching a given altitude, the aeronaut could adjust by venting gas with the valve to descend or by discarding ballast to rise. Three or four manila ropes attached to the concentration ring normally tethered the balloon to the ground. The ropes, some as long as five thousand feet, were normally fed out and held manually by the ground crew.

What made Lowe's balloons useful was the relative ease with which they could be moved in coordination with the army and this stemmed from the mobility and reliability of Lowe's hydrogen generating apparatus. Lowe's hydrogen generators were mounted on army wagons and hauled from camp to camp. To perform an inflation, the balloon crew would start by laying out a large ground cloth on level, sheltered ground to prevent damage to the envelope.[62] The envelope was then placed on the ground cloth and connected to the hydrogen generator.

The generators were wagon-mounted wooden tanks, five feet high and eleven feet long. The tanks were lined with copper on the inside to protect the wood from the acid used in the procedure. The sides and ends of the tank were fitted with shelves to help give an even distribution of the iron filings to be placed inside. For a single inflation, about thirty-three hundred pounds of iron filings were brought in through an eighteen-inch manhole in the top of the tank and spread out on the floor and shelves. The men filled the tank to within about two feet of the top with water and then closed the manhole.

As described in Appendix 3, the addition of sulfuric acid to the iron filings would then create hydrogen gas. About sixteen hundred pounds of sulfuric acid were poured in the top of the tank through a lead-lined copper funnel, equipped with a stopcock (or valve) to regulate the flow. The acid was added slowly, usually over about two and a half to three hours, to prevent the reaction from building up too much gas pressure.

The hydrogen produced was allowed to escape from the tank through a six-inch diameter rubber hose (connected on each end by copper couplers) to a wooden box filled with water. The purpose of this box was to cool the gases, which were extremely hot as they exited the generator. As the hydrogen exited the cooler, it was fed through another rubber hose to a purifier. This was simply another wooden box, filled with lime (calcium oxide) and water, which absorbed carbonic acid and other unwanted gases. The output of the purifier was essentially pure, cool hydrogen, which was fed through a twelve-inch hose and hand pump to the envelope.[63]

Once in the air, the balloons proved useful on a number of occasions for surveillance of enemy camps and troop movements. The size of an enemy camp was normally estimated from the number of tents or campfires as compared to those in the Union camp of known size. Scattered fires denoted the position of enemy pickets. Clouds of dust on distant roads could be used to observe enemy movements, with a slow-moving cloud produced by infantry and a faster-moving cloud by cavalry.[64]

The information so obtained was communicated to the ground in one of three ways: by telegraph (with a code developed to save time), message drops, or by visual signals. Although a few photographs had been taken from balloons just before the Civil War, Lowe and his men apparently took none during their service.

The Union sent balloons aloft in two theaters of operation outside of Virginia during the war, but without the success seen there by Lowe and LaMountain. In the fall of 1861, Union forces had captured the important harbor at Port Royal, South Carolina, with an idea toward threatening Charleston and Savannah. McClellan ordered Lowe to send a balloon to the area to help in the coming operations. John Starkweather arrived with a balloon and generating equipment on 3 January 1862.[65]

Union commander Brigadier General Thomas W. Sherman received McClellan's unsolicited offering with indifference and Starkweather sat for several months without taking the balloon up. At the end of March, Sherman was succeeded by Brigadier General Henry Benham, but still Starkweather sat idle. Finally, on 11 April, the Union forces took Fort Pulaski at the mouth of the Savannah River. Benham decided that perhaps Starkweather could be of some use after all, using the captured fort as a base to observe the city of Savannah.

Soon after, Starkweather began inflating his balloon but had to stop and deflate it because of the high coastal winds. This loss of hydrogen was not trivial because of Starkweather's limited supplies (one shipment of iron and sulfuric acid sent to him had been lost in a shipwreck).[66] Finally, on 19 April Starkweather ascended with an engineering officer from the deck of the steamer *Mayflower*, three miles from Savannah. They recorded the number of Confederate boats in the harbor and noted strong earthworks protecting the city. Starkweather made several other ascents, probably of limited value, before a June gale ripped the envelope of his balloon as it was moored. At this point, Starkweather's service ended and the damaged balloon was returned to Lowe. Starkweather's work at Savannah had limited importance for two reasons. First, the winds near the shore made ballooning itself difficult and reliable observations even more so. Second, with the capture of Fort Pulaski, Savannah (though not captured) was effectively removed from the war and became a much lower Union priority.[67]

The other place where the Union put balloons to use, on an even more limited scale, was on the upper Mississippi River. In early 1862, while Starkweather sat idle, McClellan sent another unexpected present, this time to Major General John Pope. On 4 February, McClellan ordered Lowe to send a balloon and aeronaut for service with the Army of the Mississippi, then faced with the task of subduing the Confederate stronghold on Island Number 10. It seemed that a balloon might be of use here because of the island's location on a hairpin turn in the river, in a heavily wooded area.

On 24 February, John Steiner arrived for what was to be a most disappointing stint with the Army of the Mississippi.[68] In five months, Steiner was to be in the air only during one week. Steiner's reception in the West made Starkweather's reception in the South look warm. Steiner was not taken seriously and was even ridiculed, possibly because of his poor English and his heavy German accent. Steiner soon sent a letter to Lowe calling his commanders "blockheads" and said "all the officers hear [sic] are as dum as a set of asses."[69]

Though Steiner got ridiculed, he could not get pay or rations, and how he was able to survive in the field for five months is a matter of speculation. Neither Pope nor his commander, Major General Henry Halleck, seemed to have any interest in aerial reconnaissance. Sadly, such observation may have prevented the disastrous surprise of the Confederate attack at Shiloh.[70]

In March, Steiner finally found himself taken seriously by a naval man, Commodore Andrew Foote. Because of the hairpin turn in the river, U.S. boats could not make observations of Confederate batteries. In addition, there was no way to assess the effectiveness of the naval mortars being used to soften the Confederate defenses. On 20 March, Steiner and his equipment were taken onto a flatboat and by 25 March he made his first ascent. This first trip was not fruitful because of heavy smoke and haze, but on 26 March he ascended with two officers and saw immediately that the mortar fire was too long. This information was relayed upon landing and the angle of fire corrected. Island Number 10 fell twelve days later. Despite the value of his observations, Steiner and his balloon were not used again.

In the East, during the time period that Lowe and his "colleagues" were making their first trials around Washington, there was also apparently some activity in the air on the Confederate side. According to reports, aeronauts were offering their services to the Confederate government as early as May 1861.[71] There was a reported sighting from Washington of a Confederate balloon in the direction of Leesburg as early as 14 June. Other sightings were reported on 23 June and 24 June in the direction of Fairfax Court House.[72] It has not been determined whether these sightings were accurate. The commander in northern Virginia at the time was P.G.T. Beauregard, who would later prove himself amenable to unorthodox forms of warfare with the *Hunley*, so there is some reason to believe that the reports are valid.

On 22 August, General Joseph Johnston (who had joined Beauregard in command in northern Virginia) wrote to Beauregard: "...it seems to me that the balloon may be useful...Let us send for it; we can surely use it advantageously." Whether this refers to a balloon already in use nearby or one located elsewhere is uncertain. By 4 September, however, Beauregard appears to have used a balloon at Munson's Hill (near Falls Church).[73] The Confederates may have used a balloon at Edward's Ferry near Leesburg in early November.[74]

By the time the Peninsula Campaign started in the spring of 1862, Beauregard had been transferred to Tennessee (but he would use balloons again later in the war, as will be seen shortly). Johnston continued the Confederate use of balloons during the struggle up the Peninsula, as McClellan tried to take Richmond using the York and James rivers to protect his flanks. By early April 1862, the Confederates had made at least one trial ascension of a balloon (probably unmanned). Newspaper reports indicated that Lowe was not worried about the competition:

> On the 13th of April the Confederates had sent up a balloon, the first they had employed, at which Lowe was infinitely amused. He said it had neither shape nor buoyancy, and predicted that it would burst or fall apart after a week.[75]

At about this time, Johnston sent a message to Major General John Magruder asking him to provide him with a man who was familiar with the terrain around Yorktown and also knowledgeable enough with military matters to make accurate observations of troop strengths. Magruder's aide-de-camp, Captain John Randolph Bryan, received the message and decided that such an assignment would be just the thing to help him make a name for himself. He presented himself to Johnston and found to his horror that the assignment was not for a conventional scout, but for an aeronaut.

Despite his protests, Johnston refused to let him rescind his offer and thus J. R. Bryan became the first known Confederate aeronaut. Bryan described his balloon as "nothing but a big cotton bag, coated over so as to make it air-tight, and intended to be inflated with hot air..."[76] The hot air was to be provided by burning pine knots and turpentine, which were set on the ground under a flue, one end of which fed into the balloon's envelope. When filled with hot air, the balloon was released from its moorings and held by a single rope. The rope passed over and around a windlass, and then was tied to a tree. After reaching a maximum height, the balloon would have lost enough hot air to become heavier than the air around it and would begin to slowly descend.

Bryan's first ascension was quite terrifying to the young captain, as the ascent and descent were painfully slow, allowing Union batteries ample opportunities to send shells dangerously close to the balloon. In addition, the single tether rope turned constantly, making observation difficult. Bryan was able to mark some Union positions on a map, using I for infantry, C for cavalry, A for artillery, and W for wagon trains. After the ascension, Bryan and his ground crew decided on a more effective means of descent. A team of six artillery horses would be tied to the rope and brought to full gallop when Bryan gave the signal (using wig-wag flags) to descend. Bryan made another ascension using this method a day or two later.

Bryan's final trip as an aeronaut took place on a bright moonlit night in early May 1862. Johnston had received information from his scouts that the Union forces were on the move and preparing to attack his Yorktown defenses. He ordered Bryan up to get a better idea of the direction of movement of the Union forces. A large crowd of soldiers had gathered around the balloon and Bryan pushed his way to the basket, a little more eager to make this ascent than the previous two because of the safety afforded by the darkness.

Bryan gave the order to rise and took off normally up to about two hundred feet. Suddenly the balloon shot quickly upwards to an altitude he estimated as two miles. On the ground a soldier in the crowd had gotten his leg tangled in the tether rope as it was being played out and began to scream in pain. A quick-thinking friend had grabbed an axe and cut the rope, saving the soldier's leg but releasing Bryan. Bryan was now "absolutely helpless, with no idea of how to manage my runaway steed."[77] Bryan was flying out of control, just as Fitz-John Porter had done nearby a week or two earlier.

Bryan was first blown over Union lines and then blown back above the Confederate-held territory, but far from the spot from which he had ascended. He was losing hot air fast and began to move rapidly downwards as well as horizontally. He passed overhead of the camp of the Second Florida, whose soldiers thought he must be a Yankee spy and gave chase, yelling and taking potshots at him. To Bryan's temporary relief, he was blown away from the angry Confederates, but soon saw that he was going to land in the middle of the York River.

To avoid drowning, Bryan decided to disrobe but found that the basket was too cramped to get his boots off, so he sliced them with his pocketknife and tossed them out of the basket. Just as he had gotten his clothes off, he realized that the wind had changed and he was being blown back to the Confederate shore.

Bryan managed to land safely in an apple orchard, got dressed, and found his way back to Johnston's headquarters. Despite his terror, Bryan had managed to get an idea of the roads upon which the Federals were approaching. Armed with this information, Johnston decided to pull back up the Peninsula, leaving McClellan holding an empty bag when he finally took Yorktown.

During the next month, Johnston continued to retreat slowly up the Peninsula towards Richmond with McClellan in sluggish pursuit. When the defensive-minded Johnston had fallen back as far as even he was willing to go, he again decided to make use of balloons for observations. Instead of the amateurish hot-air balloon Bryan used, Johnston had acquired a new balloon with a silk envelope made in Savannah, Georgia by Captain Langdon Cheves. A legend was long propagated (probably starting with the memoirs of Lieutenant General James Longstreet) that the envelope had been made from silk dresses contributed by Southern belles throughout the Confederacy. The less romantic reality was that Cheves had made the balloon from new silk, and coated it with varnish made of rubber springs dissolved in naphtha.[78]

Charge of the new balloon was given to Major E. Porter Alexander, a signal officer who had been with Beauregard in northern Virginia and Johnston all the way up the Peninsula, and had undoubtedly seen the earlier balloon or balloons in use. This was the same officer who would later in the war have premonitions about Henry Pleasants's mine at Petersburg, and whose comments regarding the demise of Union aviation were noted earlier in this chapter.

The balloon was used in a much more efficient manner than was Bryan's. Filling the envelope with coal gas at the Richmond City Gas Works and then tying it to a railroad car, the balloon could be quickly transported towards the front lines along the York River Railroad, which ran from Richmond to White House on the Pamunkey River.

In this manner, Alexander was able to observe and report on Union movements during most of the Seven Days' battles, beginning with an ascension on 27 June to observe the Battle of Gaines's Mill, again on 28 June as McClellan and his troops began their infamous "change of base" to the James River, and finally a third time to watch the Union retreat from Savage's Station to Malvern Hill on 29 June. As useful as his trips aloft had been, Alexander now had a problem. The York River Railroad was too far from Malvern Hill to make any useful observations.

The Confederates decided to approach McClellan from a different angle. Since the gas works were located next to the James River, they decided to strap the balloon to a boat, a wooden steam-powered tug with the name C.S.S. *Teaser*, and move down the river to get a better vantage point for ascensions. The Confederates apparently used the balloon from the *Teaser*'s deck on 1 July, the day of the battle at Malvern Hill. After the battle, the Union forces retreated towards Harrison's Landing. The *Teaser* and its unusual cargo followed, with disastrous results. On 4 July, the *Teaser* went aground on a sandbar. Helpless, the ship was fired on and eventually captured (along with the silk balloon) by the Union gunboat U.S.S. *Maratanza*.[79] No records exist of any further use of balloons by the Confederates in Virginia.

There was apparently one more Confederate balloon, built shortly after the demise of the balloon on the *Teaser*. Charles Cevor, a noted pre-war aeronaut in the South, completed the balloon in August 1862, again in Savannah. The balloon, made of silk like the first Savannah balloon, was sent to Richmond, possibly to replace the captured balloon, but was then sent to Charleston, South Carolina at the request of the commander there.[80] The commander was none other than P.G.T. Beauregard, who authorized funds for use of the balloon. Cevor, with his assistant A. E. Morse, appears to have made numerous ascensions during the winter of 1862–63, about six months before Beauregard would request use of the *Hunley*. As in Richmond, the Charleston balloon was inflated at the city gas works. Sometime in early 1863, the balloon appears to have been torn away from its mooring ropes and carried away by high coastal winds. Thus ended Confederate aviation.

Though the Confederates had gotten some significant benefits from their use of aerial observation, it was lack of resources and appropriate technology that doomed their efforts here as in other arenas. Without portable hydrogen generators, Confederate use of balloons in the field was necessarily limited. During the frantic Union retreat to the James River during the Seven Days' battles, three generators were left on the field by Lowe and captured by the Confederates. Strangely, the Confederates apparently never used these generators. This may have been due to lack of sufficient supplies of iron and sulfuric acid in the Confederacy to dedicate to a relatively low priority project like balloon observation. Also, until about halfway through the war, the Confederate cavalry was so superior to that of the Union that aerial reconnaissance may have seemed to be more trouble than it was worth to the Southern commanders.

There was at least one other Confederate scheme to make use of balloons, but this plan was offensive in nature. Early in the war, Isham Walker, a private from the Ninth Mississippi Infantry and stationed near Pensacola, Florida, concocted a plan to drop bombs containing poison into Union-held Fort Pickens. His letter dated 4 June 1861, to Confederate Secretary of War L. P. Walker, states that he would be willing to ascend in a balloon, tethered at an altitude of two miles above the fort, there to drop poison bombs of his own making. Isham Walker said that the total cost for the endeavor, including the balloon, copper wires for tethering, and chemicals for the bomb, would be $1200. There is no record of L. P. Walker responding to the private's letter.[81]

The Civil War period was a fertile time for invention, and the field of aeronautics was no exception. As with submarine vehicles, there were many schemes proposed, some hare-brained and some just ahead of their time. Many of these proposals took LaMountain's free ascensions one step further by looking at means of navigating through the air, instead of tethered flights or free flights made at the whim of the winds.

One common sense proposal that went nowhere came to George McClellan in the fall of 1861. William H. Helme (who had initially offered his services to the Union with James Allen) wrote to McClellan, offering to construct and demonstrate a hot-air balloon.[82] In light of the difficulties in generating hydrogen, it seems that McClellan might have been interested in such a proposal, but by this date he was in the midst of the controversy between Lowe and LaMountain, and had probably decided that he already had more balloonists than he needed.

One of the more well-known proposals to come out of the war years was that made by Dr. Solomon Andrews of Perth Amboy, New Jersey. Andrews designed and built a craft he called the *Aereon*.[83] It consisted of three eighty-foot-long (thirteen feet wide) cigar-shaped balloons fastened together, with a catwalk (twelve feet long and sixteen inches wide) suspended below. For directional control, there was a rudder on the rear of the center balloon.

When asked how the balloon was to be propelled, Andrews answered "gravitation." He apparently based his craft on principles outlined by the Italian Muzio Muzzi almost twenty years earlier. By shifting his position on the catwalk, the pilot of the *Aereon* was able to use the resistance of the air as a way of moving forward, similar to the way a sailor can tack into the wind.

Andrews made his first demonstration of the device on 1 June 1862. The final trial of the *Aereon* on 4 September was covered by a reporter from the *New York Herald*, who said the capabilities of the device "were demonstrated beyond all possibility of doubt." Soon after, Andrews met with President Lincoln, who seemed impressed with his ideas, but asked to have letters from witnesses to Andrews's flights sent to him. This Andrews did, but the letters for some reason seem not to have made it to Lincoln's desk.

Andrew's pressed on and managed to demonstrate a four-foot scale model of the *Aereon* to congressmen in the basement of the Capitol in March 1864 and to a scientific board at the Smithsonian Institution in July of that year. The board recommended that Congress make an appropriation to get Andrews into military service and Andrews received a patent for what he called a "War-Aerostat." Unfortunately, the board's recommendation got tied up in Washington red tape for so long that the Civil War ended without Congress ever acting upon it.

The patent office records from this period also show a number of proposals for heavier-than-air craft, a type of device not successfully flown for another four decades.[84] One, by Mortimer Nelson, was to be propelled by fans "driven by suitable power." Nelson showed great foresight in proposing that his craft's frame be constructed of sturdy, lightweight aluminum.

A complex design from Luther Crowell of West Dennis, Massachusetts was to have steam-driven propellers hinged so that the craft could operate horizontally but make vertical takeoffs and landings. W. F. Quinby of Stanton, Delaware proposed a craft with steam-driven rotating wings that would (if it could have gotten off the ground) have operated much like a modern helicopter. Arthur Kinsella of Cascades in the Washington Territory proposed a rocket-shaped balloon that forced gas out the back, pre-dating by about eighty years the principles of jet propulsion.

On the Confederate side, innovations were predictably few given the state of resources in the South. According to at least one report there was some sort of craft under construction in Richmond whose aim was to drop bombs on the White House and Capitol.[85] It was supposedly destroyed on the ground by high winds. Another invention, called the *Artis Avis* (or *Bird of Art*), was supposed to be able to fly when towed in a glider-like fashion behind a locomotive. It's inventor, a Professor Blank, was apparently no more than a con man. He got Confederate soldiers in Petersburg in 1864 to donate to the cause of turning the craft into an offensive weapon. After collecting his donations, Professor Blank and his bird were seen no more.

Chapter 6

War on the Wires: The Telegraph

Despite the historical significance of the *Hunley* and the observations of Thaddeus Lowe and others, it must be said that the influence of submarines and balloons on the Civil War was limited. Not until the twentieth century would warfare beneath the waves and in the skies play pivotal roles in a major conflict.

During the Civil War, a form of technology far younger than either balloons or submarines was destined to play a very significant role. In the four decades preceding the war, men had finally begun to form some limited understanding of the connection between electricity and magnetism. By 1840, the electromagnetic telegraph was a reality and in the two decades before the Civil War, a network of telegraph wires had begun to snake its way across the United States. The ability to communicate instantly across long distances would soon revolutionize the nature of military command. As with balloons and submarines, the telegraph was first used in a significant military way during the Civil War. Unlike the former technologies, however, the telegraph had a major effect on the way the war was conducted.

Antebellum Telegraphy

The electrical telegraph has been around in some form since the late 1700s. The word itself came from the Frenchman Claude Chappe, for a semaphore system used during the French Revolution, and by 1802 the word had become applied to all types of long-distance communications.[1] By 1802, several men had tried to use static electricity generated by friction to send impulses representing information. These attempts were generally unsuccessful as the results were inconsistent and the electrical signal generated was hard to insulate because of its high voltage.[2]

Around the turn of the nineteenth century, the studies of the Italian scientists Galvani and Volta led to the development of the first crude battery, the "voltaic pile." During the next decade attempts were made to make use of this method of storage of electrical charge in telegraphing information. An early version of the telegraph used the transmitted electrical signal to liberate hydrogen bubbles on the receiving end, indicating reception of the signal. An ingenious method, but fraught with so many problems that it was no more than a laboratory curiosity.

Everything began to change in 1820, the year Hans Oersted reported a remarkable discovery. While giving a lecture on electricity, he noticed that a current in a wire would cause a nearby magnetic compass needle to deflect. Thus began the study of electromagnetism, a complex subject that would not be well understood until the work of James Clerk Maxwell fifty years later. Maxwell began to develop his four elegant equations of electromagnetism in 1864, just as the Civil War was drawing to a close.

Three years after Oersted's announcement, the Englishman William Sturgeon developed the first electromagnet. By wrapping wire around an iron bar, Sturgeon created a device that could be magnetic when current ran through it and non-magnetic otherwise. This set the stage for the work of one of America's greatest scientists: Joseph Henry.

As mentioned in Chapter 5, by the time of the Civil War Henry was probably America's most prominent scientist. As secretary of the Smithsonian Institution, Henry commanded great respect and influence. His backing was enough to push Thaddeus Lowe into his position as head of the U.S. Balloon Corps. And it was his suggestion that eventually led to the widespread development of ironclad ships for the U.S. Navy.

In the 1820s, however, Henry was still a relatively unknown amateur. After hearing of Sturgeon's work, he began to pursue the idea of using an electromagnet to send a signal. He placed a battery at one end of an electrical line to provide an electrical impulse. On the other end, he placed an electromagnet and an iron bar. By using a switch to turn the current from the battery on and off, he could alternately pull the iron bar towards the electromagnet and then release it. He had invented the first practical telegraph.

In the early 1830s, Henry made two significant improvements in his system. First, he greatly improved upon Sturgeon's electromagnet by wrapping much more wire around the iron core and by meticulously insulating it with cloth.[3] Henry's electromagnet provided almost one hundred times as much magnetic pull as Sturgeon's. Second, he realized that his battery was not of sufficient power to send signals across long distances, due to the high electrical resistance of the wire. In 1835, he invented the electrical relay.[4] He found the distance in which the current had weakened to the point that the electromagnet on the far end could just move a small iron key. He used the movement of this key to close a second circuit, connected to a nearby battery, which would then operate with full power as had the first circuit. Using a series of such relays, the original signal could be projected as far as one wished.

After giving several demonstrations of his device, Henry accepted a professorship at Princeton. This would bring to an end his connection to the telegraph, however, at least as far as the American public would see things. For in the late 1830s, a struggling artist would take Henry's device as his own and steal Henry's well-deserved fame. Samuel F. B. Morse was not a scientist, but after hearing of work by Henry and others he had become fascinated with the idea of the telegraph.

In 1836, Morse began naive attempts to build his own telegraph. He called often on Henry for advice, and Henry was more than willing to give it. Henry had not patented his telegraph because he thought scientific ideas should benefit all mankind. After getting his device to work, and without giving any credit to Henry, Morse patented the electromagnetic telegraph in 1840.

In 1843, Morse asked for and was granted an appropriation of $30,000 for the construction of a telegraph line that would span the forty-mile distance between Baltimore and Washington, D.C. Morse obtained permission from the Baltimore and Ohio Railroad to run his line along its right-of-way, beginning a close association between telegraph and railroad that would last for many years.[5] He first attempted to lay his line as a buried cable but found that his insulation was not up to the job. He then decided to run the wire over wooden poles. The only important points for insulation were then those places where the line touched a pole and current could leak to the ground. He placed glass insulators at these points.

By May 1844, the complete line, running from Pratt Street Station in Baltimore to the Supreme Court Chamber in Washington, was ready to be tested. On 11 May, Morse sent his first message: "Everything worked well." He sent the message using a code of long and short bursts of electricity. This code, with combinations of short and long bursts standing for different letters of the alphabet, was Morse's only real contribution to the whole enterprise, and still bears his name today. Because the receiving apparatus was set up in such a way that the electromagnet moved a pencil, recording the bursts of electricity as short or long lines, the components of the Morse code came to be known as dots and dashes.

On 24 May, Morse gave a public demonstration of the device and transmitted what is usually noted in history books as the first telegraphic message: "What hath God wrought?" The wo·d of the demonstration spread quickly, and almost overnight America became electrified, in both senses of the word.

The exponential growth of telegraph lines across the United States during the next decade was truly amazing. At the beginning of 1846, the total telegraph mileage in the United States was not much more than the forty miles Morse had strung between Washington and Baltimore. By 1848, the mileage had grown to more than two thousand and by 1850 to more than twelve thousand miles. By 1852, this total had almost doubled again, reaching 23,283 miles.[6]

The rise of the telegraph in the 1840s was similar in some ways to the rise of the Internet in the 1990s. After appropriating the cash for Morse's line in 1844, the federal government stepped aside and let private enterprise run the show. As with the Internet, the resulting growth of the telegraph network was phenomenal and without centralized regulation. A variety of small local companies controlled the many miles of telegraph wire, with rates for transmission and the quality of operation varying wildly across the country.

As mentioned above, the telegraph and the railroad grew up together. Unlike carriages on a road, two trains traveling in opposite directions on a track could not occupy the same right-of-way. Thus, reliable, synchronized timetables and instantaneous communication across long distances became crucial to the development of railway systems. The two technologies, railroad and telegraph, were often in the hands of the same people.[7]

The highest concentrations of lines emerged in New England and in the upper Midwest. There were also two main lines heading south. One ran from Washington through Richmond, Raleigh, and Columbia, South Carolina. Spurs ran off the main line to Savannah and Charleston, while the main line continued on to New Orleans. The other southern route ran from Louisville to Nashville and then through Mississippi to New Orleans.

During this time period there were also some technical modifications. Telegraph poles were being made from heavy cedar and cypress logs and being set more deeply, greatly increasing the durability of the lines. Instead of copper wire, many lines were now being made from iron which, though not as good a conductor as copper, was cheaper and stronger. The substance gutta percha, similar to natural rubber but tougher, was found to serve as adequate insulation for submarine crossings of rivers.

As with the Internet, the telegraph began to have a significant effect on daily life. Though many rural folk feared the appearance of the "lightning lines" at first, even the most non-technical farmer soon found that he could get a better price for his crops by use of telegraphic reports; bankers, brokers, and all types of business-men found the telegraph a great aid in conducting various trans-actions; medical doctors were able to communicate with distant colleagues; Mississippi River men in the South were able to check the state of the ice on the northern part of the river during the spring. For people of all types, the telegraph also became an alter-native to the much slower written mail for sending the most mun-dane personal communications.

Messages that had taken days, weeks, or months to reach their destination were now being sent almost instantly. In America, a sig-nificant by-product of the network was the establishment of a new national cohesiveness. The different regions of the country, which had before been so isolated as to almost stand as separate nations themselves, were now in constant hourly contact.[8] The exchange of goods, services, and ideas was unprecedented. The Northern states, formerly well insulated from the South, were now in much closer proximity to their slave-holding cousins.

By the 1850s, the telegraph was spreading not only across the United States, but also throughout the world. By the end of 1852, there were almost as many miles of wire in Europe as in the United States. A submarine cable completed in June 1852 linked London across the English Channel to most of the major continental capitals.

Between 1852 and the beginning of the Civil War, a much needed consolidation of the various telegraph companies took place. As messages were sent across long distances, frustrated customers of-ten found that the signal had been delayed or lost altogether at a junction point between the lines of two of the many telegraph com-panies. Smaller companies began to be bought up by larger ones, and by 1860 only six major companies remained. Among these six, two had grown to giants. The American Telegraph Company cov-ered the eastern seaboard from the Atlantic provinces of Canada down to Florida, with connections to New Orleans. The Western Union Telegraph Company extended from the eastern states above the Mason-Dixon Line westward to the upper Midwest.

The other four companies, while nominally independent, relied heavily on the American and Western Union for their operation. The New York, Albany, and Buffalo Company had rights to much of New York state; the Atlantic and Ohio Company (the majority of the stock in the company was actually owned by Western Union stockholders) had rights to most of the state of Pennsylvania; the Illinois and Mississippi Company controlled parts of the upper Mississippi valley; and the New Orleans and Ohio Company governed the lower Mississippi valley.

The Civil War would cause changes in the power base of the telegraph industry. Western Union, with lines running mainly from east to west, would thrive. Its main competitor, the American Telegraph Company, whose lines ran generally north to south, would be torn apart. During the war, all the companies found themselves in the curious position of trying to loyally serve their nations while simultaneously trying to survive or even profit from the conflict. By the spring of 1866, Western Union had bought out its chief rival and many smaller companies and stood alone as a telegraph monopoly.

As the nation prepared for inevitable war in 1861, the telegraph lines were busy. The news of Fort Sumter's fall flashed across the country and Northern governors received by wire President Lincoln's call for seventy-five thousand volunteers. Newspaper correspondents used the lines greedily, filling up two or three pages per day with telegraph news.[9] Businessmen on both sides of the Mason-Dixon Line rushed to settle business before the lines of communication were broken.

During the war, North and South would find similar uses for the telegraph, but the North, with more existing lines and more resources to build additional lines, would use the technology to a greater extent. The Union army, in particular, would pioneer the large-scale use of the field telegraph, enabling a remote commander to micromanage tactics in various parts of a battlefield.

The first military use of the electromagnetic telegraph came in the Crimean War in the 1850s. The use of the telegraph in that war was extremely limited, however, and served mainly to link one headquarters to another. There is no historical note of tactical use in the Crimean War. There was some use of a field telegraph by the British in their Indian campaign of 1857–58. The wire was moved to advance posts on rollers, but being uninsulated the wire was not often useful in the wet Indian climate. The French also used the telegraph in a limited way during their Italian campaign of 1860–1861.[10]

Just as the telegraph would revolutionize civilian communications, it would dramatically change military command. As with any innovation, most military commanders were resistant to use the telegraph, in spite of its obvious merits. St. Arnaud, commander for Napoleon III in the Crimea, thought the telegraph would be the death of generalship as it linked the battlefield with the civilian government.[11] Civil War commanders found, however, that the power offered by the telegraph to reposition forces and gather intelligence far outweighed the distractions from armchair generals on the homefront.

Union Telegraphy

As word of the attack on Fort Sumter became known, Secretary of War Simon Cameron turned almost immediately for aid in establishing control over the railroad and telegraph lines in the North. He chose Thomas A. Scott, vice-president of the Pennsylvania Railroad, who then enlisted Andrew Carnegie to help organize the railroad side of things.[12] At that time Carnegie, who had started his railroad career as a telegraph operator, was in charge of the Pittsburgh division of the Pennsylvania Railroad. Scott also transferred the railroad's best telegraph operators to Washington. Scott was commissioned as a colonel of volunteers and in August of 1861 would be appointed Assistant Secretary of War.

Scott set up a telegraph headquarters in the War Department building in Washington, and staffed it with four young operators from the railroad: David Strouse, Samuel Brown, Richard O'Brien, and David Homer Bates. Strouse was put in charge of organizing telegraph operations. The American Telegraph Company, whose wires extended from Washington north, extended its lines from its main office to the War Department, Navy Yard, Arsenal and other strategic points in the city. Curiously, no line was ever extended to the White House.[13] As a result, Abraham Lincoln would spend many hours during the course of the next four years reading and sending telegrams in the War Department office.

Edwards S. Sanford, president of the American Telegraph Company, paid the bills for the additional lines (wire, poles, instruments, and operator salaries). Congress later reimbursed the company. At this point in the war, then, the telegraph network in the North was being operated solely on the patriotic good nature of the commercial companies.

A major problem during the first days of the war was that lines were still open between North and South, especially along the wires of the American Telegraph Company. Vital information was being sent in both directions, and as one telegraph company official stated, "...the telegraph was open to everybody, for any business whatever, treason or otherwise." On 21 April, officials of the northern and southern divisions of the American Telegraph Company met on the Long Bridge over the Potomac and decided to sever the lines between Washington and Richmond. Thus began the strange situation of two divisions of the same company siding with different hostile powers during wartime.

Severing the lines heading south did not prevent government officials in Washington from having to deal with another problem. For the first time in U.S. history, information concerning wartime events could be spread almost immediately to every corner of the nation. Lincoln's cabinet then set a historical precedent by informally deciding to censor information being sent north by newspaper correspondents.[14] When the Sixth Massachusetts arrived in Washington after being mauled by a pro-secessionist crowd in Baltimore, reporters rushed to the American office only to find it guarded by a militia squad. The angry correspondents rushed to Secretary of State William Seward, who denied that censorship of messages had been ordered. By the time the reporters returned to the telegraph office, the story had changed: they were told (incorrectly) that the lines between Washington and Baltimore had been cut and no messages could be sent.

The next day, Sanford confidentially directed the managers of each of his offices to personally examine every message being sent or received. Messages about military matters or deemed harmful to the government were to be detained and sent to Secretary of the Treasury Salmon P. Chase. Any messages which appeared to be in code were to be detained unless they came from the president or other high government officials or if they were obviously business-related telegrams sent by officials of the New York Associated Press, the news-gathering organization most favored by the government. The reporters, however, were not told that their dispatches were being censored.

In retrospect, the method of censorship seems quite strange. Civilian employees were to use their discretion in intelligence matters of the highest importance. During the war, many messages were suppressed, most concerning arms for the Confederacy.[15] In May and June, some stories concerning Union troop deployments and preparations apparently still got through to the North, and Union commanding officer Winfield Scott demanded that the censors tighten up on what was allowed to pass the wires.

By 21 July, when the Battle of Bull Run was fought, a telegraph line was in operation as far westward as Fairfax Court House. From that point, a cadre of mounted couriers directed by Andrew Carnegie transferred information to and from Irwin McDowell's headquarters.[16] As Lincoln waited in the War Department office, early telegrams from McDowell were encouraging. In mid-afternoon, though, telegrams ceased. At first the assembled officials and operators were optimistic, envisioning a rout of the Confederates, with the Union advance outpacing the telegraph capability. A short time later, the clacking instrument spelled out a far different message: "Our army is retreating."

The early reports sent by newspaper reporters also caused confusion across the North. The first telegrams indicated a Union victory, leaving readers bewildered when the news that the Union army had been routed reached them. Soon after George McClellan assumed command of the Army of the Potomac (five days after the Bull Run debacle), he met with reporters and proposed a voluntary code of censorship for news sent by telegraph. On 2 August, the reporters agreed to refrain from publishing "any matter that may furnish aid and comfort to the enemy."[17] Some reporters were still provided with great leeway: a *New York Tribune* reporter, Samuel Wilkeson, was allowed to submit his reports uncensored because he was such a staunch defender of Cameron.

Censorship of the wires sometimes extended even to messages intended for President Lincoln. On 21 October 1861, a message arrived via telegraph wire to McClellan's headquarters on Fifteenth Street in Washington. The message informed McClellan of the Union disaster on the Potomac at Ball's Bluff. Crossing the Potomac and taking an untenable position at the top of a steep cliff, Union soldiers were slaughtered by the Confederates as they tried to escape to the Maryland shore. One of the dead was Colonel Edward D. Baker, U.S. senator from Oregon and a friend of Lincoln. McClellan was at the White House with Lincoln when the message arrived at headquarters. Captain Thomas Eckert rushed the telegraph across town.

McClellan had little faith in Lincoln's military judgment and glanced at the message but did not inform Lincoln of its contents. A bit later in the day, Lincoln wandered over to McClellan's headquarters and asked Eckert if any dispatches had arrived from the front. Eckert, in his appointment by Cameron, had been ordered to give all military dispatches to McClellan only. Caught in a bind, Eckert slipped his copy of the dispatch under his desk blotter, and answered Lincoln evasively that there were no new dispatches on file. But Lincoln wandered into McClellan's office and there saw a copy of the disturbing news on McClellan's desk. He then approached Eckert and asked him why he had withheld the information. Eckert's reply seemed to satisfy Lincoln, but in the latter days when he was told that there was no news he would sometimes say: "Is there not something under the blotter?"[18]

During the second half of 1861, Lincoln became increasingly disenchanted with Cameron and eventually replaced him (Cameron was "exiled" to become minister to Russia) as Secretary of War on 20 January 1862 with Edwin Stanton.[19] One of Stanton's wishes was to gain a firm grip on the dissemination of information throughout the country. Even at this early date, officials such as Stanton were learning that even though the flow of information about the war could only be slowed down and not stopped, true power resided in those who could influence how the stories were covered. The first "spin doctors" were born.

Accordingly, on 25 February 1862, control of all telegraph lines in the United States passed to the federal government, and the United States Military Telegraph was born. The USMT was not a true military organization, but a civilian bureau acting under orders from the Secretary of War. The operators were civilians, and Stanton opposed military status for them so that they would be immune to orders from army officers. In many ways, the operators and linemen of the USMT were in a quasi-military status similar to the balloonists under Thaddeus Lowe. Like the balloonists, their lack of military status would prevent the operators (whose lives, like the balloonists, were often in danger during battle) from collecting pensions after the war. Many of the telegraphers were teenagers, and some were women.[20]

A handful of supervisors in the USMT were given commissions, however, in the interest of facilitating the acquisition of needed supplies. Eleven supervisors were made captains, while Eckert (who would supervise the War Department office) was made a major and Anson Stager, who would supervise the entire USMT, was made a colonel. Sanford was named military supervisor of military dispatches, responsible for overall censorship of telegrams.

Stager, a general superintendent for Western Union, had been serving in a similar capacity for George McClellan in the Department of the Ohio. Because of his days as an observer in the Crimean War, McClellan may have been receptive to the idea of using the telegraph in wartime. Stager was given authority by McClellan to supervise telegraphic communications, facilitate business, and disrupt disloyal communications.[21] He also helped McClellan to organize a field telegraph operation so that as Union forces advanced into West Virginia in July 1861, McClellan wrote: "...the first field telegraph that ever advanced with an army in America kept pace with this one."[22]

The USMT was nominally attached to the Quartermaster's Department, so that Stager sent his annual reports to Quartermaster General Montgomery C. Meigs.[23] In reality, though, Stager and his operators were responsible only to Stanton. This arrangement caused a great deal of friction between operators on the front lines and military commanders. The operators, who received many of their messages in cipher, were sometimes unable to give the commanding general access to important information because of USMT regulations. The resultant contempt and hostility for the operators on the part of the military personnel were similar in some ways to that felt by Lowe's balloonists.[24] The operators, showing abundant common sense, usually tried to accommodate commanding officers in any request that was not directly opposed to their orders from Washington.[25]

The new arrangement did not prevent censorship at the highest levels. Lincoln would again be kept in the dark, this time when Sanford omitted part of a telegram sent to Washington by McClellan near the end of his unsuccessful Peninsula campaign. On 29 June 1862, McClellan sent a scathing message to Stanton which ended with the lines: "If I save this army now, I tell you plainly that I owe no thanks to you or to any other person in Washington. You have done your best to sacrifice this army." Sanford ordered the dispatch recopied without these lines before being delivered to Stanton. This mutilation of an official dispatch may have been considered treason in some quarters, and officers have been shot for less, but Sanford decided the omission was in the nation's best interest. The omitted lines did not become public until McClellan published them in his official report, dated 4 August 1863.[26]

Estimates of the number of employees (operators and line builders) of the USMT range from about eleven hundred to about fifteen hundred. The line builder category included foremen, wagonmakers, teamsters, messengers, battery keepers, linemen, watchmen, and other types of laborers.[27] During the course of the war, about three hundred operators fell as casualties to wounds, disease, or capture. This figure does not include any of the workers above, who were often in greater danger than the operators.

Repair of the lines was sometimes conducted under fire in battle and more often in country infested with Southern sympathizers. Many men were ambushed while performing repairs, and on at least one occasion had their bodies mutilated.[28] Conditions were so bad in Tennessee that linemen worked only under heavy escort.

The USMT used existing commercial lines throughout the North for much of its operation and constructed or repaired similar lines as Union forces retook Confederate territory. Of the 15,389 miles of lines built by the USMT during the war, only about one thousand miles were characterized as "temporary field lines." For the first part of the war, the construction of field lines would fall to a competing organization, the United States Army Signal Corps.

The Signal Corps had at one time consisted of one man, Albert J. Myer. In the 1850s, Myer was employed as assistant surgeon at Fort Duncan in Texas. Myer, who had once been a telegraph operator, had become interested in the signaling techniques used by the Plains Indians.[29] He developed a system of signaling using flags during the day and torches at night and offered to demonstrate it for the army. In 1859, a board headed by Lieutenant Colonel Robert E. Lee gave a qualified endorsement to the system and requested further testing. Myer and Second Lieutenant E. Porter Alexander (who would later fly in a Confederate balloon and stand on top of Henry Pleasant's mine at Petersburg) carried out the field tests. On 27 June 1860, Myer was appointed as signal officer of the army. He did not have a Signal Corps, however, but took on interested officers and detailed men as the occasion demanded.

Myer was summoned to Washington in June 1861, and quickly made it clear to Secretary of War Cameron that he had in mind another role for himself than waving flags and torches. In a letter he wrote, regarding his appointment:

"Under this law I am entitled to the general charge of the telegraphic duty of the army, whether such signal duty is performed by means of signals transmitted by electricity or by aerial signals..."

Myer had apparently already realized the limitations of his own system during battle. The chaos and smoke of battle would often make visual signaling ineffective, but even under the best conditions the signals were equally available to friend and foe. Cameron, perhaps due to the hectic nature of its timing, did not respond to the letter. Myer, even while performing his assigned duty of visual signaling for McDowell's army (he also had been assigned the task of supervising the early balloonists...the reader will remember Myer's impatience leading to the demise of the balloon built by John Wise as it was towed to Manassas), was giving a great deal of thought to use of the telegraph.

What he envisioned was a tactical role for the telegraph, consisting of "flying" field telegraph trains that would accompany the army on the march. These trains would allow commanders to direct troop movements and artillery fire from a central location. The whole operation would be independent of any need for commercial telegraph lines.

Myer wrote another letter to Cameron on 6 August 1861, requesting that he be allowed to organize such a train. On 17 August, Thomas Scott (now Assistant Secretary of War) wrote back, reluctantly authorizing Myer to construct "a small telegraphic train" for experimental purposes.[30] Myer's primary duty was to establish a line of communication along the Potomac, using his "telegraphic train" where ordinary visual signals were not practical.

Myer had a contingent of enlisted men and officers detailed to him, and in August 1861 he gathered them in Georgetown, D.C. in what he called the Signal Camp of Instruction. After training (in both visual and electrical telegraphy) the men were returned to their regiments, where they instructed other men in smaller local camps.

Telegraph Wire Being Set Up at Fredericksburg, Virginia

National Archives, 64-CC-59; sketch by Alfred Waud

United States Military Telegraph (USMT) Field Station

National Archives, BA-1823

At about this time, experiments by a civilian telegraphic engineer in New York, by the name of Henry Rogers, caught Myer's attention. Rogers had developed strong, flexible insulated telegraph line that could be unwound from reels at a "rapid pace across virtually any terrain."[31] This was just the sort of thing Myer needed. The line developed by Rogers was strong enough to be crossed by the heaviest artillery without being damaged. He contacted Rogers and discussed his ideas for tactical battlefield telegraphy. Myer enlisted Rogers's help in developing a practical telegraphic train to meet his needs. The experimental train, consisting of light-wheeled vehicles towing the instruments and galvanic batteries, was completed by December 1861.

A military board tentatively approved the train in January 1862, but when McClellan asked to have it at his service for the Peninsula campaign that spring, problems arose. Specifically, there was no easy way to transport and maintain the large galvanic batteries and keep them serviceable. Rogers quickly came to the rescue by finding a substitute power source. In the late 1820s, Joseph Henry had discovered electromagnetic induction, the creation of electrical power by fluctuating magnetic fields (but again Henry was slow to take credit, and it eventually went to Michael Faraday). The basis of most of our modern electrical power, induction had been put to use by George Beardslee in a generator for telegraphic purposes.

In the Beardslee telegraph, batteries were not required: power came from manually turning a crank, which rotated wires about a magnet, producing electricity. The electrical signal was used to advance an indicator needle on the receiving end to the desired letter or number. This offered significant advantages over the Morse system in training the novice. Beardslee offered two of his generators for use in Myer's telegraphic train, and on 6 May 1862 the train was sent south to the Army of the Potomac headquarters at White House on the Pamunkey River. Before being sent, Myer suggested that the whole apparatus (power source and sending unit) be enclosed in one unit. The result was the "Beardslee United States Magneto-Electric Signal Telegraph," housed in a brass-bound walnut chest and weighing about one hundred pounds.

Myer's telegraphic train saw limited service during the Peninsula campaign. On more than one occasion, the system was used in conjunction with Thaddeus Lowe's balloon observations. McClellan was impressed enough by the train's performance that on 21 July 1862, he approved a contract for two additional trains, each with two Beardslee instruments, five miles of insulated wire and two hundred lances to be used as temporary telegraphic poles. The new trains reached the Army of the Potomac in October 1862.

Setting Up Telegraph Line in the Field

Courtesy of National Archives, 165-SB-62

In December 1862, Myer's field telegraph received another test, this time at Fredericksburg. For the first time, the telegraph was used extensively in a tactical way on the battlefield. The lines were extended from headquarters to both extreme wings of the Union formation, and the trains performed well, helping the Union command to monitor events through the blanket of smoke and fog that covered the battlefield. Some problems occurred when Union soldiers cut the lines, either out of curiosity or thinking them to be some Confederate device. After instructions were passed down through the ranks to leave the lines alone, this sort of vandalism subsided. Guarding the lines during battle became a highly desirable duty for some of the less courageous soldiers.

As 1863 began, everything looked encouraging for Myer and his system. The main problem that Myer saw at this point was the constant turnover in men under his command as their regiments requested their services. At his request, the U.S. Army Signal Corps was formed on 3 March 1863.

Just as Myer was riding this crest of popularity, things began to go wrong. Despite the glowing review from 1862, there were significant problems with the Beardslee generators. One common malfunction was lack of synchronization between the sending and receiving units, causing the receiver to end up at the wrong letter. An even greater problem was lack of range. The signal generated by the Beardslee machines was fairly weak, unusable after about five miles through the lines.

The second problem became embarrassingly obvious during the next major eastern battle. At Chancellorsville the armies were spread across a much greater distance than at Fredericksburg and the Beardslee generators were not up to the job. For crucial hours, from the evening of 30 April to the afternoon of 1 May, the failure of the Beardslee telegraph system left the right wing of Major General Joseph Hooker's army in the dark.[32] In a humiliating turn of events, desperate Union commanders gave control of the field telegraph lines to civilian operators of the USMT who were on hand. With their batteries and Morse equipment, the civilians were able to bring Federal communications successfully back under control. For the first time, officials seemed to realize that use of both the USMT and the Signal Corps might have been a redundancy they could not afford. The USMT seemed to have a clear advantage.

Myer set out to remedy the problems with his system, and in so doing he sowed the seeds of his own demise. Beardslee was confident that he could increase the power of his generators and that

USMT Telegraph Train

Courtesy of Library of Congress, LC-B811-7183

he could overcome the synchronization problems by using an electromagnetic sounder (using Morse code) instead of the indicator needles. This second change would require of the Signal Corps something they had up to this point avoided: the use of skilled telegraphic operators.

In September 1863, Myer published an advertisement in *The Army and Navy Official Gazette*, calling for "expert telegraphers" who would "have...charge of the...light field telegraph lines which are under...the Signal Corps, and which, at battle or at sieges, are run out and worked on the field or in the trenches under fire."[33] The problem with this advertisement was that the main source of recruits for Myer's Signal Corps would come directly from the USMT. Stager immediately protested to Stanton. He advised Stanton that all telegraphic operations should be placed either under the USMT (Stager's obvious preference) or under the Signal Corps, but that complications were arising from having "two organizations in the same grade of service."

In light of the Signal Corps fiasco at Chancellorsville, and with Stanton's interest in promoting his own political self-preservation through the commercial telegraph companies, the decision was not too difficult. On 10 November 1863, Stanton summoned Myer to the War Department and notified him that he was to surrender his position as head of the Signal Corps and report for duty to Memphis, Tennessee. All telegraphic equipment was to be relinquished to Stager and the USMT.

For the rest of the war, the Signal Corps confined itself to flag signaling, while the civilians of the USMT coordinated all electrical telegraphy. The idea of the field telegraph was continued by the USMT, but was not used again for tactical battlefield control. Its primary purpose fell into line with that of the USMT in general: strategic and logistical communications.

The batteries used in the field by the USMT consisted of 100 cells providing 1.5 volts each, divided into modular sections to provide variable amounts of power. The batteries were carried in converted ambulance wagons.[34] Seven fine wires insulated in gutta percha formed a line less than $^1/_8$-inch in diameter.[35] The lines were wound upon reels, with about two hundred pounds weight of wire to a reel, and fed out upon the back of a pack mule.[36] While the wire unreeled, two men followed, hanging it upon fences and bushes so it would not be run over. If time permitted, the wire was attached to wooden poles set at intervals. The poles did not have to be substantial or set particularly well, as their use was generally quite temporary. As Union forces under George Meade and Ulysses S. Grant headed south across the Rapidan River in 1864, the wire was laid out in such a manner at the rate of about two miles an

USMT Battery Wagon
Courtesy of Library of Congress, LC-B817-7934

hour. Where the lines ran through land unoccupied by Union infantry, cavalry patrols kept an eye out for sabotage. The local inhabitants were held responsible for the safety of the line...anyone caught tampering with it was to be shot on the spot.

Grant probably made more use of the telegraph during the war than did any other commander. He began using the telegraph for strategic troop deployment and to keep a rein on his subordinate commanders early in 1862. In 1864, Grant was in almost daily contact with Sherman's forces in Georgia as they combined with his forces in Virginia to choke off the Confederates.[37] According to Sherman, "The value of the telegraph cannot be exaggerated, as illustrated by the perfect accord of action of the armies of Virginia and Georgia."[38] Grant attested to the industriousness and reliability of the USMT men in his memoirs: "No orders ever had to be given to establish the telegraph. The moment troops were in position to go into camp, the men would put up their wires." Aside from Grant and Meade in Virginia and Sherman in Georgia, the field telegraph was also used extensively during Banks's disastrous trip up the Red River in 1864 (see Chapter 2).

Telegraph Attached to Battery Wagon

Operator in tent is working instrument, now connected to battery wagon.

Photographic History of the Civil War

Another major Union telegraphic feat, this time involving the commercial system, came after the defeat at Chickamauga in September 1863. Thomas Scott used the telegraph and the railroads to coordinate the movement of twenty-three thousand soldiers from Meade's forces in Virginia on a roundabout journey of twelve hundred miles to Chattanooga, Tennessee in eleven days. Lincoln had been pessimistic that the forces could be gotten to Washington in that amount of time.

There were equally dramatic stories on a smaller scale. William R. Plum tells the story of two Union soldiers captured during Hunter's raid up the Shenandoah Valley in 1864.[39] Their captors threatened the pair with death unless they joined the Confederate forces. The two agreed, hoping to escape, a feat they accomplished a short time later. Now they found themselves captured by Union forces and sentenced to death as traitors. A priest at Harper's Ferry telegraphed Abraham Lincoln, explaining the soldiers's story. Lincoln's reply, pardoning the soldiers, was delivered by horseback just as the firing squad were leveling their rifles.

By the time the war had ended, the USMT had constructed many thousands of miles of wire, including seventy-six miles of underwater cable.[40] About six and a half million messages were sent by the USMT during the war, at a direct cost to the government of $2,655,500, about forty cents per message.[41] After the war, the USMT supervised the restoration of commercial telegraph lines throughout the South. Lines constructed by the USMT in the South during the war were given to commercial companies, while those north of the Ohio River were sold.

On 30 November 1865, the USMT was disbanded and most of the operators and laborers returned to jobs with Western Union and the American Telegraph Company (Stager and Eckert retained their positions until mid-1866 and one operator remained in the War Department office until 1869).[42] A few of the most prominent operators were given silver watches engraved "United States Military Telegraph."[43] On 28 July 1866, Congress reinstated Albert Myer as head of the Army Signal Corps and gave control of all telegraph communications to that unit.

Confederate Telegraphy

The role of the telegraph in the Confederacy was important, but for lack of resources was more limited than that in the North. The word of secession traveled quickly by wire throughout the South as did the triumphant news regarding the attack on Fort Sumter.[44] The Confederate government communicated with military commanders by telegraph, and newspapers devoted much of their space to telegraphic battle reports. Still, lack of wire and battery materials made field telegraphy only a dream for the Confederates. With very few exceptions, the Confederates were limited to using commercial lines already in place.

Most of the commercial lines in the South belonged to the American Telegraph Company or, further west, the Southwestern Telegraph Company. West of the Mississippi, the Arkansas State Telegraph Company operated small network of lines, and isolated in Texas was the Texas Telegraph Company.

On 24 April 1861, James Dowell, superintendent of the American lines in the South, wired Dr. William S. Morris of Lynchburg,

Virginia asking Morris to meet with him in Richmond for a confer-
ence. Dowell convinced Morris, the only southern director of the
company, that in the interests of the company a Southern resident
should take control of affairs in the southern half of the company's
network. This arrangement, with Morris in control of the southern
lines, was confirmed in a meeting with President Edwards Sanford
in Washington on 11 May. For the remainder of the war, Morris
would be looking out simultaneously for American Telegraph interests and those of the Confederacy. In September 1861, the stockholders of the American in the South voted to change the name
there to the Confederated Telegraph Company, though throughout the war the firm was commonly called the Southern Telegraph
Company.

At about this time, the Confederate Congress in Montgomery,
Alabama had authorized Jefferson Davis to assume control of all
telegraph lines in the South. Confederate Postmaster General John
H. Reagan had been given the duty of supervising the telegraph
operation. Morris hurried to Montgomery and assured authorities
there of his loyalty to the Confederacy and his desire to operate his
company's lines for the public good. Apparently impressed with
Morris's devotion to the cause, Reagan appointed Morris as man-
ager of Confederate telegraphs.

During the next four years, Morris would discharge his duties
admirably, but he would never miss a chance to further the interests of his parent company. At Morris's request, Jefferson Davis
ordered in September 1862 that all the lines of the Southwestern
Telegraph Company (the American's largest rival in the South) be
placed under Morris's supervision. The Southwestern had also been
torn in two by the war, with its lines in Kentucky being operated
independently of those in the South. The Southwestern directors
were not about to lie down for what they considered nothing more
than a takeover attempt by Morris. They corresponded bitterly with
Reagan and finally traveled from Nashville to Richmond in November 1862. There they were finally able to get the order rescinded.

In October 1863, Morris clamped down when operators met at
Augusta to form a union. Complaining of long hours and insuffi-
cient pay, the operators called a strike. Morris immediately threatened any employees who chose to remain as members of the union
with dismissal and conscription into the army. The only strike in
the history of the Confederacy broke in a little more than a week.[45]

Despite losing all lines north of Richmond and both lines between Mobile and New Orleans early in the war, Morris was able to
keep the volume of information flowing throughout the South at
high levels.[46] Workers began reconstruction of an American line from

Lynchburg to Chattanooga and added a third line between Richmond and Charleston. In his August 1862 report to the American stockholders, Morris reported that "business in the aggregate is not very much less than it was at a corresponding period of the last year."[47]

At the beginning of the war, there were no factories for manufacturing glass (for insulators) or wire in the South, and there was little extra wire or battery acid on hand. Morris, showing some kinship to George Rains, showed great resourcefulness in obtaining materials. He obtained sulfuric acid from all across the Confederacy and Mexico and began operation of a wire factory at the Tredegar Iron Works in Richmond. Laboratories were organized to produce copper sulfate for batteries and many other materials were shipped through the blockade.[48]

As mentioned above, Confederate military use of the telegraph was limited mainly to strategic information. Jefferson Davis wired Joseph Johnston to reinforce Beauregard at Manassas in July 1861, and continued to use the telegraph to move his forces like chessmen throughout the conflict. Robert E. Lee kept in close touch with Davis through all his Virginia campaigns. Not surprisingly, Beauregard (who, as we have seen in Chapters 4 and 5, was open to exploiting any technological advantage) kept his telegraph lines busy. The only Confederate general who seemed truly upset with Morris's handling of telegraphy was Braxton Bragg. In 1862, Bragg apparently tried to assume control of lines within his territory, but he was rebuffed by authorities in Richmond.[49]

Though the Confederates did not have an official field telegraph service, temporary lines were sometimes strung for observation purposes, putting young operators in jeopardy. Lee Daniel, working from a shack in the woods along the Mississippi River, risked his life to report the approach of a Union flotilla towards Vicksburg.[50] His warning on Christmas Eve 1862 helped Vicksburg's defenders repel a surprise attack, helping that city to hold out for another seven months.

Morris and his subordinates were able to keep communications open almost to the end of the war. Not until the spring of 1865 did the lines between Richmond and the Deep South completely break down, mainly due to Sherman's advance. Still, linemen did the best they could to keep intermediate cities connected, patching important lines with wire from less important connections. Morris continued to serve his company as well, managing to pay stockholders until January 1865.

As the end of the war brought Confederate telegraph operations to a close, the managers of the Southern Telegraph Company restored all property to the American Telegraph Company. The American, as mentioned earlier, was then merged with Western Union in 1866.

Telegraph Security

Though much more secure than flag signaling, telegraph messages were not immune to interception. Telegraphers were employed by both sides to tap enemy lines. Pocket-size telegraph keys, capable of sending or receiving messages, were used before the war for testing lines. During the war, they were often used for espionage. Inserting the key into an enemy telegraphic line enabled the operator to monitor messages flowing through the line or to send false messages. Union telegraphers intercepted many Confederate messages in this way as Sherman's forces marched to Savannah.[51] Sherman stated that his men had become so skillful at tapping the wires "that by cutting the wire they could receive a message with their tongues from a distant station."[52]

Confederate telegraphers probably did more tapping than their Union counterparts. This was due to the much greater mileage of Union wire available. In July 1862, Ed Saville tapped into Union lines for four days, intercepting a number of important messages. Apparently unable to contain his pride, Saville cut into the flow of Union messages with one of his own: "Hurrah for Jeff Davis." Union operators recognized Saville from his telegraphic style or "fist" (which was apparently unique to each operator) but it was too late and he vanished without being caught.

Charles Gaston, under orders from General Lee, tapped in to Grant's line from Petersburg to Richmond and listened in from mid-August 1864 until October of that year.[53] Gaston ran an inconspicuous line from the main line in to some woods and had other Confederates nearby disguised as civilian woodcutters to alert him whenever Union troops came near. Gaston intercepted many messages during this period, but his heroics didn't do much good since most of the messages were in code. He sent his transcriptions to Richmond, but no one there was able to decipher them.

Because of the rampant tapping of lines, both sides resorted to sending messages in code or cipher. This was especially important to the Confederates, who sent virtually all their messages across commercial lines. The Civil War was the first war in which electrically transmitted messages were encoded.[54]

Union telegraphers used different levels of cryptography, depending on the sensitivity of the message. Some were quite easy for the Confederates to decipher, but they never broke the route cipher system designed by Anson Stager. The Confederates got so

Confederate Cipher Machine Captured in Mobile, 1865

National Archives, 106435

desperate that they printed tapped Union messages in Southern newspapers, hoping a civilian might be able to decipher the code. Stanton entrusted the cipher books used by the Union only to the operators.[55] They were off-limits even to the military command-ers. By the end of the war, the books contained twelve pages of "route" indicators and thirty-six pages of code words.

In the route cipher system, the message was imbedded in a rectangle of words, with a key word indicating the size of the col-umn and certain prearranged words indicating the end of a column. The receiver could then rewrite the text into the form of a rectangle. The key word also indicated the "route" through the rectangle (for example, up the first column, then down the third column, etc.). Many of the words in the message, especially those frequently used, were replaced with code words.

The results for Confederate cryptographers were mixed. In-stead of having a standardized system, there were several in circu-lation throughout the war. With little cryptographic experience, the Confederates tended to use older, established systems for their messages. The main system used by the Confederate government was known officially as the Virgenere Tableau, but was usually called the Vicksburg Square.

There were two major problems with the system. First, the system depended on a key phrase to decipher the message, and only three phrases were used during the war: MANCHESTER BLUFF, COMPLETE VICTORY and near the end COME RETRIBUTION. The messages themselves were encoded in a meaningless jumble of letters. This often caused problems as operators frequently missed or incorrectly transmitted a letter. This was not a problem in the Union system, which used common words even in the cipher. In one case, an officer under General Kirby Smith got so frustrated after trying for twelve hours to read a garbled message that he jumped on his horse and rode completely around the Union lines to find out what the sender was trying to say.[56]

Three of the young men in the Union War Department telegraph office became adept at deciphering Confederate messages. David Bates, Albert Chandler, and Charles Tinker were known as "The Sacred Three" for their work, and President Lincoln often looked over their shoulders as they spent long hours sifting meaning from Confederate transmissions.

Other deceptions were sometimes used to gain information from the telegraph. The easiest way to gain information (but the most dangerous) was to place an operative in the enemy telegraph office. J. O. Kerby did this for the Union and an unidentified Confederate worked for a brief time in Grant's office.[57] Another way to mislead the enemy was to send false messages over the lines. A good number of these hoaxes were pulled during the war. A humorous one occurred during J.E.B. Stuart's raid at Burke Station just south of Washington. Replacing the Union operator with his own, Stuart had his operator listen in on Union messages and then send his famous message to the U.S. Quartermaster's office complaining about the quality of horses he was capturing from Union cavalry.

In a more serious vein, General O. M. Mitchel was able to capture two Confederate trains because of a fake message sent by his operator to Huntsville, Alabama. George Ellsworth, a telegrapher who rode with Confederate Colonel John Hunt Morgan on his famous Kentucky raid in July 1862,[58] gained important information from wiretaps and caused confusion in Union troop movements by sending false messages through Union lines.[59] Finally, there is a possibility that the reason Sherman bypassed Augusta and its powder works was due to a telegraphic hoax. There is at least one report that the Confederates, knowing that the Union forces had their lines tapped, sent a bogus message intimating that Augusta was strongly held and that the Southern forces were prepared to defend it to the last.[60] If this report is true, it may have influenced Sherman into his mode of thinking described in Chapter 4: if bypassed to the north, Augusta was taken out of the war as effectively as if it had been captured.

Appendix 1

Buoyancy

Buoyancy is a concept that runs as a common thread through a number of chapters in this book. Thus, it seems wise to include here a short primer on the topic. To begin, consider a glass of water. Further, picture an imaginary "cube" of this water sitting motionless in the middle of the glass of water.

One of the basic laws of physics is that an object that is not changing its state of motion must be acted on by forces which balance one another. This must be true for our cube of water. But what forces act on the cube? There are two main types of forces acting here. First is the force exerted on the cube by the surrounding water. Second is the pull of the Earth's gravity on the cube.

The pressure (pressure is the amount of force applied to a given area, in this case a particular face of the cube) exerted by a fluid (gas or liquid) increases as you go further below its surface. Hence, the pressure at the bottom of the deep end of a swimming pool is greater than that at the bottom of the shallow end. Another example is that the air pressure at Baltimore is greater than at Denver because Baltimore is further down in the ocean of air we call our atmosphere.

Why must pressure be greater at greater depth? We can see by looking again at our cube of water. Let's assume that the forces on the four vertical faces will balance since they are all at the same depth, and so we will ignore them in the following discussion. This leaves us to consider the forces on the top and bottom faces of the cube. Remember that the cube is motionless and forces on it must balance. Recall also the presence of our second type of force, the downward pull of gravity on the cube (i.e., the weight of the cube of water). It follows that the force on the bottom of the cube is greater by an amount equal to the weight of the cube of water. Since all forces balance, the cube of water is said to have *neutral buoyancy* when immersed in the surrounding water. The amount by which the force on the bottom face exceeds the force on the top face (i.e., the weight of water in the cube) is called the *buoyant force.*

What happens if we replace our cube of water with a cube of the same size made of a different material? If the material is less dense than water (i.e., a similar cube of this material would weigh less than the cube of water), then all forces will stay the same except the weight of the cube itself and there will now be an overall upward force on the cube. The cube is said to have *positive buoyancy* and will rise upwards through the water. This would be the case for a cube made of cork or Styrofoam, for example.

What if we place into the water an identically sized cube made of lead, which is more dense than water (i.e., a cube of lead would weigh more than a cube of water of the same size)? Again, all forces remain the same except for the weight of the cube. There is now an overall downward force and the cube sinks to the bottom of the glass of water. The cube is said to have *negative buoyancy.*

Appendix 2

Antebellum Submarines

Humans have been exploring the ocean depths for many thousands of years. Ancient relics tell of divers around 4000 B.C. submerging to depths of a one hundred feet in search of sponges, oysters, coral, shells, and treasure.[1] The first artificial aid to diving was probably a hollow reed used as a snorkel. Descent in an enclosed compartment may have also been attempted in ancient times—legends exist of Alexander the Great (356–323 B.C.) descending in a glass barrel lowered by chains. Alexander almost certainly made use of underwater warfare when his divers destroyed an underwater barricade at the siege of Tyre.[2]

The Arabian historian Bohaddin, who lived about A.D. 1150, reports of a submarine device being used to transport a messenger into a city besieged by the Crusaders.[3] Leonardo da Vinci made sketches of a submarine in the early Renaissance, though no record exists of its construction. The first "modern" record of human descent in a semi-enclosed compartment was a diving bell demonstrated in 1538 in the Tagus River in Toledo, Spain. The principle behind the diving bell is quite simple. If a container (open at the bottom) is lowered straight down into water, water will not enter the chamber because the air is occupying the enclosed space. This can be easily demonstrated with a glass of water in a sink. The problem with diving bells is that any departure from the vertical will cause water to immediately rush in to the compartment as the air rushes out and bubbles up to the surface.

Despite this inherent flaw, diving bells were of great interest to many in the sixteenth and seventeenth centuries, and several interesting modifications were made. In 1616, Franz Kessler in Germany invented a diving chamber that was not lowered by ropes. The diver carried heavy weights for descent and released the weights when he desired to rise. This technique made use of the interplay between buoyant force and weight crucial to all submarine vehicles.

As described more fully in Appendix 1, the buoyant force on an object in water is constant if its size does not change and is equal to the weight of the amount of water which would fill the space now occupied by the object. The buoyant force is directed upwards and thus acts to counterbalance the downward force of the object's weight. If the object's weight and the buoyant force are equal in size, then the object will stay at a constant depth and is said to have *neutral buoyancy*. If the object's weight exceeds the buoyant force, then the object will sink and is said to have *negative buoyancy*. If the buoyant force is greater than the weight, the object has *positive buoyancy* and will rise through the water until enough of the object's volume has come out of the water to reduce the buoyant force so that it is equal to the object's weight.

In 1690, Edmund Halley (more famous as an astronomer) devised a method that would supply divers in a diving bell with fresh air for long periods of time.[4] Barrels (empty except for air) were floated on the water's surface. Each barrel had two holes in it. From the top hole a hose ran down through the water and up through the open bottom of the bell. Seawater entered through the barrel's bottom hole and pushed air through the hose to the divers. Halley and four others thus submerged for an hour and a half at a depth of about sixty feet.[5]

Yet even with these improvements, diving bells were quite dangerous because of the open bottom. Many felt that the future of submarine travel would have to lie in enclosed vehicles. William Bourne, an English naval officer, is credited with the first recorded design for an undersea boat in 1578. The boat (never built) was to be made of wood and covered with leather. Buoyancy was to be controlled by leather chambers on either side of the hull. The chambers could be extended to let water in (thus making the boat heavier and giving it negative buoyancy) or compressed to force water out and make the boat rise. This idea was the primitive ancestor of what would become known as ballast tanks in more modern submarines. The idea for ballast tanks may have come from observing fish, whose swim bladders operate on the same principle.

The history of submarine navigation is really the history of the efforts of many men towards the solution to a group of technical problems.[6] These problems reside mainly in the following five areas: (1) making a vessel which can submerge and rise to the surface, all the time resisting changes in water pressure; (2) making a vessel which is stable in three dimensions while operating submerged and also has adequate performance on the surface; (3) making a vessel which can be inhabited with no connection to the atmosphere; (4) making a vessel which can be propelled efficiently both submerged and on the surface; and (5) making a vessel which can deliver offensive weapons.[7]

The first working submarine boat was probably that built in 1620 by Cornelis Drebbel, a Dutch scientist living in England.[8] Drebbel's boat was wooden, covered with leather and grease to make it watertight, and was propelled by twelve oarsmen. The oars projected out of the boat through leather sleeves. Drebbel demonstrated his seventy-two-foot-long craft beneath the surface of the Thames River several times and tried (unsuccessfully) to sell it to the British navy as a weapon of war. Drebbel also claimed to have invented a method for purifying the air in the vessel, but the state of chemical knowledge at the time makes this seem unlikely.[9] In any event, his craft was certainly large enough to hold sufficient air for his crew for several hours.

A few years later, in 1653, a Frenchman named De Son, invented the first submarine to be powered artificially.[10] A large paddle wheel was installed in the center of the craft, its blades protruding into the water. The wheel was connected to a clockwork mechanism.

During the American Revolutionary War, David Bushnell of Saybrook, Connecticut, built the first American submarine of which there is record. Bushnell was a mechanically inclined inventor and student at Yale (where the library certainly contained works describing the previous accomplishments in submarine work) before the war broke out.[11] Once the British began to control the colonial ports, Bushnell began to plan a way for the Americans to retaliate. Specifically, he wanted to destroy British ships with underwater mines delivered by a submersible vehicle. The vehicle, which Bushnell called the *Turtle*, was built of wooden sections held together by iron straps. The vehicle was seven and a half feet high and five and a half feet wide[12] and designed for one man.[13]

The *Turtle* was propelled by a screw propeller operated by a hand crank and had a second propeller on a vertical shaft (also operated by a hand crank) to help the boat ascend. For buoyancy changes, Bushnell installed ballast tanks. Water was let in by a foot-operated valve and pumped out with a foot-operated pump. These ballast tanks were located at the bottom of the craft to help keep it upright. Two brass snorkels with check valves were used to admit fresh air and expel stale air. A glass tube closed at the top and leading to the outside served as a depth gauge. As depth increased, greater water pressure forced more water up into the tube. A compass and hand-operated rudder were used for directional control. Both depth gauge and compass were coated with foxfire (phosphorescent glow given off by certain types of fungi found on decaying timber) for viewing in the dark.

The *Turtle* was very sophisticated for its time and required the pilot to spend a great deal of time practicing the various controls. As the air inside was only sufficient for about thirty minutes, Bushnell designed the *Turtle* to be operated mainly near the surface with its snorkels and conning tower above water. When nearing a target, the operator would close the snorkel valves and admit enough water ballast to submerge slightly.

The mine was an egg-shaped wooden cask containing one hundred and fifty pounds of powder and detonated by a clockwork timer. The mine was attached to the submarine by a bolt. Withdrawing the bolt released the mine and started the timer. Before release, the operator (as if he didn't have enough to do) drove an auger, connected to the mine by a rope, into the hull of the target ship.

Bushnell, whose health was not good, selected and trained his brother Ezra to pilot the *Turtle*. Ezra obtained leave from the Seventh Connecticut Regiment, and began training. In late summer 1776, after months of training, Ezra Bushnell was ready to make the world's first submarine attack, when disaster occurred—he became seriously ill. General George Washington, who had given David Bushnell the authority to build the submarine, was anxious that it be used in New York Harbor as soon as possible. So it was that on the night of 6 September, Sergeant Ezra Lee, with only a minimal amount of training, piloted the *Turtle* off the tip of Manhattan Island towards the anchored British fleet.

After about two and a half hours, Lee reached the British fleet and pulled up near the man-of-war H.M.S. *Eagle*. After submerging underneath the *Eagle*, Lee found that he could not get the auger to penetrate the bottom of the boat. This was for many years thought to be due to copper sheathing on part of the wooden hull,[14] but it now appears that the *Eagle* was not sheathed until 1782.[15] A more likely possibility is (as Bushnell thought) that Lee was striking the heavy iron bar connecting the rudder fitting to the stern post.[16] It may also be possible that carbon monoxide poisoning weakened Lee or that he was simply unable to exert enough pressure from underneath the ship to get the auger started into the wood. With his air running out and daylight approaching, Lee decided to head back (a distance of about four miles). Near Governor's Island, British soldiers sighted him and a boat was sent out to investigate. When they came within about fifty yards, Lee let released his mine. This so frightened the British that they headed back to the island. After drifting a little past the island, the mine exploded in the water, throwing up a huge plume of water.

A few nights later, Lee made another attempt on a ship in the North River, but was noticed while trying to attach the mine and was forced to leave.[17] On 9 October, the British fleet drove the Americans further up the Hudson River and the sloop hauling the *Turtle* was sunk. Bushnell salvaged the submarine later in the war, but it was never used again. It was probably destroyed after Washington's defeat at White Plains to keep it out of British hands.

In 1800, the American Robert Fulton built a submarine that had many features from the *Turtle* as well as some innovative features. A foldable sail was used to propel the craft on the surface. To increase the crew's endurance while submerged, compressed air was stored in the boat. Horizontal rudders were used to help the submarine rise and descend and a lead keel improved stability. Fulton's design also may have included a rotating periscope. The copper-sheathed boat, called the *Nautilus*, was shown by Fulton to the French government at Rouen where he submerged in the Seine River for forty-five minutes,[18] and in another demonstration at Brest he was able to successfully destroy an old ship by using the *Nautilus* to deliver a copper mine containing twenty pounds of gunpowder.[19] The *Nautilus* was a little over twenty-one feet long and about six and a half feet in the beam and was designed for a crew of three men.[20] The French were impressed but noncommittal, so Fulton tried a more impressive display. He had the boat towed to Le Havre and he and his two crewmates attempted unsuccessfully to attack British ships in the English Channel. After the French lost interest, Fulton tried to sell the idea to the British, who also declined.

Fulton returned to America and began his more famous work on steamboats, but he never forgot the submarine. During the War of 1812 he launched a small submarine at New London, Connecticut which used a mine to damage, but not sink, the H.M.S. *Ramilies*.[21] For two years before his death in 1816, he worked on an eighty-foot-long submarine called the *Mute*, which was meant to be propelled by steam and carry a crew of a hundred men.[22] It was never finished.

Through the first half of the nineteenth century, work on submarines continued, with little real progress except for increasing size. In 1856, Wilhelm Bauer constructed a fifty-two-foot-long submarine (powered by a screw propeller worked by foot power),[23] called *Le Diable Marin*, for Russian use in the Crimean War.[24] To deliver a mine to an enemy ship, a crew member worked through rubber gloves extended through the hull and observed through a glass porthole.[25] Though Bauer reportedly made 134 dives between 1856 and 1858 at depths as great as one hundred and fifty feet, the craft never saw military action.[26]

At the time of the U.S. Civil War, the main problems of submarine technology which still eluded inventors were how to achieve mechanical propulsion under water, how to provide a long-term atmosphere for the crew, and how to effectively deliver offensive weapons. The problems of descending and ascending had been successfully solved through the use of ballast tanks and stability was taken care of through the use of diving fins and a weighted keel.

For propulsion, steam engines could not be used when submerged because they required oxygen. Electrical motors powered by batteries were first used to effectively power a submarine in 1886 (some pioneering attempts had been made in France as early as 1855 (Marie-Davy) and 1861 (Riou) and by the American Alstitt in 1863,[27] but the submarine had only a limited range of about eighty miles before the batteries needed to be recharged.[28] In France in 1863 (where peace gave inventors the luxury of time to experiment), Charles Brun built the *Plongeur*, a 146-foot submarine which had its propeller driven by compressed air.[29] The submarine was, unfortunately, very difficult to control and was scrapped after two years of testing. The first truly effective modern submarine was developed with the advent of the internal combustion engine in the 1890s. These submarines used gasoline (and later diesel) engines for propulsion on the surface and also to run a generator which recharged the batteries for the motor. When submersion was necessary, the submarine used the electric motor.

Through World War II most submarines were forced to operate mainly on the surface unless attacking or under attack. Only the advent of nuclear-powered submarines in the 1950s allowed submarines to stay submerged for long periods of time. Nuclear fission reactions, unlike combustion, do not need oxygen. These prolonged periods of submersion required more sophisticated solutions than the snorkel for the crew's breathing: oxygen is typically produced on modern submarines by electrolysis of water; absorbent filters remove carbon dioxide.[30]

For the delivery of mines against enemy ships, a variety of methods had been tried through the Civil War, ranging from direct attachment by auger or by hand to towed mines. The great problem with all of these methods was the need for the attacking submarine to get in dangerous proximity to the target ship. The solution came only three years after the end of the Civil War. The British engineer

Robert Whitehead invented the self-propelled torpedo in 1868. A forty-horsepower engine (running on compressed air) which turned twin screw propellers drove the torpedo.[31] If the Confederates had been able to develop such a device, the Civil War on the sea might have had a dramatically different outcome!

Appendix 3

Antebellum Aircraft

The desire of humans to leave behind the bonds of gravity and fly is surely an ancient one. That successful flight seems to have come so late in human history is interesting, because the principles are not difficult and men have observed objects floating and rising in the air for thousands of years.

Because the flight of objects heavier than air requires lift forces generated by moving airfoils at high speeds, attempts to emulate the flight of birds were doomed to failure until the advent of the powerful internal combustion engine in the late nineteenth century. Thus, the first successful human flights were achieved by creating objects lighter than the air around them. Objects lighter than air will rise due to buoyant forces (see Appendix 1) just as a cork will rise when placed in water.

In 1670, Franceso de Lana, a Jesuit monk, reasoned that "no air" must be lighter than "some air."[1] He came up with a scheme in which an apparatus consisting of four copper spheres would be evacuated of air and be buoyed up by the air around it.[2] Though de Lana was on the right track, this sort of device would not be successful. Even if sufficiently powerful vacuum pumps had been available in his day, copper spheres thick enough to enclose a near vacuum would certainly be too heavy to float.

A scheme more likely to succeed would be one that would involve filling a very lightweight vessel with a gas which was considerably lighter than the air around it. Nearly a hundred years would pass from de Lana's time before scientists would isolate a gas lighter than air, so in the meantime prospective aeronauts would need to be more creative. From ancient times, men have stared at fires and watched smoke rise from the flames. Perhaps an inverted bag or container placed over a fire would capture the smoke and rise also.

We now know that smoke rises as it is carried by warm air away from the fire. The warm air rises because it is less dense than the cooler air surrounding it. Before Joseph Priestly discovered oxygen in 1774, and the subsequent understanding of combustion as a chemical reaction, many believed that fire involved the release of a substance called phlogiston from an object. Hence, the earliest attempts at lighter-than-air flight were likely attempts at capturing phlogiston and riding upward with it.

Though there is a possibility that the Chinese may have flown balloons as early as the 1300s, the first reliable evidence for successful flight comes from Europe.[3] In 1709, Bartolomeu Laurenco de Gusmao demonstrated several small balloons in Portugal. The small paper balloons held a suspended earthen bowl containing fire. There is also evidence that a balloon constructed of hides and containing "evil smelling smoke" was flown in Russia in 1731, and may have been the first manned flight.[4]

Travel through the air on a regular basis began in France in 1783. The two Montgolfier brothers, Joseph Michel and Jacques Etienne, had been working on small balloons for several years. On 5 June 1783 at Annonay, they demonstrated for a large crowd a much larger balloon. Suspended between two wooden poles, their balloon was made of paper and was seventy feet high and forty-six feet in diameter when filled with heated air.[5] Beneath the balloon was a smoky fire of wet straw and sheep's wool.[6] When inflated, the brothers cut the balloon loose. The delighted and amazed crowd watched as the device rose more than a mile in the sky and traveled a mile and a half from its launching point.[7]

Later that summer, another significant launch took place in France. Natural philosopher Jacques Alexandre Cesar Charles, assisted by John and Noel Robert, released a balloon from the Champs de Mars in Paris (now the site of the Eiffel Tower) on 27 August. The thirteen-foot balloon was not lifted by the buoyancy of hot air, but by that of hydrogen (called "inflammable air" at the time), discovered by Henry Cavendish in 1766. The balloon flew for more than forty-five minutes before touching down near the village of Gonesse, some fifteen miles distant. There a group of frightened peasants attacked and tore apart the invader from the sky.[8]

In the large crowd gathered for the launching was American Benjamin Franklin, leader of the American diplomatic contingent in France. When a bystander asked Franklin what good was a device such as the balloon, Franklin responded, "What is the use of a newborn babe?"[9]

Indeed, Charles's balloon heralded the infancy of practical travel through the sky, for hydrogen has a major advantage versus hot air for lifting objects: it has only about one-eleventh the weight of an equal volume of air. If we consider an outside environment of thirty-two degrees Fahrenheit air at sea level, a typical hot-air balloon will provide about seventeen to twenty pounds of lift for every one thousand cubic feet of enclosed volume (i.e., a sphere with a diameter of about eighteen feet). The same balloon filled with hydrogen provides about seventy-five pounds of lift.[10] Thus hot-air balloons must be considerably larger than hydrogen-filled balloons to achieve the same lifting power.

As the early aeronauts found, hot air does retain some advantages over hydrogen, however. Though hydrogen lifts more easily than hot air, it is easier to quickly change one's altitude in a hot-air balloon. By extinguishing the source of heat (usually a propane-fueled heater in modern hot-air balloons), the air in the balloon quickly cools and contracts, causing the balloon to slow in its ascent. To slow the ascent of a hydrogen balloon, one must release some of the enclosed hydrogen by opening a valve located at the top of the balloon. The response time of this method is slower than that of a hot-air balloon.

Another major disadvantage of hydrogen is that it is extremely flammable. Using helium in place of hydrogen eventually solved this problem, but not until after several disasters occurred, including the Hindenburg tragedy in 1937. Helium is not flammable, and will in fact extinguish a fire, but is heavier than hydrogen and was not discovered in substantial quantities on Earth until the early twentieth century.

Finally, producing a sufficient amount of hydrogen to fill a large balloon was difficult. It took Charles and his assistants four days to inflate their balloon. The most typical way to generate hydrogen at the time was to mix iron filings with sulfuric acid, and collect the hydrogen gas produced by the chemical reaction,

$$2Fe + 3(H_2SO_4) = Fe_2(SO_4)_3 + 3H_2$$

in which iron is oxidized and hydrogen is reduced. To generate a sufficient amount of hydrogen gas required thousands of pounds of iron and sulfuric acid. Still, the superior lifting capabilities of hydrogen would lead most early air pioneers to opt for it instead of hot air.

Nineteenth-century balloonists who were to ascend in an urban area could often opt for another source of buoyancy. Coal gas (mostly methane), released during the dry distillation of coal, was being used widely by the mid-1800s as a source of lighting in large cities. Many Civil War balloonists (and all Confederate balloonists) would tap into the city gas mains through which the coal gas was piped to homes and businesses. The lifting power of coal gas, while not equal to that of hydrogen or helium, is superior to hot air and its ready availability made it a good choice for balloonists located near a large city.

After Charles's exhibition, the Montgolfier brothers decided to take the next step and attempt an ascension with passengers. Concerned that the upper atmosphere might be filled with toxic substances (perhaps unbreathable phlogiston), they decided to use animals first. On 19 September 1783, they launched a balloon with a straw basket attached. In the basket were the world's first known air passengers, a sheep, a duck, and a rooster. The passengers returned safely to the ground after a trip to an altitude of about fifteen hundred feet[11] (The U.S. Balloon Corps of the early twentieth century wore an insignia of the three animals on their uniforms).[12]

Finally, it was time for a human to go skyward. The man of fate was Jean Francois Pilatre de Rozier, an acquaintance of the Montgolfiers. De Rozier had been the first man on the scene at the recovery of the three animals in September.[13] Though de Rozier was quite willing to fly, he had an obstacle in his way. King Louis XVI was opposed to the idea of men flying, perhaps because it would lessen the apparent power of his royal position (Louis XVI would find in several years that his power over his subjects was far weaker than he suspected at the time). Only through the intervention of Marquis d'Arlandes, a friend of de Rozier's and cousin of the king, was de Rozier finally able to get permission to fly. At first, Louis only relented to the point of giving permission to take a criminal aloft, to be set free if he survived. D'Arlandes, however, was able to convince the monarch that it would look better for France if a free citizen made the first ascent.

In October, de Rozier made two tethered ascents to several hundred feet in a hot-air balloon built by the Montgolfiers. During these trials, it became obvious that a second passenger would be needed for an untethered flight, to help balance the basket and to help stoke the fire, which was contained in a pan suspended below the mouth of the balloon. De Rozier's friend d'Arlandes was a willing volunteer.

On 21 November 1783, the two men climbed into the wicker basket and took off. After a low-altitude flight of some twenty-five minutes covering about five miles, the men descended safely, the first humans to safely fly above the earth. De Rozier would later claim another honor, this one more dubious. On 15 June 1785, de

Rozier, along with Pierre Romain, became the first men to die in an aerial accident. De Rozier decided to combine the lifting power of a hydrogen balloon with the quick maneuverability of a hot-air balloon by constructing a double balloon device.[14] Unfortunately, he ignored warnings from Charles about hydrogen's flammability. At a height of about seven hundred feet, the flame from the hot-air balloon ignited the hydrogen balloon, sending both men plummeting to their deaths.[15]

Word of these first balloon flights rapidly spread across the Atlantic to the new-born United States. The first American to leave the ground was thirteen-year-old Edward Warren, who volunteered on 24 June 1784 in Baltimore to go up in a tethered balloon built by Peter Carnes. The first American to make an untethered ascent was John Jeffries, who accompanied the Frenchman Jean Pierre Blanchard in a two-hour flight above London on 30 November 1784 and then joined Blanchard in the first trip across the English Channel from Dover to France in three hours on 7 January 1785.[16] This last trip was a semi-comic affair that ended with the two men only avoiding a hard crash at the end by urinating to remove the last possible bit of weight from the balloon.[17] Blanchard made the first untethered ascent in the United States in Philadelphia on 9 January 1793.

Not long after the first balloon flights, men on both sides of the Atlantic began to ponder the possibilities of using these devices in military situations. On 20 October 1783, after joining de Rozier in one of his tethered ascents, Andre Firaud de Vilette wrote in the Journal de Paris: "...I was convinced that this apparatus, costing but little, could be made very useful to an army for discovering positions of its enemy, his movements, his advances, and his dispositions, and that this information could be conveyed to the troops operating the machine." Englishman Thomas Martyn in 1784 suggested a scheme for aerial signaling for use in military situations.[18] Ben Franklin in a letter dated 16 January 1784 discusses the military advantage to be gained by quickly transporting large numbers of men by balloon. A letter written a month later by Thomas Jefferson states: "...the discovery seems to threaten the prostration of fortified works...the destruction of fleets."[19]

A decade would pass before balloons would first be used in a military setting. With the coming of the French Revolution, the young French republic found itself threatened on all sides by land-hungry nations (mainly England, Austria, and Holland) looking to take advantage of their neighbor's internal chaos. In such desperate times, the French sought any means possible to improve their military situation. In 1793, the revolutionary committee first sought

Joseph Montgolfier. Montgolfier realized that for military purposes, balloons would need to stay aloft for hours at a time, something much more easily accomplished at that time with a hydrogen balloon than with a hot-air balloon. Not being familiar with the construction of hydrogen balloons, Montgolfier referred the committee to a chemist, Jean Marie-Joseph Coutelle.[20]

Coutelle completed his balloon in the spring of 1794. On 2 April 1794, the revolutionary leaders passed a law forming the world's first military air company, with Coutelle as captain. The twenty-five men in the company were selected for their particular skills: masons, carpenters, chemists, fishermen, and an artist. The carpenters were needed to make and repair the balloon's basket; the chemists were to aid in producing the hydrogen and to test varnishes with which to seal the balloon's surface; the fishermen's job was to construct and repair the balloon's rigging; and the artist, of course, was to handle the task of sketching the enemy's works.

The masons were needed because Coutelle was being forced to generate hydrogen in a new way. Since sulfur was desperately needed for manufacturing ammunition, the old way of adding sulfuric acid to iron scraps was not possible. Instead, Coutelle heated iron until it was white-hot and then sprayed water on it. The heat was sufficient to break the water into its hydrogen and oxygen components, with the hydrogen then collected for use in the balloon. The job of the masons was to construct and maintain the furnace.[21]

At the inception of the air company, the revolutionary leaders had three missions in mind for the unit: reconnaissance and observation, signaling between friendly units, and spreading propaganda pamphlets. When Coutelle and his men arrived in Maubege at the end of May, his immediate task was to find the strength of the Austrians opposing the French. The French command needed to know whether they should retreat or if they had sufficient strength to hold out until reinforcements arrived. On 2 June 1794, Coutelle made history's first military reconnaissance. Tethered at about twelve hundred feet, he saw that much of the Austrian camp was empty and that many of the tents had been set up merely as decoys.

After receiving this information, the French commanders decided not only to stay but also to attack the main Austrian force at the nearby town of Charleroi. The French put the town under siege. On 24 June, Coutelle ascended once again and saw that the Austrians were outmanned. The demoralized Austrians, who saw the balloon as some sort of evil omniscient eye, surrendered the next day. Unbeknown to the defenders of Charleroi, Austrian reinforcements had been on the way and met the French two days later at the battle of Fleures. During the battle, Coutelle stayed aloft for nine hours, dropping weighted notes detailing Austrian deployments. Just as the French troops were losing heart, Coutelle dropped a note informing them that the Austrians were in retreat.

Obviously a success, the air company continued to assist the French army during the rest of the campaign as they drove their attackers from the country. Impressed, the revolutionary council set up a second company and in October of 1794 they authorized the formation of the first flight training school.[22] Both companies saw service until 1796, when the first company was captured at the Battle of Wurzburg (they were released in early 1797).

Despite these early successes, the French balloon companies soon went into decline. Although Napoleon took a balloon company with him to Egypt in 1797, he did not put them to military use and apparently was not much interested in using them in future campaigns. By early 1799, the companies had been disbanded and authorities closed the aeronautics school.[23]

The military history of balloons between the time of the French Revolution and the U.S. Civil War consists of a few scattered attempts, none very successful. In 1807, a Dane named Kolding attempted to break a British blockade with a balloon using some sort of propulsion system. The attempt failed, but the Danes did make use of balloons the next year when they sent small balloons bearing propaganda pamphlets floating above the coast of their enemy, Sweden. The pamphlets apparently had little effect as they were quickly seized and suppressed by Swedish police.[24]

In that same year of 1808, a Major Lhomond attempted to revive the French balloon service by proposing to Napoleon that the French invade England with immense hot-air balloons, each capable of carrying a thousand men, two cannons, twenty-five horses, and provisions for ten days. Napoleon was understandably skeptical and nothing came of Lhomond's idea. The French did apparently make use of a balloon several decades later when Jean Margat made at least one flight aloft in support of troops in Algeria in 1830. The flight was apparently made under fire and the general staff praised Margat.[25] Louis and Eugene Godard continued the French use of balloons in 1859 during the campaigns against Italy.[26] Just after the U.S. Civil War, the French made important use of balloons during the siege of Paris in 1870. During a four-month period, using sixty-six balloons fueled by the heated gases given off by burning coal, the French airlifted 167 men and more than three million letters out of the beleaguered city.[27]

During Napoleon's campaign against Russia in 1812, Alexander I had a large fish-shaped balloon built with the intent of bombing Napoleon's headquarters. Designed by a German engineer named Leppig, the balloon was inflated over a five-day period, but never raised.[28] During the Crimean War, the Russians used aerial observers in balloons during the siege of Sebastopol.[29]

The British, who were besieging Sebastopol, had also considered using balloons for observation there but didn't act on the idea. The year before, the British had also considered, but ultimately rejected, a plan to bomb Cronstadt by air with a balloon as the delivery vehicle.[30]

During the siege of Milan in 1848, the captive Austrians sent up paper hot-air balloons carrying propaganda pamphlets. The pamphlets were released from the balloons by burning timed fuses. The next year, during the siege of Venice, the Austrians went a step further. They used small balloons to determine wind direction and then released many larger balloons carrying bombs. In addition to the balloons released by the army, some were released from boats anchored nearby. The bombs, released by timed fuses, did no significant damage.[31]

There were two pre-Civil War situations which did lead the U.S. command to at least ponder the possibility of using balloons. The first was in the Seminole War in Florida, which began in 1835. The purpose of the war was to remove the Seminoles to the West, but by 1840 the U.S. forces had still not completed the task. Their biggest problem was in locating their elusive enemy in the thickly wooded country. The military leaders were beginning to feel intense pressure from politicians to get the job done.

In September 1840, Colonel John Sherbourne sent a letter to Secretary of War Joel Poinsett in which he outlined a plan for using balloons in an attempt to end the conflict. By making night ascensions, the U.S. troops could locate Seminole campfires and use the information to surround and surprise them. A month later Sherbourne notified Poinsett that Charles Durant (one of America's first professional aeronauts) had agreed to construct an appropriate balloon and all necessary equipment for $600.[32] Poinsett was intrigued and decided to consult with General W. K. Armistead, the commander in Florida.

Armistead saw no use for the plan. He felt that the terrain was not suitable for balloon operations and refused to have anything to do with the scheme. Undaunted, Sherbourne continued to press Poinsett and submitted the plan again in late 1841 as the war continued to drag on. This time Poinsett asked the opinion of General

Edmund P. Gaines, who had once been in command in Florida and was now commanding the Western Division of the Army. Gaines was more favorable to the idea, but cautioned the War Department not to underestimate the intelligence of the Seminoles. He raised the possibility that the Seminoles would soon figure out what was happening and would begin to set false fires as decoys and ambush the U.S. forces.[33] Poinsett decided to hold off on pushing the plan. In early 1842, the hostilities were finally brought to a close without the plan ever being put into action.

The second pre-Civil War situation that almost led to the use of balloons in combat occurred during the Mexican War in 1846. In the final thrust toward Mexico City, the U.S. commanders considered the submission of Vera Cruz a crucial preliminary step. The city was well protected by the imposing castle of San Juan de Ulua, which had guns trained on all possible directions of attack. The balloonist John Wise of Lancaster, Pennsylvania devised a plan to assault the castle from an unexpected direction: the air. To test his ideas before submitting the plan to the U.S. command, Wise first had an outline of the scheme published in a Lancaster newspaper.

Wise planned to construct an immense balloon, one hundred feet in diameter, capable of lifting a net load of twenty thousand pounds. The load would consist of eighteen thousand pounds of percussion torpedoes, with two thousand pounds reserved for crew and ballast.[34] The balloon would ascend out of range of the Mexican fort and then be maneuvered along a five-mile-long cable to a height of five thousand feet above the fort. As bombs were dropped, a constant height would be maintained by releasing gas from the balloon. Wise believed the fort would surrender in short order.

The published article received a large public response, much of it favorable. Encouraged, Wise submitted his plan to the War Department on 10 December 1846.[35] There is no evidence that the letter was ever answered and U.S. forces under General Winfield Scott eventually took Vera Cruz.

So, between the time of the French Revolution and the U.S. Civil War, there were no major successes for aerial warfare. This seems to be mainly due to mistrust of the devices by veteran officers and also to the inconvenience of using the devices in the field. Hot-air balloons of the time could not stay aloft long enough to render important service and it was difficult to generate sufficient amounts of hydrogen in the field for gas balloons.

During this same time period, however, civilian ballooning had become increasingly sophisticated and almost commonplace. During the first two decades of the nineteenth century, there were sporadic balloon exhibitions and experiments. Most of these flights were unmanned. Large balloons were occasionally inflated for parades and several groups of college students released small balloons that traveled fairly long distances.[36] Not until the 1820s, however, did manned ascensions occur regularly in the United States. To make a career of ballooning, a prospective aeronaut had to be assured of consistently large crowds. It was not until the 1820s that there were enough population centers in reasonable proximity to each other to make the endeavor profitable. It was also not until that time that sufficient supplies of materials like sulfuric acid could be obtained to generate gas on a regular basis.

Charles F. Durant was probably the first professional American aeronaut, beginning his career in 1829 and continuing through the 1830s with eight ascents in New York, two in Baltimore, and three in Boston.[37] By the time Durant retired in 1834, at the request of his new bride, he had been seen flying by many thousands of people. Many others followed Durant's lead in taking to the air. The most experienced aeronauts of the 1840s included William Paullin of Philadelphia, Louis Lauriat of Boston, and especially John Wise.

Wise, in addition to being a showman, was interested in the science of the atmosphere. Among other observations, Wise noted what seemed to be a persistent west to east air current in the upper atmosphere. As early as 1842, Wise was pondering the possibility of riding this current across the Atlantic to Europe (financial problems would keep Wise from making good on this dream). In addition to meteorological experiments, Wise made an important improvement in balloon design when he developed the rip panel, a panel of cloth which could be quickly ripped away upon landing, deflating the balloon and keeping the balloon from being dangerously dragged across the ground by high winds.

Wise and others made many exhibition flights around the country, mainly in the northeast, during the 1840s and the 1850s. Two other prominent aeronauts of the 1850s, James Allen of Rhode Island and Samuel A. King of Tirricum, Pennsylvania, joined Wise in studying the atmosphere. William H. Helme of Providence, Rhode Island and J. William Black, a leading Boston photographer, made the first photographs from the air in the U.S.[38] By the late 1850s, ballooning had also become fairly common in the South, with Alexander J. B. DeMornat in New Orleans and Charles Cevor in Savannah, Georgia being the most prominent aeronauts.

Ballooning had become so widespread by the late 1850s that paying audiences required more than a mere ascension for

entertainment. Eugene Godard, a transplanted Frenchman, became among the most celebrated of aerial entertainers. Godard
often did acrobatics on a trapeze suspended from the balloon's
basket, and on several occasions his wife controlled the balloon
from the basket while Godard rode on the back of a horse suspended from the balloon. In one such ascent, the Godards and
the horse made a twelve-mile trip before anchoring the balloon
in the top of a grove of trees where the horse contentedly
munched on the tree tops until the balloon was brought to
earth.[39] By 1859, Godard had returned to France where he and
his brother Louis made several aerial surveillances for Napoleon III in his Italian campaign against Austria.

Balloonists just before the Civil War were also amusing themselves and their audiences by engaging in balloon races and long-
distance free ascensions. The ultimate dream of the most experienced aeronauts was a crossing to Europe across the Atlantic, riding
the high west to east currents noted earlier in this appendix. Wise
and a young apprentice, John LaMountain, formed the Trans-Atlantic Balloon Corporation in 1858 and decided to test their ideas by
making a flight from the Midwest to the East Coast. Leaving Saint
Louis on 1 July 1859, Wise, LaMountain, O. A. Gager (an investor in
the venture), and a local reporter ascended to such a height that
Wise nearly passed out from lack of oxygen. They eventually crash-
landed in a storm near Lake Ontario at Henderson, New York. During the chaos of trying to land safely, Wise and LaMountain argued
violently about the best course of action, beginning a feud which
would last throughout their Civil War service.

The most serious rival to LaMountain and Wise in attempting
an Atlantic crossing turned out to be Thaddeus Lowe of New Hamp-
shire. Making his first flight in 1856, he quickly became a popular
performer and saved enough money to construct an enormous balloon in 1859. The envelope was two hundred feet tall and one hundred thirty feet in diameter. He had great trouble getting the balloon
inflated (the coal gas he was using leaked almost as fast as the city
of New York could provide it) and during an inflation on 8 September 1860, the giant envelope burst (it was later used as a ground
cloth for inflation of Lowe's military balloons). Still, Lowe was hope-
ful that an Atlantic attempt could be made successfully and gained
the favor of one of America's most well-known scientists, Joseph
Henry. Henry suggested the trial flight from Cincinnati (described
in Chapter 5) which landed Lowe in hot water in South Carolina just
after the surrender of Fort Sumter.

As America went to war in the spring of 1861, tethered ascensions were commonplace and free ascensions were beginning to become somewhat controllable. No one had yet been successful in developing a truly navigable balloon which could travel under its own power, but air currents in the atmosphere were becoming less of a mystery. On the dark side, however, serious rivalries had already developed among three of the men destined to play a part in the Union war effort: John LaMountain, Thaddeus Lowe, and John Wise.

Notes

CHAPTER 1

1. Archibald Gracie, "Gen. Archibald Gracie," *Confederate Veteran* 5 (8): 431 (1897).
2. Noah Trudeau, *The Last Citadel* (Baton Rouge: Louisiana State University Press, 1991), 23.
3. Ibid., 33.
4. Bruce Catton, *A Stillness at Appomattox* (Garden City, New York: Doubleday and Company, 1953), 187.
5. William C. Davis, *Death in the Trenches* (Alexandria, Virginia: Time-Life, Inc., 1986), 44.
6. Ibid., 53.
7. Shelby Foote, *The Civil War—A Narrative*, 3 vols. (New York: Random House, 1963), vol. 2, 409.
8. Catton, *Stillness at Appomattox*, 220.
9. Foote, *The Civil War*, vol. 2, 261.
10. Jerry Korn, *War on the Mississippi* (Alexandria, Virginia: Time-Life, Inc., 1985), 148.
11. Davis, *Death in the Trenches*, 67.
12. Catton, *Stillness at Appomattox*, 223.
13. Trudeau, *The Last Citadel*, 105.
14. *War of the Rebellion: A Compilation of the Official Records of the Union and Confederate Armies*, (Washington: Government Printing Office, 1880-1901), ser. 1, vol. 40, pt. 1, 557. (Hereafter cited as *Official Records*.)
15. Trudeau, *The Last Citadel*, 105.
16. Henry Pleasants, Jr. and George H. Straley, *Inferno at Petersburg* (Philadelphia: Chilton Company, 1961), 71.
17. *Official Records*, ser. 1, vol. 40, pt. 2, 610.
18. Pleasants, Jr. and Straley, *Inferno at Petersburg*, 70.
19. Trudeau, *The Last Citadel*, 100.
20. "Capt. George B. Lake," *Confederate Veteran* 2 (5): 153 (1894).
21. George N. Saussy, "Generals Lee and Gracie at the Crater," *Confederate Veteran* 17 (4): 160 (1909).

22. *Official Records*, ser. 1, vol. 42, pt. 1, 883.

23. Robert Underwood Johnson and Clarence Clough Buel, eds., *Battles and Leaders of the Civil War*, 4 vols. (New York: T. Yoseloff, 1956), vol. 4, 546.

24. Pleasants, Jr. and Straley, *Inferno at Petersburg*, 77.

25. Richard Wayne Lykes, *Campaign for Petersburg* (Washington, D.C.: National Park Service, 1970), 29.

26. Trudeau, *The Last Citadel*, 107.

27. Pleasants, Jr. and Straley, *Inferno at Petersburg*, 101.

28. Larry George, "Battle of the Crater: A Combat Engineer Case Study," *Military Review* 64 (2): 43 (1984).

CHAPTER 2

1. Ludwell H. Johnson, *Red River Campaign: Politics and Cotton in the Civil War* (Kent, Ohio: Kent State University Press, 1993), 7.

2. Ibid., 13.

3. Alvin M. Josephy, *War on the Frontier: the Trans-Mississippi West* (Alexandria, Virginia: Time-Life, Inc., 1986), 47.

4. Johnson, *Red River Campaign*, 45.

5. Frank L. Church, *Civil War Marine, A Diary of the Red River Expedition, 1864*, ed. James P. Jones and Edward F. Keuchel (Washington, D.C.: U.S. Marine Corps, 1975), 50.

6. Michael C. Robinson, *Gunboats, Low Water, and Yankee Ingenuity: A History of Bailey's Dam* (Baton Rouge: F.P.H.C., Inc., 1991), 16.

7. Church, *Civil War Marine*, 9.

8. *Official Records of the Union and Confederate Navies in the War of the Rebellion* (Washington: Government Printing Office, 1892-1922), ser. 1, vol. 26, 138. (Hereafter cited as *Official Navy Records*.)

9. Robert Underwood Johnson and Clarence Clough Buel, eds., *Battles and Leaders of the Civil War*, 4 vols. (New York: T. Yoseloff, 1956), vol. 4, 358. (Hereafter cited as *Battles and Leaders*.)

10. Shelby Foote, *The Civil War—A Narrative*, 3 vols. (New York: Random House, 1974), vol. 3, 78.

11. Foote, *The Civil War*, vol. 3, 78.

12. *Battles and Leaders*, vol. 4, 359.

13. Robinson, *A History of Bailey's Dam*, 41.

14. *Official Navy Records*, ser. 1, vol. 26, 130.

15. Robinson, *A History of Bailey's Dam*, 37.

16. Foote, *The Civil War*, vol. 3, 81.

17. Robinson, *A History of Bailey's Dam*, 39.

18. Ibid.

19. *Official Navy Records*, ser. 1, vol. 26, 135.

20. Robinson, *A History of Bailey's Dam*, 50.

21. *Official Navy Records*, ser. 1, vol. 26, 142.

22. *War of the Rebellion: A Compilation of the Official Records of the Union and Confederate Armies* (Washington: Government Printing Office, 1880-1901), ser. 1, vol. 34, pt. 3, 512. (Hereafter cited as *Official Records*.)

23. *Official Navy Records*, ser. 1, vol. 26, 131.

24. *Official Records*, ser. 1, vol. 34, pt. 3, 544.

25. Robinson, *A History of Bailey's Dam*, 52.

26. Ibid., 59.

27. Foote, *The Civil War*, vol. 3, 88.

28. *Official Records*, ser. 1, vol. 34, pt. 3, 546-48.

29. Johnson, *Red River Campaign*, 282.

30. *Official Navy Records*, ser. 1, vol. 26, 160.

31. Foote, *The Civil War*, vol. 3, 83.

32. *Official Navy Records*, ser. 1, vol. 26, 130-32.

33. Biographical information on Bailey is from Robinson's book and from Ezra Warner, *Generals in Blue* (Baton Rouge: Louisiana State University Press, 1964), 14.

CHAPTER 3

1. Bell Irvin Wiley, *Embattled Confederates* (New York: Harper and Row, 1964), 108.

2. Arthur Pine Van Gelder and Hugo Schlatter, *History of the Explosives Industry in America* (New York: Arno Press, 1972), 30.

3. Tenney Davis, *The Chemistry of Powder and Explosives* (London: John Wiley and Sons, 1941), 45.

4. Van Gelder and Schlatter, *History of the Explosives Industry*, 107.

5. *War of the Rebellion: A Compilation of the Official Records of the Union and Confederate Armies* (Washington: Government Printing Office, 1880-1901), ser. 4, vol. 1, 555. (Hereafter cited as *Official Records*.)

6. Jefferson Davis, *The Rise and Fall of the Confederate Government* (New York: D. Appleton and Co., 1881), 407.

7. E. Merton Coulter, *The Confederate States of America 1861-1865* (Louisiana State University Press, 1950), 200.

8. Coulter, *Confederate States of America*, 201.

9. J. W. Mallet, "Work of the Ordnance Bureau," *Southern Historical Society Papers* 37, (1909): 2.

10. Maurice Melton, "A Grand Assemblage: George W. Rains and the Augusta Powder Works," *Civil War Times Illustrated* 7 (7): 28 (1968).

11. Ibid.

12. Frank E. Vandiver, *Ploughshares into Swords* (Austin: University of Texas Press, 1952), 268.

13. Ezra J. Warner, *Generals in Gray* (Baton Rouge: Louisiana State University Press, 1959), 112.

14. Mallett, "Ordnance Bureau," 1.

15. Clement Eaton, *A History of the Southern Confederacy* (New York: Macmillan, 1954), 134.

16. George Washington Rains, *History of the Confederate Powder Works* (Newburgh, New York: Newburgh Daily News Print, 1882), 7.

17. Rains, *Confederate Powder Works*, 6.

18. *Official Records*, ser. 1, vol. 6, pt. 1, 776.

19. Theodore P. Savas, "The Life Blood of the Confederate War Machine," *Journal of Confederate History* 5 (1990): 90.

20. *Official Records*, ser. 1, vol. 1, pt. 4, 557.

21. Florence Fleming Corley, *Confederate City* (Columbia: University of South Carolina Press,1960), 53.

22. Rains, *Confederate Powder Works*, 10.

23. Ibid., 11.

24. Ibid., 7.

25. Ibid., 8.

26. Melton, "Augusta Powder Works," 30.

27. Charles D. Ross, personal observations of Powder Works sketches by C. Shaler Smith, Augusta-Richmond County Museum, Augusta, Georgia.

28. Ross, personal observations.

29. Ibid.

30. Ibid.

31. Eaton, *Southern Confederacy*, 134.

32. "How the Confederacy Armed its Soldiers," *Confederate Veteran* 30 (1): 10 (1922).

33. Davis, *Confederate Government*, 409.

34. Mallet, "Ordnance Bureau," 10.

35. Davis, *Confederate Government*, 274.

36. Melton, "Augusta Powder Works," 33.

37. Savas, "Confederate War Machine," 99.

38. Melton, "Augusta Powder Works," 33.

39. Savas, "Confederate War Machine," 105.

40. Rains, *Confederate Powder Works*, 25.

41. Fitzgerald Ross, *Cities and Camps of the Confederate States* (Urbana: University of Illinois Press, 1958), 142.

42. Frank Daniel, "Sherman Bypassed City for Military Reasons," *Civil War Times Illustrated* 1 (1): 19 (1962).

43. Corley, *Cities and Camps*, 59.

44. Ibid.

45. Peggy Robbins, "Bomb Brothers," *Civil War Times Illustrated* 36 (4): 46 (1997).

46. Rains, *Confederate Powder Works*, 24.

47. Corley, *Cities and Camps*, 59.

48. Rains, *Confederate Powder Works*, 23.

49. Corley, *Cities and Camps*, 59.

50. Rains, *Confederate Powder Works*, 11.

51. Melton, "Augusta Powder Works," 37.

CHAPTER 4

1. Raimondo Luraghi, *A History of the Confederate Navy* (Annapolis: Naval Institute Press, 1996), 251.

2. Louis H. Bolander, "The Alligator First Federal Submarine of the Civil War," *United States Naval Institute Proceedings* 64 (6): 847 (1938). (Hereafter cited as *USNI Proceedings*.)

3. James L. Christley, "The Alligator : The North's Underwater Threat," *Civil War Times Illustrated*, 19 (10): 26 (1981).

4. Scott Rye, *Men and Ships of the Civil War* (Stamford, Connecticut: Longmeadow Press, 1995), 106.

5. Ibid., 107.

6. Ibid.

7. Christley, "The Alligator," 27.

8. Edwin Mustard, "The Submarine in the Revolution and Civil War," *The Social Studies* 37 (5): 206 (1946).

9. Sir Henry John Newbolt, *A Note on the History of Submarine War* (New York: George H. Doran, 1917), 4.

10. Christley, "The Alligator," 26.

11. Rye, *Men and Ships*, 110.

12. Phillip Van Doren Stern, *The Confederate Navy* (New York: Bonanza Books, 1962), 88.

13. Rye, *Men and Ships*, 110.

14. *Official Records of the Union and Confederate Navies in the War of the Rebellion* (Washington: Government Printing Office, 1892–1922), ser. 1, vol. 7, 501. (Hereafter cited as *Official Navy Records.*)

15. Christley, "The Alligator," 30.

16. *Official Navy Records*, ser. 1, vol. 7, 523.

17. Ibid., 525.

18. Ibid., 526.

19. Bolander, "First Federal Submarine," 853.

20. Christley, "The Alligator," 31.

21. Ibid.

22. Bolander, "First Federal Submarine," 31.

23. Burke Davis, *The Civil War: Strange and Fascinating Facts* (New York: Wing Books, 1960), 176.

24. Rye, *Men and Ships*, 115.

25. *They Fought under the Sea* (Harrisburg: Stackpole, 1962), ed. the editors of *Navy Times*, 23.

26. Patricia A. Gruse Harris, "The Great Lakes' First Submarine: L. D. Phillips' Fool Killer," *Inland Seas* 39 (3): 163 (1983).

27. Patricia A. Gruse Harris, *The Great Lakes' First Submarine: L. D. Phillips' Fool Killer* (Michigan City, Indiana: Michigan City Historical Society, Inc., 1982), 36.

28. *They Fought under the Sea*, 15.

29. Ibid., 16.

30. *The Blockade: Runners and Raiders* (Alexandria, Virginia: Time-Life, Inc., 1983), ed. the editors of Time-Life, 10.

31. *The American Heritage Picture History of the Civil War* (New York: American Heritage Publishing, Inc., 1960), ed. the editors of American Heritage (narrative by Bruce Catton), 170.

32. *The Blockade: Runners and Raiders*, 161.

33. Mark Ragan, *The Hunley: Submarines, Sacrifice, & Success in the Civil War* (Miami/Charleston: Narwhal Press, 1995), 15.

34. *Official Navy Records*, ser. 1, vol. 7, 363.

35. Milton Perry, *Infernal Machines* (Baton Rouge: Louisiana State University Press, 1965), 92.

36. *Official Navy Records*, ser. 1, vol. 7, 347.

37. Ibid., 346.

38. Ibid., 349.

39. Ibid., 349.

40. Ibid., 350.

41. Luraghi, *Confederate Navy*, 252.

42. Perry, *Infernal Machines*, 92.

43. Ibid., 93.

44. *Official Navy Records*, ser. 1, vol. 9, 411.

45. *Official Navy Records*, ser. 1, vol. 22, 104.

46. James E. Kloeppel, *Danger Beneath the Waves* (Orangesburg, South Carolina: Sandlapper Publishing, Inc., 1987), 6.

47. Ibid., 7.

48. David Whittet Thomson, "Three Confederate Submarines," *USNI Proceedings* 67 (1): 40 (1941).

49. George Hagerman, "Confederate Submarines," *USNI Proceedings* 103 (9): 74 (1977).

50. Kloeppel, *Danger Beneath the Waves*, 8.

51. Louis S. Shafer, *Confederate Underwater Warfare: An Illustrated History* (Jefferson, North Carolina: McFarland and Company, Inc., 1996), 105.

52. Ibid., 105.

53. Hagerman, "Confederate Submarines," 74.

54. Ragan, *The Hunley*, 18.

55. H. S. Mazet, "Tragedy and the Confederate Submarines," *USNI Proceedings* 68 (5): 664 (1942).

56. Kloeppel, *Danger Beneath the Waves*, 9-19.

57. Richard K. Wills, "The Confederate Privateer Pioneer and the Development of American Submersible Watercraft," *The Institute for Naval Archaeology Quarterly* 21 (1-2): 12-19 (1994).

58. *Official Navy Records*, ser. 1, vol. 22, 288.

59. Sidney H. Schell, "Submarine Weapons tested at Mobile during the Civil War," *Alabama Review* 45 (3): 164 (1992).

60. Carvel Hall Blair, "Submarines of the Confederate Navy," *USNI Proceedings* 78 (10): 1115 (1952).

61. Schell, "Submarine Weapons," 170.

62. Ragan, *The Hunley*, 22.

63. Virgil Carrington Jones, *The Civil War at Sea* (New York: Holt, Rinehart and Winston, 1962), 118.

64. Ragan, *The Hunley*, 22.

65. Ibid.

66. Ibid.

67. Thomson, "Three Confederate Submarines," 40.

68. Ragan, *The Hunley*, 24.

69. Perry, *Infernal Machines*, 97.

70. Ragan, *The Hunley*, 26.

71. W. A. Alexander, "Thrilling Chapter in the History of the Confederate States Navy," *Richmond* (Virginia) *Dispatch*, (21 July 1902).

72. Mark M. Newell, "The C.S.S. *H. L. Hunley*: Solving a 131-Year-Old Mystery," *Civil War Regiments*, 4 (3): 78 (1994).

73. Ragan, *The Hunley*, 30.

74. *War of the Rebellion: A Compilation of the Official Records of the Union and Confederate Armies* (Washington: Government Printing Office, 1880-1901), ser. 1, vol. 28, pt. 2, 265. (Hereafter cited as *Official Records*.)

75. Kloeppel, *Danger Beneath the Waves*, 28.
76. Ragan, *The Hunley*, 40.
77. Ibid.
78. C. L. Stanton, "Submarines and Torpedo Boats," *Confederate Veteran* 22 (9): 398 (1914).
79. Ragan, *The Hunley*, 54.
80. *Official Navy Records*, ser. 1, vol. 15, 693.
81. Kloeppel, *Danger Beneath the Waves*, 43.
82. Ibid.
83. P. G. T. Beauregard, "Torpedo Service in the Harbor and Water Defences of Charleston," *Southern Historical Society Papers* 5 (1878): 154.
84. Ragan, *The Hunley*, 90.
85. Shafer, *Confederate Underwater Warfare*, 122.
86. *Official Navy Records*, ser. 1, vol. 15, 229.
87. *Official Navy Records*, ser. 1, vol. 15, 233.
88. R. Thomas Campbell, *Gray Thunder: Exploits of the Confederate States Navy* (Shippensburg, Pa.: Burd Street Press, 1996), 166.
89. Harry Von Kolnitz, "The Confederate Submarine," *USNI Proceedings* 63 (1): 1456 (1937).
90. Ragan, *The Hunley*, 108.
91. Alexander, "Thrilling Chapter."
92. Kloeppel, *Danger Beneath the Waves*, 58.
93. "South Carolina Confederate Twins," *Confederate Veteran* 33 (9): 328 (1925).
94. William E. Beard, "The Log of the C.S. Submarine," *USNI Proceedings* 42 (1916): 1556.
95. Ragan, *The Hunley*, 156.
96. A net search for "Hunley" will turn up a number of sites. A good place to start is with the University of South Carolina's Institute of Archaeology and Anthropology (SCIAA) at http://www.cla.sc.edu/sciaa/hunley4.html#one.
97. See the SCIAA site on the World Wide Web noted above.
98. Schell, "Submarine Weapons," 177.
99. Ibid.
100. Perry, *Infernal Machines*, 183.
101. Arthur W. Bergeron, *Confederate Mobile* (Jackson: University Press of Mississippi, 1991), 169.
102. Rye, *Men and Ships*, 115.
103. Joseph T. Durkin, *Stephen Mallory: Confederate Navy Chief* (Chapel Hill: University of North Carolina Press, 1954), 280.
104. Peter M. Chaitin, *The Coastal War* (Alexandria, Virginia: Time-Life, Inc., 1984), 141.
105. Ragan, *The Hunley*, 167.

CHAPTER 5

1. Robert V. Bruce, *Lincoln and the Tools of War* (Indianapolis: Bobbs-Merrill Co., 1956), 86.
2. F. Stansbury Haydon, *Aeronautics in the Union and Confederate Armies* (Baltimore: Johns Hopkins Press, 1941), 40.
3. Ibid., 42.

4. Ibid., 57.

5. Ibid., 161.

6. Ibid., 163.

7. Ibid., 45.

8. Ibid., 60.

9. Ibid., 90.

10. Ibid., 170.

11. Ibid., 172.

12. Ibid., 61.

13. June Robinson, "The United States Balloon Corps in Action in Northern Virginia During the Civil War," *Arlington Historical Magazine* 8 (2): 5 (1986).

14. Tom D. Crouch, *The Eagle Aloft* (Washington: Smithsonian Press, 1983), 346.

15. Haydon, *Aeronautics*, 175.

16. Ibid., 156.

17. Ibid., 183.

18. Ibid., 190.

19. Wilbur S. Nye, "The First Aeronaut of the War was an Engineer," *Civil War Times Illustrated* 3 (6): 19 (1964).

20. Haydon, *Aeronautics*, 51.

21. Ibid., 66.

22. J. David Truby, "War in the Clouds: Balloons in the Civil War," *Mankind* 2 (11): 66 (1971).

23. Haydon, *Aeronautics*, 73.

24. Herman Hattaway, "America's First Air Force," *American History Illustrated* 19 (4): 28 (1984).

25. William H. Hassler, "John Wise: Lincoln's Hard Luck Spaceman," *Civil War Times Illustrated* 1 (1): 18 (1962).

26. Crouch, *Eagle Aloft*, 354.

27. *War of the Rebellion: A Compilation of the Official Records of the Union and Confederate Armies* (Washington: Government Printing Office, 1880-1901), ser. 1, vol. 2, pt. 1, 1005. (Hereafter cited as *Official Records.*)

28. Haydon, *Aeronautics*, 97.

29. Richard Pindell, "The Technological Inheritance," *Civil War Times Illustrated* 26 (4): 54 (1987).

30. Haydon, *Aeronautics*, 105.

31. Crouch, *Eagle Aloft*, 355.

32. Ibid., 361.

33. Haydon, *Aeronautics*, 113.

34. Ibid., 115.

35. Daniel T. Davis, "The Air Role in the War between the States," *Air University Review* 27 (5): 13-29 (1975).

36. Haydon, *Aeronautics*, 123.

37. *Official Records,* ser. 1, vol. 5, pt. 1, 982.

38. Crouch, *Eagle Aloft*, 366.

39. Ibid., 371.

40. Juliette Hennessy, "Balloons and Airships in the United States Army, 1861-1863," *Aerospace Historian* 16 (4): 47 (1969).

41. Crouch, *Eagle Aloft,* 375.

42. Henry Steele Commager, *The Blue and the Gray*, 2 vols. (Indianapolis: Bobbs-Merrill Co., 1950), vol. 1, 311.

43. Crouch, *Eagle Aloft*, 380.

44. Ibid., 386.

45. George Alfred Townsend, *Rustics in Rebellion* (Chapel Hill: University of North Carolina Press, 1950), 97.

46. Crouch, *Eagle Aloft*, 391.

47. Ibid., 398.

48. "The Balloon in the Civil War," unclassified document, United States Air Force Historical Archives, Maxwell Air Force Base, Alabama.

49. *Official Records*, ser. 3, vol. 3, 252-319.

50. Crouch, *Eagle Aloft*, 407.

51. Ibid., 408.

52. Dr. Jay Luvaas and Col. Harold W. Nelson, ed., *The U.S. Army War College Guide to the Battles of Chancellorsville and Fredericksburg* (New York: Harper and Row, 1989), 309.

53. Jay Luvaas, "The Role of Intelligence in the Chancellorsville Campaign, April-May 1863," *Intelligence and National Security* 5 (2): 111 (1990).

54. Steven W. Sears, *Chancellorsville* (Boston: Houghton Mifflin Co., 1996), 244.

55. Crouch, *Eagle Aloft*, 411.

56. Robert Underwood Johnson and Clarence Clough Buel, eds., *Battles and Leaders of the Civil War*, 4 vols. (New York: T. Yoseloff, 1956), vol. 3, 358.

57. Dr. Francis A. Lord, "U.S. Balloon Corps Potential Unrealized," *Civil War Times* 3 (3): 23 (1961).

58. William Normyle, "Balloon Warriors and Their Craft," *Civil War Times* 1 (4): 9 (1959).

59. Lord, "U.S. Balloon Corps," 23.

60. Truby, "War in the Clouds," 67.

61. Haydon, *Aeronautics*, 232.

62. Ibid., 310.

63. Ibid., 249.

64. Ibid., 314.

65. Ibid., 378.

66. Ibid., 383.

67. Shelby Foote, *The Civil War—A Narrative*, 3 vols. (New York: Random House, 1963), vol. 1, 352.

68. Haydon, *Aeronautics*, 387.

69. Ibid., 388.

70. Ibid., 393.

71. Ibid., 188.

72. Ibid., 188.

73. Ibid., 218.

74. Ibid., 360.

75. Joseph Jenkins Cornish III, *The Air Arm of the Confederacy* (Richmond: Richmond Civil War Centennial Committee, 1963), 30.

76. J. R. Bryan, "Balloon Used for Scout Duty," *Southern Historical Society Papers* 33 (1905): 33.

77. Ibid., 39.

78. Cornish, *Air Arm of the Confederacy*, 35.

79. *Official Records of the Union and Confederate Navies in the War of the Rebellion* (Washington: Government Printing Office, 1892-1922), ser. 1, vol. 7, 543.

80. Cornish, *Air Arm of the Confederacy*, 48.

81. Bell T. Wiley, "Drop Poison Gas from a Balloon: A Confederate Proposal," *Civil War Times Illustrated* 7 (4): 40 (1968).

82. Crouch, *Eagle Aloft*, 368.

83. Helen Shultz, "The Magnificent Aereon," *Civil War Times Illustrated* 19 (8): 26 (1980).

84. Al Gross, "Not Quite Flying Machines," *Civil War Times Illustrated* 13 (10): 20 (1975).

85. Ashley Halsey, Jr., *Who Fired the First Shot?* (New York: Hawthorn Books, Inc., 1963), 79.

CHAPTER 6

1. Bill Bryson, *Made in America* (New York: William Morrow and Co., 1994), 90.

2. Robert Thompson, *Wiring a Continent* (Princeton: Princeton University Press, 1947), 3.

3. Isaac Asimov, *Asimov's Biographical Encyclopedia of Science and Technology*, 2nd ed. rev. (Garden City, New York: Doubleday and Co., Inc., 1982), 503.

4. Ibid.

5. Thompson, *Wiring a Continent*, 21.

6. Ibid., 503.

7. Martin van Creveld, *Technology and War* (London: The Free Press, 1987), 157.

8. Thompson, *Wiring a Continent*, 252.

9. Ibid., 353.

10. William R. Plum, *The Military Telegraph During the Civil War in the United States*, 2 vols. (Chicago: Jansen, McClurg and Co., 1882), vol. 1, 26.

11. John Keegan, *The Mask of Command* (New York: Elisabeth Sifton Books, 1987), 210.

12. David Homer Bates, *Lincoln in the Telegraph Office* (Lincoln: University of Nebraska Press, 1995), 20.

13. Edward Rosewater, "The War between the States: Reminiscences of Edward Rosewater, Army Telegrapher," *American Jewish Archives* 9 (2): 135 (1957).

14. Richard B. Kielbowicz, "The Telegraph, Censorship, and Politics at the Outset of the Civil War," *Civil War History* 40 (2): 97 (1994).

15. Kielbowicz, "Telegraph, Censorship, and Politics," 99.

16. Bates, *Lincoln in the Telegraph Office*, 88.

17. Kielbowicz, "Telegraph, Censorship, and Politics," 100.

18. Bates, *Lincoln in the Telegraph Office*, 96.

19. Shelby Foote, *The Civil War—A Narrative*, 3 vols. (New York: Random House, 1958), vol. 1, 244.

20. Thomas C. Jepsen, "Women Telegraph Operators on the Western Frontier," *Journal of the West* 35 (2): 75 (1996).

21. Thompson, *Wiring a Continent*, 385.

22. Ibid., 385.

23. *War of the Rebellion: A Compilation of the Official Records of the Union and Confederate Armies* (Washington: Government Printing Office, 1880-1901), ser. 1, vol. 52, pt. 1, 479. (Hereafter cited as *Official Records*.)

24. Frances Miller, ed., *The Photographic History of the The Civil War*, 10 vols. (New York: Review of Reviews Co., 1911), vol. 8, 344.

25. Ibid.

26. Bates, *Lincoln in the Telegraph Office*, 111.

27. P. J Scheips, "Union Signal Communications: Innovation and Conflict," *Civil War History* 9 (4): 403 (1963).

28. Miller, *Photographic History*, 360.

29. Stephen Siemsen, "The Aerial Telegraph," *Military Images* 12 (3): 22 (1990).

30. Raymond W. Smith, "Don't Cut! Signal Telegraph," *Civil War Times Illustrated* 15 (2): 19 (1976).

31. Smith, "Don't Cut! Signal Telegraph," 25.

32. Stephen W. Sears, *Chancellorsville* (Boston: Houghton Mifflin Co., 1996), 196.

33. Scheips, "Union Signal Communications," 33.

34. Wilbur S. Nye, "The U.S. Military Telegraph Service," *Civil War Times Illustrated* 7 (7): 34 (1968).

35. Alexander Gardner, *Gardner's Photographic Sketch Book of the War* (New York: Dover Publications, 1959), plate 73.

36. Thomas C. Jepsen, "Crossed Wires," *Civil War Times Illustrated* 33 (5): 60 (1994).

37. Keegan, *Mask of Command*, 210.

38. Miller, *Photographic History*, 368.

39. Plum, *Military Telegraph*, 124.

40. Richard Pindell, "The Technological Inheritance," *Civil War Times Illustrated* 26 (4): 47 (1987).

41. Scheips, "Union Signal Communications," 419.

42. Ibid.

43. Plum, *Military Telegraph*, 350.

44. Bell Irvin Wiley, *Embattled Confederates* (New York: Harper and Row, Inc., 1964), 138.

45. J. Cutler Andrews, "The Southern Telegraph Company, 1861–1865: A Chapter in the History of Wartime Communication," *Journal of Southern History* 30 (3): 340 (1963).

46. Ibid.

47. Ibid.

48. Ibid.

49. *Official Records*, ser. 1, vol. 17, pt. 2, 673.

50. "The Telegraph in Warfare," *Confederate Veteran* 24 (11): 506 (1916).

51. Charles J. Brockman, Jr., ed., "The John Van Duser Diary of Sherman's March from Atlanta to Hilton Head," *Georgia Historical Quarterly* 53 (2): 220–40 (1969).

52. Keegan, *Mask of Command*, 211.

53. John Bakeless, *Spies of the Confederacy* (Philadelphia: J. B. Lippincott Company, 1970), 309.

54. Donald E. Markle, *Spies and Spymasters of The Civil War* (New York: Hippocrene Books, 1994), 39.

55. Francis A. Lord, "The Military Telegraph was Communications Workhorse," *Civil War Times Illustrated* 3 (3): 17 (1964).

56. *Spies, Scouts and Raiders*, (Alexandria, Virginia: Time-Life, Inc., 1985), ed. the editors of Time-Life, 67.

57. Markle, *Spys and Spymasters*, 36.

58. George A. Ellsworth, "Gen. Morgan's Telegraph Operator," *Confederate Veteran* 6 (4): 174 (1898).

59. Michael B. Ballard, "Lightning Ellsworth's Electronic Warfare: Deceit by Telegraph," *Civil War Times Illustrated* 22 (6): 22-27 (1983).

60. H. W. Graber, "Why Sherman did not go to Augusta," *Confederate Veteran* 22 (7): 319 (1914).

APPENDIX 2

1. Frank Ross, Jr., *Undersea Vehicles and Habitats* (New York: Thomas Crowell, 1970), 1.

2. Ibid., 5.

3. Ibid., 10.

4. Alex Roland, *Underwater Warfare in the Age of Sail* (Bloomington: Indiana University Press, 1978), 45.

5. Roland, xvi.

6. Sir Henry John Newbolt, *A Note on the History of Submarine Warfare* (New York: George H. Doran Company, 1917), 4.

7. *International Military and Defense Encyclopedia*, 6 vols. (Washington: Brassey's Inc., 1993), vol. 5, 2590.

8. Ross, *Undersea Vehicles*, 14.

9. *They Fought under the Sea* (Harrisburg: Stackpole, 1962), ed. the editors of *Navy Times,* 5.

10. Ross, *Undersea Vehicles,* 15.

11. Roland, *Underwater Warfare,* 79.

12. Ross, *Undersea Vehicles,* 17.

13. *Encyclopedia Americana*, 30 vols. (Danbury, Connecticut: Grolier, Inc., 1992), vol. 25, 821. A nice sketch of the *Turtle* can be found on the Internet at http://www.connix.com/~crm/graphics/turtlebig.JPG.

14. Benson Lossing, *The Pictorial Field Book of the American Revolution*, 2 vols. (Rutland, Vt.: Charles E. Tuttle, Inc., 1972), vol. 2, 608.

15. Roland, *Underwater Warfare*, 81.

16. Dan Higginbotham, *The War of American Independence* (Bloomington: Indiana University Press, 1977), 63.

17. Edwin Mustard, "The Submarine in the Revolution and Civil War," *The Social Studies* 37 (5): 205 (1946).

18. Ralph Hill, *Robert Fulton and the Steamboat* (New York: Random House, 1954), 46.

19. Clara Ingram Johnson, *Boat Builder* (New York: Charles Scribner's Sons, 1940), 92.

20. Cynthia Phillip, *Robert Fulton- A Biography* (New York: Franklin Watts, 1985), 79.

21. *They Fought under the Sea,* 13.

22. Ibid.

23. Ibid., 15.

24. E. B. Potter, ed., *The United States and World Sea Power* (Englewood Cliffs, N.J: Prentice-Hall, Inc., 1955), 258.

25. *They Fought under the Sea,* 15.

26. Roland, *Underwater Warfare,* 130.

27. Edward V. Lewis and Robert O'Brien, *Ships* (New York: Time Inc., 1965), 128.

28. Newbolt, *History of Submarine Warfare*, 10.
29. Philip Van Doren Stern, *The Confederate Navy: A Pictorial History* (New York: Bonanza Books, 1962), 173.
30. *McGraw-Hill Encyclopedia of Science and Technology*, 20 vols. (New York: McGraw-Hill, 1987), vol. 17, 520.
31. *They Fought under the Sea*, 25.

APPENDIX 3

1. *Encyclopedia Brittanica, International Edition*, 29 vols. (Danbury, Connecticut: Grolier Inc., 1993), vol. 3, 115.
2. Tom D. Crouch, *The Eagle Aloft* (Washington: Smithsonian Institution Press, 1983), 20.
3. Don Dwiggins, *The Complete Book of Airships - Dirigibles, Blimps and Hot-Air Balloons* (Blue Ridge Summit, Pennsylvania: TAB Books, Inc., 1980), 12.
4. Crouch, *Eagle Aloft*, 21.
5. Kurt R. Stehling and William Beller, *Skyhooks* (Garden City, New Jersey: Doubleday and Company, Inc., 1962), 10.
6. Dwiggins, *Airships*, 15.
7. *Encyclopedia Brittanica*, vol. 3, 116.
8. Crouch, *Eagle Aloft*, 14.
9. Ibid.
10. Ed Newman, *Hot Air and Gas: The Basics of Balloons* (Roseland, Virginia: Greenway Publishing Co., 1992), 17.
11. Crouch, *Eagle Aloft*, 26.
12. Hugh Allen, *The Story of the Airship*, 8th ed. (Akron: Goodyear Tire and Rubber Co., 1932), 5.
13. Crouch, *Eagle Aloft*, 30.
14. Lynn Poole, *Ballooning in the Space Age* (New York: McGraw-Hill, 1958), 48.
15. Stehling and Miller, *Skyhooks*, 30.
16. *A Narrative of the Two Adventures of Doctor Jeffries with Mons. Blanchard* (London: 1786).
17. Crouch, *Eagle Aloft*, 82.
18. F. Stansbury Haydon, *Aeronautics in the Union and Confederate Armies* (Baltimore: The Johns Hopkins Press, 1941), 3.
19. Dwiggins, *Airships*, 16.
20. Stehling and Miller, *Skyhooks*, 33.
21. Ibid., 37.
22. Haydon, *Aeronautics*, 11.
23. Ibid., 15.
24. Ibid., 16.
25. Ibid., 17.
26. Crouch, *Eagle Aloft*, 336.
27. Stehling and Miller, *Skyhooks*, 142.
28. Haydon, *Aeronautics*, 16.
29. Crouch, *Eagle Aloft*, 337.
30. Haydon, *Aeronautics*, 20.
31. Ibid., 18.

32. Crouch, *Eagle Aloft*, 122.
33. Ibid., 157.
34. Ibid., 340.
35. Ibid., 225.
36. Ibid., 122.
37. Ibid., 144-146.
38. Ibid., 339.
39. Ibid., 225-226.

Bibliography

A Narrative of the Two Adventures of Doctor Jeffries with Mons. Blanchard. London, 1786.

Alexander, W. A. "Thrilling Chapter in the History of the Confederate States Navy." *Richmond (Virginia) Dispatch* (21 July 1902).

Allen, Hugh. *The Story of the Airship*, 8th ed. Akron: Goodyear Tire and Rubber Co., 1932.

The American Heritage Picture History of the Civil War. Edited by the editors of American Heritage Publishing. New York: American Heritage Publishing, Inc., 1960.

Andrews, J. Cutler. "The Southern Telegraph Company, 1861–1865: A Chapter in the History of Wartime Communication." *Journal of Southern History* 30 (3): 319-44 (1963).

Asimov, Isaac. *Asimov's Biographical Encyclopedia of Science and Technology.* 2nd ed. rev. Garden City, New York: Doubleday and Co., Inc., 1982.

Bakeless, John. *Spies of the Confederacy.* Philadelphia: J. B. Lippincott Company, 1970.

Ballard, Michael B. "Lightning Ellsworth's Electronic Warfare: Deceit by Telegraph." *Civil War Times Illustrated* 22 (6): 22-27 (1983).

"The Balloon in the Civil War." Unclassified document, United States Air Force Historical Archives, Maxwell Air Force Base, Alabama.

Bates, David Homer. *Lincoln in the Telegraph Office.* Lincoln: University of Nebraska Press, 1995.

Beard, William E. "The Log of the C.S. Submarine." *United States Naval Institute Proceedings* 42 (1916): 1545-57.

Beauregard, P.G.T. "Torpedo Service in the Harbor and Water Defences of Charleston." *Southern Historical Society Papers* 5 (1878): 145-61.

Bergeron, Arthur W. *Confederate Mobile.* Jackson: University Press of Mississippi, 1991.

Blair, Carvel Hall. "Submarines of the Confederate Navy." *USNI Proceedings* 78 (10): 1115-21 (1952).

The Blockade: Runners and Raiders. Edited by the editors of Time-Life. Alexandria, Virginia: Time-Life, Inc., 1983.

Bolander, Louis H. "The Alligator First Federal Submarine of the Civil War." *United States Naval Institute Proceedings* 64 (6): 847-54 (1938).

Brockman, Charles J., Jr., ed. "The John Van Duser Diary of Sherman's March From Atlanta to Hilton Head." *Georgia Historical Quarterly* 53 (2): 220-40 (1969).

Bruce, Robert V. *Lincoln and the Tools of War.* Indianapolis: Bobbs-Merrill Co., 1956.

Bryan, J. R. "Balloon Used for Scout Duty." *Southern Historical Society Papers* 33 (1905): 32-42.

Bryson, Bill. *Made in America.* New York: William Morrow and Co., 1994.

Campbell, R. Thomas. *Gray Thunder: Exploits of the Confederate States Navy.* Shippensburg, Pa.: Burd Street Press, 1996.

"Capt. George B. Lake." *Confederate Veteran* 2 (5): 153 (1894).

Catton, Bruce. *A Stillness at Appomattox.* Garden City, New York: Doubleday and Company, 1953.

Chaitin, Peter M. *The Coastal War.* Alexandria, Virginia: Time-Life, Inc., 1984.

Christley, James L. "The Alligator : The North's Underwater Threat." *Civil War Times Illustrated* 19 (10): 26-31 (1981).

Church, Frank L. *Civil War Marine, A Diary of the Red River Expedition, 1864.* Edited by James P. Jones and Edward F. Keuchel. Washington, D.C.: U.S. Marine Corps, 1975.

Commager, Henry Steele. *The Blue and the Gray.* Vol. 1. Indianapolis: Bobbs-Merrill Co., 1950.

Corley, Florence Fleming. *Confederate City.* Columbia: University of South Carolina Press, 1960.

Cornish, Joseph Jenkins III. *The Air Arm of the Confederacy.* Richmond: Richmond Civil War Centennial Committee, 1963.

Coulter, E. Merton. *The Confederate States of America 1861-1865.* Louisiana State University Press, 1950.

Crouch, Tom D. *The Eagle Aloft.* Washington: Smithsonian Press, 1983.

Daniel, Frank. "Sherman Bypassed City for Military Reasons." *Civil War Times Illustrated* 1 (1): 19 (1962).

Davis, Burke. *The Civil War: Strange and Fascinating Facts.* New York: Wing Books, 1960.

Davis, Daniel T. "The Air Role in the War between the States." *Air University Review* 27 (5): 13–29 (1975).

Davis, Jefferson. *The Rise and Fall of the Confederate Government.* New York: D. Appleton and Co., 1881.

Davis, Tenney. *The Chemistry of Powder and Explosives.* London: John Wiley and Sons, 1941.

Davis, William C. *Death in the Trenches.* Alexandria, Virginia: Time-Life, Inc., 1986.

Durkin, Joseph T. *Stephen Mallory: Confederate Navy Chief.* Chapel Hill: University of North Carolina Press, 1954.

Dwiggins, Don. *The Complete Book of Airships—Dirigibles, Blimps and Hot-Air Balloons.* Blue Ridge Summit, Pennsylvania: TAB Books, Inc., 1980.

Eaton, Clement. *A History of the Southern Confederacy.* New York: Macmillan, 1954.

Ellsworth, George A. "Gen. Morgan's Telegraph Operator." *Confederate Veteran* 6 (4): 174 (1898).

Encyclopedia Americana. Vol. 25. Danbury, Connecticut: Grolier, Inc., 1992.

Encyclopedia Brittanica, International Edition. Vol. 3. Danbury, Connecticut: Grolier, Inc., 1993.

Foote, Shelby. *The Civil War—A Narrative.* New York: Random House, 1963.

Gardner, Alexander. *Gardner's Photographic Sketch Book of the War.* New York: Dover Publications, 1959.

George, Larry. "Battle of the Crater: A Combat Engineer Case Study." *Military Review* 64 (2): 35–47 (1984).

Graber, H. W. "Why Sherman did not go to Augusta." *Confederate Veteran* 22 (7): 319–20 (1914).

Gracie, Archibald. "Gen. Archibald Gracie." *Confederate Veteran* 5 (8): 429–33 (1897).

Gross, Al Gross. "Not Quite Flying Machines." *Civil War Times Illustrated* 13 (10): 20–24 (1975).

Hagerman, George. "Confederate Submarines." *United States Naval Institute Proceedings* 103 (9): 74-75 (1977).

Halsey, Ashley, Jr. *Who Fired the First Shot?* New York: Hawthorn Books, Inc., 1963.

Harris, Patricia A. Gruse. "The Great Lakes' First Submarine: L. D. Phillips' Fool Killer." *Inland Seas* 39 (3): 163-66 (1983).

Harris, Patricia A. Gruse. *The Great Lakes' First Submarine: L. D. Phillips' Fool Killer.* Michigan City, Indiana: Michigan City Historical Society, Inc., 1982.

Hassler, William H. "John Wise: Lincoln's Hard Luck Spaceman." *Civil War Times Illustrated* 1 (1): 19 (1962).

Hattaway, Herman. "America's First Air Force." *American History Illustrated* 19 (4): 24-29 (1984).

Haydon, F. Stansbury. *Aeronautics in the Union and Confederate Armies.* Baltimore: Johns Hopkins Press, 1941.

Hennessy, Juliette. "Balloons and Airships in the United States Army, 1861-1863." *Aerospace Historian* 16 (4): 41-47 (1969).

Higginbotham, Dan. *The War of American Independence.* Bloomington: Indiana University Press, 1977.

Hill, Ralph. *Robert Fulton and the Steamboat.* New York: Random House, 1954.

"How the Confederacy Armed its Soldiers." *Confederate Veteran* 30 (1): 10-11 (1922).

International Military and Defense Encyclopedia. Vol. 5. Washington: Brassey's Inc., 1993.

Jepsen, Thomas C. "Crossed Wires." *Civil War Times Illustrated* 33 (5): 56-60 (1994).

Jepsen, Thomas C. "Women Telegraph Operators on the Western Frontier." *Journal of the West* 35 (2): 72-80 (1996).

Johnson, Clara Ingram. *Boat Builder.* New York: Charles Scribner's Sons, 1940.

Johnson, Ludwell H. *Red River Campaign: Politics and Cotton in the Civil War.* Kent, Ohio: Kent State University Press, 1993.

Johnson, Robert Underwood, and Clarence Clough Buel, eds. *Battles and Leaders of the Civil War.* New York: T. Yoseloff, 1956.

Jones, Virgil Carrington. *The Civil War at Sea.* New York: Holt, Rinehart and Winston, 1962.

Josephy, Alvin M. *War on the Frontier: the Trans-Mississippi West.* Alexandria, Virginia: Time-Life, Inc., 1986.

Keegan, John. *The Mask of Command.* New York: Elisabeth Sifton Books, 1987.

Kielbowicz, Richard B. "The Telegraph, Censorship, and Politics at the Outset of the Civil War." *Civil War History* 40 (2): 95–118 (1994).

Kloeppel, James E. *Danger Beneath the Waves.* Orangesburg, South Carolina: Sandlapper Publishing, Inc., 1987.

Korn, Jerry. *War on the Mississippi.* Alexandria, Virginia: Time Life, Inc., 1985.

Lewis, Edward V., and Robert O'Brien. *Ships.* New York: Time, Inc., 1965.

Lord, Francis A. "The Military Telegraph was Communications Workhorse." *Civil War Times Illustrated* 3 (3): 16–17 (1964).

Lord, Dr. Francis A. "U.S. Balloon Corps Potential Unrealized." *Civil War Times* 3 (3): 23 (1961).

Lossing, Benson. *The Pictorial Field Book of the American Revolution.* Vol. 2. Rutland, Vt.: Charles E. Tuttle, Inc., 1972.

Luraghi, Raimondo. *A History of the Confederate Navy.* Annapolis: Naval Institute Press, 1996.

Luvaas, Dr. Jay. "The Role of Intelligence in the Chancellorsville Campaign, April-May 1863." *Intelligence and National Security* 5 (2): 99–115 (1990).

Luvaas, Dr. Jay, and Col. Harold W Nelson., ed. *The U.S. Army War College Guide to the Battles of Chancellorsville and Fredericksburg.* New York: Harper and Row, 1989.

Lykes, Richard Wayne. *Campaign for Petersburg.* Washington, D.C.: National Park Service, 1970.

Mallet, J. W. "Work of the Ordnance Bureau," *Southern Historical Society Papers* 37 (1909): 1–20.

Markle, Donald E. *Spies and Spymasters of The Civil War.* New York: Hippocrene Books, 1994.

Mazet, H. S. "Tragedy and the Confederate Submarines." *United States Naval Institute Proceedings* 68 (5): 662–68 (1942).

McGraw-Hill Encyclopedia of Science and Technology. Vol. 17. New York: McGraw-Hill, 1987.

Melton, Maurice. "A Grand Assemblage: George W. Rains and the Augusta Powder Works." *Civil War Times Illustrated* 7 (7): 28–37 (1968).

Miller, Frances Miller, ed. *The Photographic History of the Civil War.* New York: Review of Reviews Co., 1911.

Mustard, Edwin. "The Submarine in the Revolution and Civil War." *The Social Studies* 37 (5): 204-10 (1946).

Newbolt, Sir Henry John. *A Note on the History of Submarine War.* New York: George H. Doran, 1917.

Newell, Mark M. "The C.S.S. H. L. Hunley: Solving a 131-Year-Old Mystery." *Civil War Regiments* 4 (3): 77-87 (1994).

Newman, Ed. *Hot Air and Gas: The Basics of Balloons.* Roseland, Virginia: Greenway Publishing Co., 1992.

Normyle, William. "Balloon Warriors and Their Craft." *Civil War Times* 1 (4): 9 (1959).

Nye, Wilbur S. "The First Aeronaut of the War was an Engineer." *Civil War Times Illustrated* 3 (6): 19 (1964).

Nye, Wilbur S. "The U.S. Military Telegraph Service." *Civil War Times Illustrated* 7 (7): 28-34 (1968).

Official Records of the Union and Confederate Navies in the War of the Rebellion. Washington: Government Printing Office, 1892-1922.

Perry, Milton. *Infernal Machines.* Baton Rouge: Louisiana State University Press, 1965.

Phillip, Cynthia. *Robert Fulton—A Biography.* New York: Franklin Watts, 1985.

Pindell, Richard. "The Technological Inheritance." *Civil War Times Illustrated* 26 (4): 42-47 (1987).

Pleasants, Henry Jr., and George H. Straley. *Inferno at Petersburg.* Philadelphia: Chilton Company, 1961.

Plum, William R. *The Military Telegraph During the Civil War in the United States.* Vol. 1. Chicago: Jansen, McClurg and Co., 1882.

Poole, Lynn. *Ballooning in the Space Age.* New York: McGraw-Hill, 1958.

Potter, E. B. Potter, ed. *The United States and World Sea Power.* Englewood Cliffs, N.J: Prentice-Hall, Inc., 1955.

Ragan, Mark. *The Hunley: Submarines, Sacrifice, & Success in the Civil War.* Miami/Charleston: Narwhal Press, 1995.

Rains, George Washington. *History of the Confederate Powder Works.* Newburgh, New York: Newburgh Daily News Print, 1882.

Robbins, Peggy. "Bomb Brothers." *Civil War Times Illustrated* 36 (4): 40-46 (1997).

Robinson, June. "The United States Balloon Corps in Action in Northern Virginia During the Civil War." *Arlington Historical Magazine* 8 (2): 5-17 (1986).

Robinson, Michael C. *Gunboats, Low Water, and Yankee Ingenuity: A History of Bailey's Dam.* Baton Rouge: F.P.H.C., Inc., 1991.

Roland, Alex. *Underwater Warfare in the Age of Sail.* Bloomington: Indiana University Press, 1978.

Rosewater, Edward. "The War between the States: Reminiscences of Edward Rosewater, Army Telegrapher." *American Jewish Archives* 9 (2): 128-38 (1957).

Ross, Fitzgerald. *Cities and Camps of the Confederate States.* Urbana: University of Illinois Press, 1958.

Ross, Frank Jr. *Undersea Vehicles and Habitats.* New York: Thomas Crowell, 1970.

Rye, Scott. *Men and Ships of the Civil War.* Stamford, Connecticut: Longmeadow Press, 1995.

Saussy, George N. "Generals Lee and Gracie at the Crater." *Confederate Veteran* 17 (4): 160 (1909).

Savas, Theodore P. "The Life Blood of the Confederate War Machine." *Journal of Confederate History* 5 (1990): 87-110.

Scheips, P. J "Union Signal Communications: Innovation and Conflict." *Civil War History* 9 (4): 399-421 (1963).

Schell, Sidney H. "Submarine Weapons tested at Mobile during the Civil War." *Alabama Review* 45 (3): 163-83 (1992).

Sears, Steven W. *Chancellorsville.* Boston: Houghton Mifflin Co., 1996.

Shafer, Louis S. *Confederate Underwater Warfare: An Illustrated History.* Jefferson, North Carolina: McFarland and Company, Inc., 1996.

Shultz, Helen. "The Magnificent Aereon." *Civil War Times Illustrated* 19 (8): 26-28 (1980).

Siemsen, Stephen. "The Aerial Telegraph." *Military Images* 12 (3): 22-26 (1990).

Smith, Raymond W. "Don't Cut! Signal Telegraph." *Civil War Times Illustrated* 15 (2): 19-25 (1976).

"South Carolina Confederate Twins." *Confederate Veteran* 33 (9): 328 (1925).

Spies, Scouts and Raiders. Edited by the editors of Time-Life. Alexandria, Virginia: Time-Life, Inc., 1985.

Stanton, C. L. "Submarines and Torpedo Boats." *Confederate Veteran* 22 (9): 398-99 (1914).

Stehling, Kurt R., and William Beller. *Skyhooks.* Garden City, New Jersey: Doubleday and Company, Inc., 1962.

Stern, Phillip Van Doren. *The Confederate Navy.* New York: Bonanza Books, 1962.

"The Telegraph in Warfare." *Confederate Veteran* 24 (11): 506-7 (1916).

They Fought under the Sea. Edited by the editors of *Navy Times.* Harrisburg: Stackpole, 1962.

Thompson, Robert. *Wiring a Continent.* Princeton: Princeton University Press, 1947.

Thomson, David Whittet. "Three Confederate Submarines." *United States Naval Institute Proceedings* 67 (1): 39-47 (1941).

Townsend, George Alfred. *Rustics in Rebellion.* Chapel Hill: University of North Carolina Press, 1950.

Truby, J. David. "War in the Clouds: Balloons in the Civil War." *Mankind* 2 (11): 64-71 (1971).

Trudeau, Noah. *The Last Citadel.* Baton Rouge: Louisiana State University Press, 1991.

Van Creveld, Martin. *Technology and War.* London: The Free Press, 1987.

Vandiver, Frank E. *Ploughshares into Swords.* Austin: University of Texas Press, 1952.

Van Gelder, Arthur, and Hugo Schlatter. *History of the Explosives Industry in America.* New York: Arno Press, 1972.

Von Kolnitz, Harry. "The Confederate Submarine." *United States Naval Institute Proceedings* 63 (1): 1453-68 (1937).

Warner, Ezra J. *Generals in Gray.* Baton Rouge: Louisiana State University Press, 1959.

War of the Rebellion: A Compilation of the Official Records of the Union and Confederate Armies. Washington: Government Printing Office, 1880-1901.

Wiley, Bell Irvin. *Embattled Confederates.* New York: Harper and Row, 1964.

Wiley, Bell T. "Drop Poison Gas from a Balloon: A Confederate Proposal." *Civil War Times Illustrated* 7 (4): 40-41 (1968).

Wills, Richard K. "The Confederate Privateer Pioneer and the Development of American Submersible Watercraft." *The Institute for Naval Archaeology Quarterly* 21 (1-2): 12-19 (1994).

Index

12